The Crystal Textbook

The Language of Light was Written...

Within these pages you will find, as did I, the answers to your enlightenment when you understand why you have been attached to the light in a way you have not yet dreamed.

Dream then with me as you read this clear work directly from source through pen and mind of Roger Joyeux.

Be prepared to think.
Be prepared to lay the book down to ponder the significances.
Be prepared to cry with your own sweet soul in gratitude for this gifting of these pages unto the waiting hands of humanity.
Be prepared to thank your own sweet angels for putting this book in your consciousness.
And be prepared to feel forth more radiant Light, more precious Love, more gratitude within your opening heart.

You stand then on the threshold of this time of the Great Awakening along with the escorts of Roger—along with those gems you have gathered.

Blessed be the Light has come.

SanandaMagdalene / Peggy of the Pleiades
Channel for *In That Vibration of the Christing*

ii

Books by S. Roger Joyeux

The Story of Light, Path to Enlightenment

The Story of Light, Through Heaven's Gate

The Crystal Textbook

www.thestoryoflight.com
www.thecrystaltextbook.com

For the online gallery of crystal images go to:
www.thecrystaltextbook.com/gallery.php

The Crystal Textbook

S. Roger Joyeux

The Crystal Textbook

Antara Publishing

Library and Archives Canada Cataloguing in Publication

Joyeux, S. Roger (Summermoon Roger), 1952-
    The crystal textbook / S. Roger Joyeux.

ISBN 978-0-9686521-3-8

1. Crystals--Psychic aspects. I. Title.

BF1442.C78J68 2012 133'.2548 C2012-903132-1

A definitive body of knowledge about how crystals work with divine light.

www.thecrystaltextbook.com

This Book is dedicated to my wife, Judy.

Table of Contents

PART ONE
WORKING WITH LIGHT AND CRYSTALS

PART TWO
CRYSTALS

Acknowledgements

We are all One, and this needs acknowledgement. As One, we have all created *The Crystal Textbook*. Each of us is a channel for light in the same way as crystals channel light. You, too, can, as do I, acknowledge your part in the crystalline grid that is moving the Earth ever closer to enlightenment and full absorption into the all-encompassing Oneness of the vast and heavenly universe. Love and accept all the light within. You are the One.

First, thank you to all those who have purchased this book. I am honoured that you have the confidence in my work to bring it into your life.

I wish to acknowledge all those individuals who have taken my *Crystal's Light Workshop*. Teaching about the crystals and how they work with the light and the various parts of the physical and subtle bodies has honed and expanded my understanding from the channelled information first given to me by my guides, the Councilate of the Ascended-Light. The kind and honest suggestions that my students have provided to me over the years have not only shaped the presentation of the workshop, they have contributed significantly to the presentation of *The Crystal Textbook*. I especially acknowledge those individuals who have graduated from the practicum, having learned how to conduct crystal layouts. Working with the combinations of crystals that others have intuited for their clients has lead to an explosion of understanding for both my students and myself. All so exciting for me to watch! Dare I suggest that the practicum might be the foundation for a future workbook on layouts and crystal combinations?

I wish to acknowledge two groups of writers to which I belong, Calgary Authors and IPAC (Independent Publishers Association of Canada, Calgary chapter). Both groups have been a great support in the process of bringing this book to print. Calgary Authors was formed around a spiritual theme with the intimacy of a small group. The option to speak with other members one-to-one or at our casual meetings has been a real awakening to the many sides of writing, editing, cover graphics, webdesign, social media, dealing with distributors, grant applications, promotion, expo booths, marketing, and just plain sharing. IPAC stands equally to offer a slight variation on many of these same themes. Although there is no specific spiritual flavour, IPAC has always been a very positive place of sharing and support.

In particular, I wish to first acknowledge Brandon Royal. His selfless sharing of his extensive knowledge of the publishing industry with both groups mentioned above has truly made him a bright star in the night sky of authors' heaven. I wish to thank Karen Gillespie and Kellie Jo Conn, GG (the crystal deva) for permission to use the registered name of Boji® Stones. I wish also to thank all those who provided testimonials, in particular Helena Kalivoda, Rosemarie Wrobel, and Serah Roer. A very heartfelt thank you goes to my good friend and mom in a past life, Peggy of the Pleiades, Peg Watson. Her 'The Language of Light was Written' passage on page ii raises the vibration of *The Crystal Textbook*.

Most of all, I wish to acknowledge and thank my wife, Judy. She is the answer to my prayers to the universe for support in getting my books to the printer. Without her, I would not have had the opportunity to put my gratitude to her in black and white herein. You, the reader, would not have a book from which to learn about the crystals. Partners like Judy are a rare find. She, too, is an author, having written, *Earth Wisdom Meditations: 111 Contemplations for People that Love the Earth*, available at Amazon. Thank you Judy, I love you.

As always, last but not least, I wish to acknowledge my guides, the Councilate of the Ascended-Light. They are my connection to the source of all knowledge, wherever it may reside in the great enlightened heavens.

Thanks be to All.
Most humbly,
S. Roger Joyeux

Introduction

Welcome to *The Crystal Textbook*.

So, you want to learn about crystals!

First introductory snippet of joy—crystals work with light. Almost all crystals work directly with light. A very few work indirectly with light. Pyrite, for example, works with the etheric magnetic field. Stilbite, as another example, works with the emotional body. In turn, the etheric magnetic field and the emotional body work directly with light.

Second introductory snippet of joy—light does all the work. Light does the healing, balancing, empowering, cleansing, reconditioning, and more. Light stands ahead of the crystals in the fulfillment of the mission to bring enlightenment to Earth. The general role of the crystals is to help bring the light. Crystals bring light to our Solar System, planet, geographical region, dwellings, bodies, organs, cells, and molecules. Crystals set up our bodies to receive light and, in many cases, to remove blockages and density that otherwise prevent the enlightenment process from taking place.

The Crystal Textbook is laid out in two parts. Part I is "Working with Light and Crystals", which establishes a foundation of how light works, along with asserting the need for discernment in understanding how crystals work. Part II, "Crystals" discusses individual crystals. It is set up alphabetically, thus providing the reader with an easy way to go directly to the discussion of a particular crystal. Ideally, the reader reads section one outright, then delves into crystals of interest at his leisure.

Because the light does the work, some confusion naturally arises around which crystals contribute to which tasks. The sections on healing and negativity work toward an understanding of the qualities of light that could lead to the misconception that all crystals are healers and that all crystals work with negativity. True enough perhaps, but crystals are specialized.

A section entitled, "Crystal Specialization" is included to

clarify the specific roles that crystals play by addressing the concept of specialization. Light is central to any understanding of how crystals work, so there is a section in Part I entitled, "Basic Characteristics of Light". Densification, fragmentation, and splitting are a few of the difficulties that happen to light frequencies as they take on physical density. Light has a number of basic characteristics that need to be explained before making sense of the way particular crystals work. Although my first two books, *The Story of Light, Path to Enlightenment*, and *The Story of Light, Through Heaven's Gate,* cover the characteristics of light and light frequencies quite thoroughly, *The Crystal Textbook* carries sufficient explanations of the relevant characteristics of light at the appropriate places to ensure that it stands alone. The spiritual devotee is well advised to read both volumes of *The Story of Light*, but does not need to do so to acquire the advanced understanding of how crystals work with light herein.

As part of "Working with Light and Crystals", I have included a section on the 'Eleven-Chakra' system. Having this background information will help in synthesizing the knowledge of the Light Body layout and the roles played by Hematite, Kyanite, Calcite, and Selenite. Also included are sections on the rules of thumb for crystal colours, the nature of creativity, and the shortfall that plagues the quality of crystals. Not all aspects of crystals are so straight-forward that background information can be omitted. While most discussions of a given crystal are complete unto themselves, "Working with Light and Crystals" was placed at the front of the book because of its importance in fleshing out the reader's inventory of background knowledge. This section could have been included as an appendix, but would then have been after-the-fact.

The section on cleansing, clearing, and empowering crystals is also placed in the introduction to similarly elevate its importance and prevent its being missed. Unless the reader has attended my "Crystals' Light Workshop", references to the role of ions in water is likely to offer a new understanding of how crystals are cleansed.

Ions are not the only topic in this section.

The carpenter (remember Joseph, father of Jesus), politician, rocket scientist, truck driver, and biologist are highly specialized occupations. Each discipline bears its own very unique set of skills. One of the primary themes running throughout *The Crystal Textbook* is that crystals are also highly specialized. Each crystalline vibration is unique, and therefore, each crystal works in its own very specialized way.

Each of the carpenter, politician, rocket scientist, truck driver, and biologist can very easily create new life to become a father or mother. They have a number of other common possibilities as well. Crystals, too, have common possibilities in the sense that the same light frequency can be attracted by a number of different crystals. Attributing the quality or action of the common frequency to one of the crystals, but not the others, provides only a partial truth. There is some crossover of qualities and actions because the light frequencies involved can crossover between different crystals. The complete story revolves around what else the crystals do. The complete story points to the specialization and uniqueness inherent to every different crystal.

By far, the majority of content in *The Crystal Textbook* discusses a list of the most popular, interesting, or common crystals found on the market in new age crystal shops. In each section, immediately under the crystal's name is a mnemonic tag. The tag is a means by which to remember the chief characteristic or function of the crystal. For example, Fuchsite is called the 'Millennium Reconditioner'. Fuchsite is a new age stone that has come during the current millennium. Its role is to recondition the physical body in preparation for receiving many of the unfamiliar light frequencies that are very high and subtle, and very new to the physical plane. Without reconditioning, the light is too high for the body to assimilate.

Each species of crystal has the physical properties at the top of the page with the discussion of the metaphysical properties immediately following. Part of the emphasis on discernment points to the principle that each unique crystal works with a specific range of light frequencies, along with a specific part of the physical or subtle body, and in its own way. Which light frequencies are involved? Which parts of the body are involved? How is the crystal manipulating the light to fulfill its role?

Quite often, the crystal is working, not merely with the physical and subtle bodies, but with the soul or other places in the universe where light is created. Perhaps, as with Smoky Quartz, the Godhead is providing divine light directly. Perhaps, as with Apatite, Earth is the source that created the stone and the light. The excitement arises with the realization of what the Angelic Ones had to do to help the Godhead's light make its way into Smoky Quartz.

Excitement also arises with the way numerous other crystals work with light. For example, which crystal uses the technique of splitting light frequencies into their negative and positive aspects? More exciting still, what does splitting light do for the person using the crystal? As another example, which crystal translates the 'language of light' into symbols, ideas, and concepts that the intellect can grasp? If the 'language of light' arrives in the mind's intuition as a ninth dimensional vibration, how could the intellect possibly grasp what is meant without translation?

The crystals have shared with me an amazing wealth of insights into crystals, the nature of our world, and the light that goes with it. I am deeply honoured to be in a position to pass their wisdom on to you the reader.

Love and light,
S. Roger Joyeux

PART ONE

WORKING WITH LIGHT AND CRYSTALS

Basic Characteristics of Light

"To understand crystals, first understand light."

This quotation has been one of the promotional pieces of wisdom for the "Crystals' Light" workshop—almost since the beginning. Crystals and light go hand-in-glove. Without light, crystals can have no effect. Without crystals, light is almost unaffected. Light will do the job it came to do—crystals or not. The significance is that light does the work of enlightenment, not crystals. Crystals are a significant help, but their role is to bring light to the place where the work of enlightenment can move forward. Crystals do not do the work of the light[1].

The High-Low Sliding Scale

To begin, **divine light frequencies** have high vibration and low vibration. On Earth, some light frequencies vibrate at the high end of the sliding vibrational scale, while other frequencies vibrate at the low end. High third dimensional frequencies exist near the threshold to the fourth dimension and could easily accelerate out of the third and into the fourth dimension. Enlightened

---

1   For the purposes of understanding crystals in this volume, this section, along with accompanying sections and information within the text of each crystal, is sufficient to provide clarity. If the reader wishes to delve further into the nature of divine light and light frequencies, *The Story of Light, Path to Enlightenment* and *The Story of Light, Through Heaven's Gate* have much to offer.

masters work with the Earth's high light frequencies. Low third dimensional frequencies exist near the threshold to the second dimension. If their density increases, there is a very good chance that they will slip down into the second dimension. Third dimensional vibration is quite stable at this point in Earth's history, otherwise the highest and lowest physical objects would easily pass into the higher and lower dimensions respectively.

The high and low vibrational model can be applied to most scenarios involving light. The **chakras**, for example, work with high and low vibrations of light. First, the crown chakra works with the highest frequencies that the human body can assimilate. Although the crown works with all light frequencies in its role of light distribution, its range of activity also includes the assimilation of light from the highest levels of the higher-self. Frequencies of the higher-self vibrate at a rate slightly above the range that is within reach of the third eye. The third eye, therefore, works with a lower range than the highest frequencies coming through the crown chakra. The range of frequencies related to the throat chakra is below the vibration rate of the third eye, but above the vibration rate of the heart. The base chakra works with lower light frequencies than does the pelvic chakra. Each chakra from top to bottom works with a set range of frequencies that are progressively higher from the base chakra up.

The high-low scale can be applied to the chakras as a group, but can also be applied to individual chakras and to crystals. Within the frequencies for each chakra is a high and low range. For example, Rose Quartz works with the mid-range of heart chakra frequencies, while Rhodochrosite works with the high ranges of the heart. As another example, the second or pelvic chakra works with the vibrations of sex and anger. Sex is at the high end of the scale of vibrations within the second chakra, while anger is at the low end. Because Red Garnet resonates with the frequencies of anger, its range of activity is generally limited to the lowest frequencies in the second chakra.

The physical body itself reflects the ranges of the high and low frequencies of the chakras. Because the chakras have a role in distributing light to adjacent **organs and body parts**, lower ranges of frequencies find their way to the body's lower organs and parts. For example, the second chakra distributes light to the bladder, kidneys, testes, ovaries, and reproductive system. Higher ranges of frequencies emanate from the upper chakras to those parts of the body that have higher vibration. The third eye chakra distributes light to the brain, nervous system, eyes, and ears.

Beyond the body and chakras, some **geographical locations** on Earth carry higher vibrations, while other locations carry lower vibrations. Numerous new age, shamanic, and religious sources refer to 'power places' on the planet. Mecca and Jerusalem are the centres of the Muslim, Jewish, and Christian faiths. The Hindi people look to the ashrams of their gurus as places of pilgrimage. Natural sites, such as Mount Shasta, Banff, and Sedona are celebrated as light stations[2] among the devotees of the new age. In contrast, there are numerous locations that vibrate at the low end of the scale. The Abu Ghraib and Lubyanka prisons, along with the Auschwitz death camp, are representative of stations of darkness.

Looking to the universe beyond the Earth, the vibration of **the solar system** can also be tagged to the sliding scale of high and low light vibration. The Earth, whose focus is primarily on the third dimension, is the lowest of the planetary vibrations within our solar system. Venus is somewhat higher, as its focus is currently in the fifth dimension, or two levels above the Earth's. Mercury might be compared to the crown chakra of the human body in the respect that its primary role involves light distribution[3]. As such,

---

2   Chapter 12 of *The Story of Light, Through Heaven's Gate* is entitled: "Light Stations". It discusses light stations in detail from their inception and empowerment, along with how they serve the process of enlightenment.

3   Please see Chapter 10, "Expansion into our Solar System", section 10.1, "Mercury-Sun-Arcemedus Alignment", and Chapter 11, "Solar

it works with the full range of frequencies common to our solar system. The light it sends to Mars carries much lower ranges of frequencies than the frequencies it sends to Jupiter or Saturn.

The principle that light vibration can be scaled as either high or low applies wherever light exists and in whatever circumstance. Crystals, then, work with light in the vibration range for which they were designed. Crystals that work with the frequencies of the high ranges are highly unlikely to work with the frequencies of the low ranges. Sugilite, which is purple and intimate with the soul, works with the third eye. It does not resonate with the throat, heart, or lower chakras. Red Garnet, as previously mentioned, works with the vibrations of anger in the second chakra, but not with the vibrations of love in the heart chakra.

The above section concerning the sliding scale of high and low light vibrations is indicative of the crystal user's need to be discerning. Not all crystals do the same job. Truly, few crystals work in ways that are similar to other crystals.

Individual Frequency Fragmentation

The next section deals with the highs and lows of the individual light frequency. The model to envision is that an individual light frequency exists on many, if not all, dimensional levels. Light that was created within the Godhead and has come to Earth exists as vibration at all levels between the Earth and the Godhead. In comparison, a light frequency that was created on the 19th dimension, for example, and has also come to Earth, exists at all dimensional levels between the 19th dimension and Earth. Its vibration is not high enough to exist above the 19th dimension. Similarly, a frequency that has not descended to Earth remains in

---

System's One Consciousness", section 11.1.02, "Mercury" in *The Story of Light, Through Heaven's Gate* for discussion on Mercury's role in the distribution of light throughout our local solar system.

the heavens above Earth's level of vibration[4].

Light frequencies may not exist in a particular dimension because they are either too high or too low to be compatible with that dimension. Because Earth is at the bottom end of the vibrational scale of creation, most of the light in the vast universe cannot descend to take up a place on the physical plane. Its vibration is simply too high. Truly, only a very minute portion of the light of creation has any chance of assuming the extremely dense vibrations of the physical plane to be on Earth.

Even when an individual light frequency finds its way into physical density, the vast majority of the frequency's vibration is too high to come to the Earth. A tiny portion, which is invariably the lowest aspect of the frequency, enters the Earth's physical plane. Most of the frequency remains in the higher realms. The frequency actually splits apart or fragments, with only the lowest

---

4   Author's Note: Because so many spiritual sources are advocating that our planet and its inhabitants are rising to become a fifth dimensional vibration, a comment needs to be made. First, the fifth, tenth, twentieth, or eighth dimensions are third dimensional concepts. Humanity is at the bottom of the consciousness scale. The mind needs third dimensional symbolism to grasp meaning. Meaning itself is locked into reason, which dominates the third dimension. On the third dimension, reason dictates that there is a need to define the qualities and characteristics that go along with a given dimension. Beyond the third dimension, reason is not required. I am. Being is enough. Therefore, reason does not apply above the third dimension. The fifth dimension, at the level of what we perceive to be the fifth dimension, does not need a label. Further, there is some thought that humanity and the Earth are about to 'ascend' to the fifth dimension. When humanity and the Earth are ready to leave the third dimension, which is synonymous with ascending, why, in heaven's name, would there be a need to ascend to only the fifth dimension? The Earth and each of its inhabitants made a contract at the level of the soul or higher-self to participate in the enlightenment of the physical plane. Fulfilling a third dimensional contract as a fifth dimensional being is a contradiction. A fifth dimensional being cannot have a presence on the physical plane in physical form.

aspects entering physical density. The fact that the light frequencies available to the spiritual devotee on Earth are among the lowest frequencies in the universe, along with the fact that they are split, fragmented, and incomplete, has tremendous implications for humanity's understanding of reality.

Understanding what is—the truth—depends upon the illumination given to the mind by the quality of the light frequencies it receives. What can humanity know with only the lowest light in the universe available? Further, the mind works with the lowest aspects of any given light frequency, while the higher aspects remain unavailable in the heavens. Thought-forms that arise from frequencies at the low end of the scale produce perceptions, world views, and concepts that are also at the low end. High and low, however, are relative terms. The highest frequencies on Earth are still among the lowest frequencies in the universe. As good as human understanding can be, it is at the bottom of the scale. When viewing the sliding high-low scale only within the context of Earth, the highest thought-forms are quite near to the fourth dimension and could very easily impress the human mind.

Much of the work of the crystals is focused on helping light frequencies to bring more of their higher aspects into the physical plane. The process has always been incremental, continuous, and steadily rising. With more and higher light frequencies, along with higher aspects of individual frequencies, the march towards the enlightenment of the planet and its inhabitants is relentless.

Duality and the Nature of Light

Discerning the ways of the light is not complete without the discussion about duality. Man-woman, up-down, hard-soft are recognizable examples of duality on Earth. Light frequencies, also on Earth, are constructed with an inherent duality. Each frequency consists of a negative and a positive aspect. Yin and yang are the common spiritual terms used to denote negative and positive. Light, then, consists of its yin, or feminine aspect, and its yang, or masculine aspect. In a whole and complete light frequency, yin and yang are united in polar balance.

Working with a whole light frequency, as opposed to an incomplete frequency can make a serious difference to the perceptions of the human mind. If the mind contemplates a subject, honesty for example, and has only the positive aspect of the frequencies of honesty available, the person may think everyone on Earth is honest. Thinking and the thought-forms that are generated by the mind are skewed to the positive, and therefore quite off-balance. 'Crazy' might be the colloquial term for such an imbalance . The clinical diagnosis might use the term 'dementia'. In contrast, if the mind has only the negative aspect of the light of honesty available, the whole world might appear to be corrupt and dishonest. "No one can be trusted!"

Light on Earth is not always whole and complete with both yin and yang aspects united in balance. Although seldom overwhelming enough to result in the view that everyone is either honest or dishonest, individual light frequencies are often missing their yin or yang aspects to some degree.

In the previous section, discussion pointed out that the high and low aspects of individual frequencies usually fragment with the higher aspects remaining in the heavens, and the lower aspects descending to Earth. The inherent assumption is that the fragmented frequency maintains its unity regarding its polarized yin and yang structures. However, frequencies are very often fragmented into their yin and yang aspects as well. The yin aspect can be floating around within the Earth's etheric magnetic field quite separate from the yang aspect, which can also be floating in the etherics. Polar separation precludes the wholeness of light.

Fragmentation into polar opposites is not the problem it may seem to be. Polarity aside, the lowest aspects of a whole and complete frequency actually do descend onto the physical plane. Gradually, the higher aspects adjust, and more of the same frequency comes to Earth. The separation of the yin and yang polar opposites has a somewhat different implication. Splitting frequencies produces an incomplete frequency that is not subjected to the same scrutiny on the part of the etheric magnetic field. The etherics serve to filter light by attracting the desirable and repelling the undesirable frequencies. The prerequisite for effective filtering is that the frequency being filtered is whole and complete. Polarized aspects of a light frequency that have split away are unaffected by the etherics. They cannot be filtered out because the etheric field cannot attune to their extreme polarity. The yin aspect of a light frequency can bypass the Earth's and a person's etheric magnetic field as easily as the yang aspect. A light frequency that cannot otherwise come to Earth can come as a partial frequency in the form of the yin or yang aspect[5].

Arrival on Earth as a partial frequency does not mean that it can be used to participate appropriately in the Earth's and humanity's enlightenment process. Yin aspects produce negative thought-forms, and yang aspects produce positive thought-forms. Neither thought-form results in a balanced world-view. However, the polarity inherent to each aspect implies that the separated aspects will attract each other and eventually unite into a whole and complete frequency. Sending light to Earth, separated into yin and yang aspects, is a crucial and important innovation in the quest to bring light to Earth.

Understanding that light frequencies are not always in balance, that they can be broken down into negative and positive aspects, and that their polarity always brings the separate parts together in unity has significant implications for the way a few of the crystals work with light. Among the crystals of interest,

---

5   Using duality to bring light to Earth is one of the great innovations discovered early in the planet's lifespan. Please see *The Story of Light, Path to Enlightenment*, Chapter 1, section 1.9, entitled "Innovating Physical Duality".

whenever the splitting of light is involved, is Malachite, Herkimer Diamond, Azurite, and Black Tourmaline.

Reaching Discernment

Invariably, crystals work with light, whether directly or indirectly. Each light frequency is unique and each group or range of frequencies is unique as well. The differences between one frequency or range of frequencies and another frequency or range of frequencies can be minor or extreme. Further, when polarity is involved, frequencies can actually split into separate aspects and create unchallenged imbalances. Further still, light frequencies can be tagged somewhere on the sliding scale of high and low vibration. They can also be tagged with breadth and depth of vibration in mind. Finally, divine light frequencies come from individual sources of creation somewhere in the vast enlightened universe. There are millions more sources of creation than there are stars in the clear night sky.

Although a crystal works with light, it cannot be expected to have the diversity and flexibility to work with all frequencies in both polarities and from every part of the vast enlightened universe. A person using a crystal for whatever purpose needs to be discerning as to which portion of the light spectrum the crystal works. Light is specialized, and therefore, crystals are specialized.

The Specialization of Crystals

The previous section pointed out the diversity of light and the need to be discerning about the qualities of the light involved in using crystals. Discussion also pointed out that crystals are specialized because the light itself is specialized. Using crystals involves another factor. What do they act upon?

As is light, humanity is diverse. Some people are polarized to the negative or positive side. Some people are high in vibration and others low. Some people work more or less with their spirit, mind, and body. Examples that can be tagged to different attributes might include body-builders, monks, brick-layers, academics philosophers, criminal gang members, sea captains, accountants, writers, priests and rabbis, and many more. Which individual has a life path focused on the body, the mind, or the spirit? Which individual has high vibration, and which has low? Which individuals project a negative vibration and which are positive?

Crystals work with the diversity of light frequencies, but they also work with the diversity of humanity as vested in persons using them. Beyond the diversity of humanity as a whole is the diversity of the human body, mind, and spirit. The physical body is the sum of its parts. The brain has a very specialized job to do, as does the heart, kidneys, and ankle joint. Each organ in the body carries its own unique vibration and specialized function. Light frequencies acting on the physical eyes react very differently to the vibration of the muscle tissues.

The mind itself is specialized. To begin, the intuition is not the intellect, but both are part of the mind and work harmoniously and with synchronicity. For example, the person, whose mental focus is in the realm of philosophy, uses a much different part of the brain than does the person focused on an improved computer game score. The police detective works using a different intellectual approach than does the corporate financial officer. Each discipline is unique and works with a different part of the brain and intellect and with different light frequencies.

Similarly, in the realm of spirit, the shamanic discipline is different than the discipline of Catholicism. Spiritual endeavours involve vastly different sets of light frequencies. The world view of the orthodox Jew is often at violent odds with the world view of the follower of Mohammed. Whether or not all roads lead to God, Allah, Shiva, or the Creator, spiritual diversity is a fact. The essence of diversity is that vibration itself is diverse. The Hindu temple can work with a three foot Earth keeper crystal, while the head of the Church of England wears a crown of jewels. The light that drives one spiritual discipline is often very different than the light that drives another spiritual discipline.

When each of the diverse forms of humanity, its body, mind, and spirit are reduced to vibration, the conclusion is that vibration is diverse and unique unto itself. When crystals are added to the equation, diversity takes another completely different direction.

What action does a crystal perform?

The partial list of how crystals act on vibration includes balancing, empowering, cleansing, healing, creating, enhancing, facilitating, expanding, accelerating, connecting, interpreting, translating, aligning, reconditioning, illuminating, transmuting, polarizing, and more.

What does a crystal act upon?

The partial list of the vibrations that crystals act upon includes forms (physical or otherwise), light frequencies, general bodily essence, chakras, the etheric magnetic field, emotional body, consciousness, conscious body, mind, intellect, intuition, Light Body, higher-self, aura, truth, vision, compassion, density, love, and more.

Succinctly, crystals perform a significant array of actions upon an equally significant array of unique and diverse vibrations.

Both the actions and the vibrations acted upon are specialized. While there is crossover between crystals regarding actions and vibrations acted upon, the overlap is rooted in the light. Some crystals work with frequencies or ranges of frequencies that are the same or similar to the frequencies or ranges of frequencies that other crystals work with. The overlap, however, may not be at all significant. Specialization is the rule. For example, a crystal that works with the soul does not work with the second chakra. A crystal that enhances creativity does not interpret the language of the light. Crystals that heal are not illuminating. Crystals that facilitate opening the chakras do not contribute to a person's connection to his higher self. Aligning is not expansion. Balancing is not specifically healing, and clearly not polarizing. Crystals that work with the heart do not work with the throat. Crystals that work with the conscious body do not work with the chakras. Crystals that work with the etheric magnetic field do not work with the general bodily form.

There are many places to which crystals bring light and many ways that they do so. While there is some crossover between actions, the light involved, and the objects upon which the light acts, specialization of crystals is the greater reality.

Creativity from the Perspective of Light

The artist gently applies a softer tone of brown with highlights of orange and grey to accent the dramas of the sunset that he[1] is creating on his canvas. There is no difficulty grasping the creativity that an artist invests in a painting. He has the love of painting on canvas at heart. He understands colour and lighting. He knows the limits of his medium and the brushes to use. Most important of all, he is focused on his work.

The focus of the mind is crucial because any creative process is dependent on the light frequencies available to produce the outcome. When the light available is unlimited, 'the sky's the limit'. Availability, however, is dependent upon the vibration of the mind and body to which the light comes. Light frequencies invariably reflect the exact vibration to which they are attracted. Otherwise, attraction is not possible.

Although the mind and conscious body can play a significant role in the creative process, creativity needs to be understood from the perspective of light and light frequencies. For example, the car design engineer, who is working on next year's car designs, has available to his mind all of the light currently on the Earth. The engineer's mind and consciousness create the attraction for the light frequencies that contribute to the car design by setting up a focused contemplation. He ponders the problems and solutions. His contemplation then sets up the appropriate etheric magnetic field within the mind to attract the exact frequencies to create

---

1   How should an author treat gender designation? In *The Crystal Textbook*, in Part I, where reference might be to he or she, odd sections will use the masculine, 'he', and even sections will use the feminine, 'she'. In Part II, every other crystal name, starting with the letter designation of 'A', is feminine, Every other letter designation starting with the letter 'B' is masculine. For example, where 'he or she' is the convention, in the section on Amethyst, Moldavite, or Sugilite, the gender designation is feminine, and 'she' is used. With Bloodstone, Lapis, or Pyrite, the gender designation is masculine and 'he' is used.

the design. As the mind synthesizes the thought-forms that bring awareness to the solutions, the car designs unfold.

If the engineer was living in 1927, the same process of focus, contemplation, and etheric field attraction for light would apply. The difference is the light available to the mind and the resulting thought-forms that lead to the final designs. The amount and quality of available light in 1927 is significantly less and of lower vibration than is present today. Car design reflects the differences between then and now.

The example of car design offers further insight. Car designs, through the years, have steadily moved forward. Every year improvements have taken place. The design process reflects a steady pattern of growth. The mind and conscious body of the individual engineer, and the engineering discipline in general, has moved forward in an equally steady pattern of growth. Every year, there is more light and higher vibrations of light available to the creative process. Every year, the engineer's mind and consciousness rises in vibration. It can then accommodate the new frequencies available.

Because creativity depends directly on the light frequencies that fuel the process, enhancing creativity amounts to attracting more and higher frequencies. The vibration of today accommodates the range and quality of light available to the mind's contemplation according to the mind's vibration. As light keeps coming, the mind's vibration rises, which means that even more and higher light can be attracted and assimilated.

The change in vibration ever upward occurs as light combines with form (physical body form, conscious body form) to create Oneness. Oneness has its own God-powers of creation. It can create more form to accommodate more light. Contributing directly to the creativity process involves the expansion of form. Bodily forms increase in light carrying capacity and quality of vibration. Whereas, for illustration purposes, bodily form accommodates 1,000 light frequencies, the increase in size and quality means the form accommodates an additional 100 frequencies of higher vibration. When the mind sets up its contemplation, the expansion of its form means that it has the original 1,000 frequencies, plus an extra 100 light frequencies of higher quality, with which to generate its insights.

With more light, the creative process takes a step forward. Problems are met with solutions having greater insight. For example, the car designer creates disc brakes as an improvement over drum and shoe brakes. As another example, each wheel gets its own independent suspension as an improvement over wheels attached to a single axle.

Crystals are involved in the creative process. They bring light to form. The resulting Oneness uses its God-powers of creation to create more form. Every incremental increase in Oneness leads to an increase in the light carrying capacity and quality of form. The form makes more light available thus enhancing the mind's creative abilities.

The essence of creativity, then, is the expansion of form.

Classic Crystal Healing

Healing can mean many things. Understanding healing can also come from numerous perspectives. What is healing to the nurse or doctor? What is healing to the wounded soldier? What is healing to the emotionally abused? What is healing to those who have suffered racism or genocide? Each form of healing takes a different path. When crystals are involved, healing involves light and light frequencies. There is crossover of course. Metaphysical healing, as was given by Jesus and scores of energy healers, has the power to transform vibration from its diseased or injured state back to its original healthy state. With enough light, healing happens.

The diseased state usually means that some part of the body has greater density of vibration than is healthy. Tissues contract, and the accompanying etheric magnetic field concentrates. Symptoms might include cancerous tumours, tense muscles or muscle spasms, areas of pain, and inappropriate behaviours due to brain dysfunction, but can also include emotional outbursts, cold hearts, and obsessions. Dense vibration is low and slow, and does not permit light to flow easily. Light is blocked, or the flow becomes distorted, and the body develops disease. Removing the problem, such as changing the body's pH balance, moving the tree that fell on a person's leg, leaving an abusive relationship, or refraining from consuming chemical-laced foods, has an effect. However, the density that remains must be changed to bring the body back to its normal healthy state.

Healing with light is the acceleration of form so that light can flow through and assimilate as needed. Slow, low, and dense vibration blocks light flow. High, fast, and accelerated vibration facilitates light flow. Anything that can accelerate dense spots contributes to the influx of light and, thereby, the outcome of healing. Light is the healer.

The category of crystals that is properly called 'healing crystals' are those crystals that accelerate form. Healing crystals are almost always green in colour. The primary exceptions to the green rule are Malachite, which splits light, but does not accelerate form, and Moldavite, which is a healer, but only as an auxiliary function. Moldavite's healing is a side-line, and not its primary purpose. Green stones such as Green Adventurine, Serpentine, Green Tourmaline, and Bloodstone are a few examples of crystal healers in the sense of accelerating form.

In every case of healing with crystals, the crystal manipulates light, and light does the healing. The inference that needs to be clear is that light does the healing, not the crystals. If the language around healing is fast and loose, one might say that, "All crystals work with light, therefore all crystals are healers." So, which crystals are healers and which are not is dependent on the definition one uses. Herein, healing means the acceleration of the density of form for the purpose of allowing more and higher vibrations of light to flow in and assimilate, thus raising form's vibration above the threshold of dis-ease. Call this 'classic healing'. Saying that all crystals are healers insults the mind of the reader, and while a truth, it is a meaningless truth.

Using the term 'classic healing' is one way to describe how crystals help light to perform healing. Because light does the healing, crystals work with light for healing, but not strictly healing, purposes. Crystals also help the soul to coordinate light in a type of healing that might be better understood as soul empowerment. Crystals that work with the soul help the soul to assess and then re-condition the body's vibration. They include, for example, Sugilite and Sodalite among others. Crystals also heal by accelerating light past blockages to heal form, as does Kyanite. However, Kyanite's healing affect is incidental and does not pay homage to its other primary and more important purposes. Further, crystals can heal by either cleaning up the quality of light, as does Malachite, or by providing exceptionally clean light, as does Herkimer Diamond. Another way the crystals work with light to raise the vibration of dense forms is to displace the form's lower light vibrations. Simply, good light goes in, bad light comes out. Any number of crystals perform this task.

Again, classic healing is the acceleration of dense form to allow more light to enter and assimilate thus raising form's vibration above dis-ease. Those crystals that accelerate form are the classic healers in *The Crystal Textbook*.

Crystals and Negativity

"All crystals work with light, therefore, all crystals work with negativity". A very similar quote was made in the previous section on healing. The truth behind this statement is equally meaningless. All light is composed of both negative and positive aspects. Using a generalized statement to claim that crystals work with negativity tells the reader very little and betrays the quality of the source.

When a frequency of light is somewhat damaged or otherwise polarized to the negative or positive polarity, confusion might arise as to what is going on. One is really pushing the envelope to say that a damaged light frequency is working with negative vibration. Can one attribute the qualities of a person as being negative because that person broke a leg? Rather, the frequency that is damaged is doing its best to accomplish its mission in spite of the damage that is giving negativity prominence. As well, polarized frequencies are usually involved in some task that brings balance or creates attraction within the bodily form. They are not working toward any purposeful articulation of negativity.

Crystals work with light, which is both negative and positive, therefore polarity and the presence of negative aspects are incidental to the crystal's purpose. With only a couple of exceptions, crystals do not purposefully work to alleviate the influence of negativity. Of the many crystals discussed in this volume, only Black Tourmaline and Azurite work directly to reduce negative vibration. Any other involvement of negatively polarized light or crystals relates to the use of imbalances to attract or repel light frequencies.

Crystal Colour Variations

Colour plays an important role in the flow of light. Red hues are penetrating, for example. Golden hues work to enhance creativity, as another example. The rainbow has seven primary colour bands, but there are numerous other colours that are not visible to the human eye and that also contribute to the enlightenment process. Each frequency or range of frequencies vibrates within one or other band of the colour spectrum of light. Each band carries its unique and specialized contribution to the flow of light on Earth.

Asserting that the colours of certain light frequencies perform certain tasks is a liberal use of the 'rules of thumb'. Particular colours generally perform particular tasks, but exceptions are not uncommon. Assigning a role to a colour is a rule of thumb because, as a rule, the colour performs the task asserted.

Here are some of the rules of thumb that can be generally applied to the colour variations of crystals.

White

White implies purity, which in turn implies high vibration. White crystals work with the higher ranges of light frequencies within particular chakras or with the higher chakras. White stilbite, for example, works with the highest chakra—the crown. As another example, Howlite, which is white with silvery inclusions, works to purify whichever vibration upon which it is placed.

White implies the involvement, or at least, the potential involvement of all light frequencies. The full spectrum of all light is vested within the white (and usually clear and cloudy) crystals. The presence of all frequencies ensures that the body's vibration has the specific frequency or frequencies it needs available to it at any given moment, and for the quality of vibration needed. On the other side of the coin, having all frequencies available also means that the quantity of any particular frequency is small.

White crystals provide purity along with minor amounts of all light frequencies.

Purple

The colour purple almost always heralds the presence of the soul. Amethyst is the 'calling card of the soul'. Sugilite is the 'soul healer'. Lepidolite involves the soul in the balancing process. Although the soul is involved, the method by which the soul is involved is quite specialized for each crystal. In addition, the work done by the soul is quite different. Balancing and healing, as mentioned, are two very different services. They also happen in two very different ways. The rule of thumb of the colour purple is that the soul is at work.

Dark or Cobalt Blue

Deep blue that reflects the night sky points to the depths of consciousness. The rule of thumb for cobalt blue stones, such as Azurite, Lapis, and Sodalite is that the mind and third eye are involved and that consciousness is in play. How the stone works with the mind, or how it manipulates light frequencies, is unique for each stone.

Sky Blue or Turquoise Blue

The sky, turquoise, or pale blue colours generally belong to the throat chakra's range of light frequencies. The throat is the chakra of truth and the expression of truth. The Turquoise stone is the primary empowerment stone for the throat. Chrysocolla, also worthy of mention, enhances the throat's vibration. The rule of thumb for sky blue or turquoise colours of crystals is that the expression of truth, usually coming through the throat chakra, is divine and uncorrupted.

Green

The rule of thumb for green crystals is that these are the classic healing crystals of the crystal world. Classic healing, as outlined in the section on healing is basically the acceleration of form to allow more light to enter. Thereafter, light does the healing. Most green crystals are related to the heart chakra in some way. Classic healing involves many different forms, and therefore, different vibrations. For example, Prehnite works with the high vibrations of the heart chakra's emotional body, but Epidote works with the frequencies of the base chakra for an entirely different purpose. Crystals that perform healing as rule of thumb are green, but almost always work with very specific vibrations and on very specific aspects of the physical or subtle bodies. Notable exceptions for the green crystals are Malachite and Moldavite, which are not classic healing crystals.

Pink or Peach

As are the green healing crystals, most pink or peach coloured crystals are also related to the heart chakra. The pink, the darker peach, and the lighter reddish colour hues reflect love and compassion, which are the two ranges of frequencies that are indigenous to the heart chakra. Love, however, has many faces. Rose Quartz works with a person's love and with divine love at the same time. Rhodochrosite, on the other hand, works with the love of the soul's heart, but also with the body's chakras. Love, at the highest levels of the heart chakra, works with the Morganite crystal. Pink Halite works with the same frequencies as Rose Quartz, and at the midranges of the heart. As a rule of thumb, the pink or peach colour hues help the heart chakra's frequencies of love and compassion to find their way to expression.

Gold and Yellow

Gold is money, is wealth, and follows the work of creating abundance. Abundance comes in many forms: love, happiness, peace of mind, prestige, money, and more. The human being creates abundance by focusing the mind in the contemplative state upon the object of desire. The mind marshals the vibrations that fulfill its contemplation. Creativity in the world of crystals and light refers to the expansion of form for the purpose of accommodating more light. The role of the crystals is to help with the expansion of form. If the form of the mind's contemplation can be expanded, the flow of abundance related to the contemplation increases. The gold and yellow varieties of crystals work to empower the forms (chakras or bodily parts), with which they resonate, to expand the presence of the Oneness within the form. The Oneness, with its powers of creativity, creates more form, which in turn accommodates more light. The rule of thumb is that the crystals of the golden and yellow hues enhances abundance. Foremost among the stones of creativity is Citrine.

Red

The rule of thumb for the red band of light frequencies and the crystals that bring red light is the rapid penetration of form. Most light frequencies resonate with only their intended forms and do not enter the space of any other form. Red light frequencies pierce form with little resistance. For example, laser beams, which first employed the red light of Ruby are well known for piercing their way through any physical form and for travelling outward for eternity. The crystals that bring the red range of frequencies bring light without frustration into physical form in the face of whatever resistance may be in place.

Black

Black light frequencies are the lowest frequencies on Earth. They are the Earth's indigenous range of light. When the planet first entered the physical plane, its vibration was so very low and slow that only the black light frequencies had any chance of assimilating into the Earth's form. Black light goes to ground—to the Earth—first. The rule of thumb for the black crystals is that they are the grounding stones of the crystal world.

This short list of the primary common colours found among the crystals is not exhaustive. The qualifier that limits the spectrum of colours to which rules of thumb apply is the human physical eye. Beyond the eye's ability to perceive ranges of colour, the variations in the tasks that crystals perform tend not to fall into classifications that can be applied to a colour grouping. Rules of thumb are also just that, rules of thumb. They can help a person to understand some general and common tendencies in the performance of a class of crystals, but there are inevitably exceptions to the rule.

The Eleven-Chakra System

The original chakra—the very first one—was a brand new experiment with only a faint hope of discovering how light could find its way into the human physical body. Following the great success that the new chakra proved to be, other experiments were tried to determine the appropriate mix and number of chakras[1]. At one point, the experiment involved chakras in almost every joint, certainly at the wrist, elbow, shoulder, and neck, as well as, the ankle, knee, hip, and spine (at the lumbar 4 position or solar plexus). The objective was to determine how the body could best attract, anchor, and assimilate the full range of light frequencies needed to achieve enlightenment.

The full range of light frequencies needed by the body are frequencies that are already on the physical plane. These frequencies have a range of activities that the high, subtle, and sensitive chakras could work with easily. Even just one of the early, and still primitive, chakras was capable of working with the full complement of available frequencies on its own. The need for a few dozen chakras was quickly dismissed as unnecessary.

Chakra specialization did not develop overnight. The first chakra soon became one of three primary chakras—crown, heart, and base chakras. With three chakras, specific roles began to surface. The crown chakra, located in the upper part of the skull, became the initial doorway for light attracted to the body. The heart chakra helped frequencies to adjust to the third dimension to become physical vibrations. It also helped the high and low vibrations within the body to come into balance. The lower or base

---

1   The discussion of the experiments that led to the creation and design of the first and subsequent chakras is provided in *The Story of Light, Path to Enlightenment*, chapter 3, "Starting from Scratch", and in particular, sections 3.2 through 3.7 of chapter 3.

chakra initially helped the physical body to adjust to its immediate environment. The base chakra worked, and still works, to bring a person into harmony with the places on Earth that are best suited to her vibration.

The three-chakra system worked well during the initial stages of the chakra experiments. Light was attracted and assimilated, and the person brightened with the infusion of new frequencies. Just as the seven-chakra system is now yielding to the eleven-chakra system, as the human body evolves, the three-chakra system yielded to the seven-chakra system. Following testing and the realization of the breadth of frequencies that each chakra could handle, the optimal number was determined to be seven chakras. With the specializations that emerged, the number of roles increased. The third eye held the intuition, the throat chakra held truth, the navel chakra worked with form expansion (creativity), and the pelvic chakra acquired a light sorting function[2]. The crown, heart and base chakras continued to perform their assigned tasks, but also took on new tasks.

The seven-chakra system provided the body with the light of empowerment in a number of diverse roles. It was able to attract, acquire, and assimilate the full range of light frequencies needed by the body. Having extra chakras became redundant. The quest to achieve enlightenment was well served with seven chakras.

In the long period between the first arrivals of humanity on the Earth and this present moment, enlightenment has always been the foremost objective of the spiritual path. As long as humanity was preoccupied with enlightenment, seven chakras was all that was needed. The journey to enlightenment has only recently become established and successful enough to allow humanity to open the door to the next quantum leap. Enlightenment is now the

---

2   The in-depth discussion concerning how each of the chakras works with its own range of specialized light frequencies can be found in volume one of *The Story of Light, Path to Enlightenment*, Chapter Four, entitled: "Empowering the Incarnation".

cornerstone for humanity's venture into co-creation. Although co-creation is easily accomplished between persons who are in harmony with each other, the real step into co-creation goes beyond individuals on Earth. It involves co-creation with the universe, the spirits of the heavens, and the Godhead. The seven-chakra system has limits. It can only take a person to the point of being ready to work with the larger enlightened universe. What is needed from this moment forward is the means to connect with the heavens and work with the higher realms directly.

Enter the eleven-chakra system!

The eleven-chakra system incorporates the original seven charas, which are basically unaffected. The original seven chakras work to empower the physical body with light. The additional four chakras connect the highest parts of the heavens, including the Godhead, with the core of the Earth. They also work to provide protective safeguards for the in-coming divine light from unwarranted frequencies, and to overcome the resistances generated by the mind, either by ego, denial, or vibrational inconsistencies.

The first of the four new chakras is the Earth chakra, or Earth-star chakra, which, on the human body, is located about a foot or so below the feet. It works to allow the light of the physical body to harmonize with the Earth, and to flow out into the Earth. It is a grounding chakra and therefore, has a simple role.

The next important chakra is the highest chakra. It is the galactic-centre chakra, and is located a foot or so above the crown chakra. It serves a role that is similar to the crown chakra. It attracts and directs light from the person's external environment to the body. The difference is that, while the person's crown chakra works with light that has already adjusted to a physical vibration, the galactic-centre chakra works with the very high and subtle frequencies of the upper heavens and Godhead. The galactic-centre is the open conduit for the highest light possible. It brings the enlightened presence of the heavens and God. The Earth-star chakra grounds that divine presence into the person's body and helps the frequencies involved find their way into the mass of the Earth.

The remaining two chakras, the stellar gateway chakra and the causal chakra, condition the body and the light for the purpose of harmonization. Godhead frequencies carry a vastly different vibration than the vibration of the human body that receives them. Harmony and compatibility are significant issues that must be resolved before the high God light and low physical body form can reconcile each other.

The stellar gateway chakra regulates the light flowing to and from the heavens and Earth. It is responsible for ensuring that the light frequencies involved are compatible. The flow of negative light frequencies[3] from the Earth is not allowed. Low, slow, and negative Earthly frequencies are stopped from moving upward into the heavens by the stellar gateway chakra. It is truly the gatekeeper. The stellar gateway also ensures that the higher soul frequencies and frequencies of the Godhead are low enough in vibration to be received by the physical body. It prevents the range of frequencies that vibrate beyond the range of the body from entering the third dimension and the personal space of the person on Earth. It is the gateway for harmonious and compatible light going in both directions, to and from the Earth and heavens.

Finally, the soul-star chakra, or causal chakra, works with the mind. The soul-star chakra is located a few inches from the base of the skull. Its role is to further harmonize the light moving through the stellar gateway with the human mind. The body cannot receive light that the mind wilfully blocks. The mind, through both the intuition and intellect, carries the final determination of which fre-

---

3   The negative polarity of a light frequency need not be judged as a bad thing. Negative aspects of vibration are best placed in context with positive aspects to be understood. However, the presence of the negative polarity is quite often problematic for spiritual growth and the evolutionary journey to enlightenment. To understand the negative aspect of light, please see the discussions in the sub-sections of chapter two, "Into the Void", in volume two, *The Story of Light, Through Heaven's Gate*.

quencies can enter the body. If light is not compatible, the mind's multi-layered etheric magnetic field will set its polarity patterns to create a blockage. The problem is that the conscious mind has an element of fickleness. The will to work with the light is easily compromised by the energies of denial and ego. Denial and ego stem from a person's life conditioning. The person's world view is patterned after her vibration, but always limited by it in one way or another. On its own, the mind is a frequent impediment to the in-coming light of the heavens.

In the human body's connection with the heavens, and in the process of invoking the Light Body, light needs to move past the mind. The causal chakra works first to bring the frequencies that are immediately harmonious and compatible into the mind, and then to bring frequencies that need only minor adjustments. It treads a middle road where, on one side, it tempers, adjusts, and re-conditions the higher light frequencies entering the person's space to make them conform to the vibration of the person, her mind, and her body. On the other side, it trims away the limitations of the mind's world view by removing undesirable light frequencies, and further adds light that has no skewed preconditioning to both the mind's intuition and its intellect. The causal chakra stops the energies of the ego from dominating the mind, and prevents the mind's willful denials from blocking the arrival of new frequencies. The causal chakra has a 'prune-and-open-strategy' that ensures that at least some of the very high and subtle frequencies from the God-head find their way past the mind and into the body.

The recent emphasis on co-creation with the higher realms in this new age absolutely requires a greater flow of the light of the heavens into the human body and mind for empowerment. The high and subtle frequencies that reach to the Earth from the heavens cannot enter dead space. A person needs to be Oneness. She needs to have fulfilled the prerequisite of enlightenment before heavenly light can flow adequately to provide the insights and energies for a person to participate in the fulfillment of the divine will to co-create on Earth. With the person fully enlightened and empowered to work in co-creation with the heavens, consciousness moves at an unprecedented rate. Indeed, we are in a brand new age. The eleven-chakra system is the facilitator.

Clearing and Cleansing Crystals

Rocks, stones, and crystals of the mineral world are among the most stable and consistent vibrations on the planet. Why, on Earth, do they need cleansing? In truth, crystals do not need cleansing. The need for cleansing belongs to the light. Light needs cleansing. It also needs empowering.

When a crystal does its work of moving light frequencies, residual and polarized aspects of the light often remain behind. The crystal is burdened with light frequencies that get stuck within its structures and create a disharmonious energetic. The objective of cleansing a crystal is to remove the debris of unwanted light frequencies and to reestablish the crystal's balance.

Light is extremely subtle. It hardly acknowledges the density of the physical plane by its existence. Cleansing light is not like shoveling mud. The subtlety dictates that cleansing be gentle. A few different methods are used. They include the Sun, water, crystal bowl or stemware, and salt.

After using a crystal for a crystal layout or by wearing it for a day, it will need both cleansing and empowerment. The easiest method is to place the crystal in the Sun for an hour or so. The rejuvenating light of the Sun cleanses the crystal by displacing the light it holds with its own fresh light frequencies. Empowerment by the Sun method is automatic. Placing the crystal in water (exceptions to the use of water follow later in this section) and in the Sun is a second method that is quite effective and gentle. Tap water is appropriate. Well water, complete with its living ground water and complement of minerals is an added bonus. The water element can also help re-balance any emotionally charged energies that may have remained in the crystal.

Adding salt to the water for cleansing makes the cleanse even more effective. The imbalances of light that the crystal holds and that need cleansing are subtle polar charges attached to the residual light frequencies. Salt in solution separates into the Na^+ ion and the Cl^- ion. These two charged ions combine with the charged light frequencies to neutralized the polar imbalances in both polarities. If sea salt is used, the ions involved add sulfate (SO_4^{2-}), magnesium (Mg^{2+}), Calcium (Ca^{2+}), Potassium (K^+), Bicarbonate (HCO_3^-), Bromide (Br^-), Borate (BO_3^{3-}), and Strontium (Sr^{2+}). Each ion works with a slightly different range of frequencies, thus giving a more thorough neutralization of the crystal's complement of charged light frequencies. As previous emphasized light is subtle. Therefore, the number of ions needs to be minimal. As a rule of thumb, use only 6-12 grains of salt in a goblet or bowl—no more! Using a quarter teaspoon is the equivalent of winter road salt rusting a car.

Cleansing can also be accomplished by using a smudge of cedar, sage, and sweetgrass, or any combination of these. Good quality incense can also be used in a pinch. Similar to the ions in water, the smoke attaches to the polarized light in the crystal. From there, it carries the imbalance up and away into the dimensions of the heavens. Smudging, of all the methods, is the quickest. If doing crystal layouts for clients one after another, smudging is the most effective cleanse in the shortest time.

Not every crystal needs cleansing or empowering, and some have special circumstances. The crystal with the most special circumstance is Malachite. Because Malachite splits light into its yin and yang aspects, its structures at the molecular level are extremely refined and delicate. Care needs to be taken with Malachite. It needs cleansing after each use. Some stones may need a little cleansing, but more importantly, they need empowering on a regular basis. For Citrine, Rose Quartz, and Carnelian, use the Sun or Sun-water-salt method after use to both cleanse and empower.

The black stones, such as Hematite and Obsidian, are very powerful grounding stones. Because they bring light to the lowest vibrations, they displace negative energies with the light they bring. Black grounding stones usually have a full complement of light frequencies within, and therefore, offer no space for negative frequencies to reside. While not perfectly cleansed all the time, black grounding stones are rarely in need of cleansing.

Stones that do not need cleansing include the following:

- Turquoise, which only holds frequencies of truth,
- Kyanite, which moves light so fast that negativity cannot attach itself,
- Black Tourmaline, which renders negativity harmless,
- Azurite, which makes negativity disappear, and
- Selenite, which is dormant when not in use, or perfectly attuned to it user.

Some crystals do not do well in water. Their soft mineral structures might deteriorate if exposed to water outside of their natural environment. Ulexite may come as a solid mass, but can also take the form of very fine filaments. If Ulexite's filaments are placed in water, they are ravaged under the mere weight of the water they are exposed to. Selenite, while not needing cleansing in any event, is often too soft for exposure to water, even though Selenite is originally formed in an hydro-thermic environment. Pink Halite, or Halite in general, is a salt that will deteriorate with exposure to water. There are other crystals not mentioned herein that are damaged in one way or another by water and should not be submersed.

Most crystals do not have special circumstances and can be cleansed using any of the methods mentioned.

Crystal Quality

Top quality crystals work the best. Physical form in top shape works the best. Whole and healthy light frequencies work the best. Each crystal, form, and frequency has its own role to fulfill. Each performs its tasks best when in its prime state of vibration. Crystals, forms, and frequencies, however, are here on Earth and within the density of the physical plane. They are not always at the peak of their vibrations.

The form aspect of any manifest object arrives on Earth before the light that gives it empowerment. How much of the form, or what portion, can actually cross from the higher dimensions? In the crossing, how much of the form's vibration is damaged by the traumas of moving from the subtle heavens into physical density? Is the form's vibration mature enough to assimilate light within a physical environment? Form is not the only vibration that may not be in top condition. Crystals and light can also be in less than stellar shape, and therefore, not up to the task of contributing to the process of enlightenment and raising vibration.

Both form and light can be present on Earth in a damaged state due to physical density. They can also both be present only partially with a significant portion of their vibrations remaining in the heavens unavailable for their Earthly purpose. The same can be said about crystals. On Earth, crystals grow. Their vibrations acquire their form and light over time to develop into fully functioning, mature crystals. The question of their quality hinges on how much they have grown. Are they mature crystals? Can they work with the full complement of frequencies for which they were intended?

At times, a crystal may not be mature enough to do the job it came to do. As an example, Azurite is often sold before its time. A mature Azurite has well developed nodules, along with a deep cobalt blue colour. In contrast, the underdeveloped Azurite is a much paler blue with a grainy surface and no distinguishable nodules. It cannot possibly perform as does the mature Azurite. The pale variety of Azurite needs to have been left in its place in the Earth to mature. It is not worth purchasing.

The simple fact that a crystal can be identified as a bona fide variety does not mean that it can do what it was intended by creation to do. To expect a child of five years old to calculate algorithms using a scientific calculator is folly. So, too, is expecting an immature crystal to carry the light as it would have done had it been allowed to grow without plucking it before its time. The clear choice to not purchase crystals until they are fully developed is the answer. The consumer need not waste his money for an item that is not working properly. As well, without a market to sell to, numerous varieties will be left to mature as creation intended.

The important theme of this section is that crystals do not always come to us as top quality vibrations. They can arrive on Earth damaged, incomplete, and unable to function. They can also be perfectly formed but too immature to perform. The crystal enthusiast needs to realize that crystal quality is not always assured. At the same time, the qualities of light frequencies, along with the qualities of the physical forms into which they come, are not always assured either. Crystals, light frequencies, and physical forms do the best job that they possibly can. The best job, however, is dependent upon their quality.

PART TWO

CRYSTALS

Amazonite

Calming the Vision to See More

Scientific Properties: (Variety of Microline, Feldspar Group)
Crystallography: Triclinic
Chemical formula: $KAlSi_3O_8$
Mohs hardness: 6-6.5
Density: 2.54 - 2.57 g/cm^3
Colour: transparent, translucent, green, bluish green, white, grey, greyish yellow, yellowish, tan, salmon-pink,

Amazonite empowers the throat chakra with the most exquisite of light frequencies. It also adds luster to a person's communication by offering a host of additional, and delicate, frequencies. Each expression of divine light, coming through the throat chakra, brings with it the descriptive conceptual language of light. This language paints the land and sea scapes of the truth as the mind sees it.

As each moment of time and space unfolds into expressions of truth, the light frequencies shaping that truth cannot enhance the expression beyond the limitations of their own characteristics. A light frequency that has come to Earth very often leaves the highest aspects of its vibration in the heavens. The truth suffers for the missing parts. The expression of truth demonstrates the qualities of the applicable light frequencies as they are, and nothing more. When Amazonite is added to the expression, the truth glows exquisitely. Amazonite contributes to the frequencies of truth their original complement of characteristics, as found in the heavens. The light frequency that comes whole, and with its higher aspects intact, expands the scenery of the vision of the truth.

Amazonite works by reducing the physical plane's resistance to frequencies coming into the third dimension. The problem, arising from the difficulty of passing through the threshold between the third and higher dimensions, causes a reduction in the total amount of vibration of any single frequency that crosses over. Many of a frequency's higher aspects are trimmed from the frequency as it enters the third dimension, and therefore must remain in the heavens beyond the reach of the physical plane. Unfortunately, crossing into physical density removes the peaks and ridges of most light frequencies. The crossing eliminates that aspect of the frequency, which cannot cross, from participating in the expression of the truth.

Amazonite goes to work in the vicinity of the threshold between the third and higher dimensions. Its presence precedes the in-coming light frequencies, for the purpose of smoothing the way. Amazonite's vibration combines with both the frequencies at the point of the inter-dimensional threshold, and the frequencies of the throat chakra intended for expression. The combined frequency vibrates in harmony with both the upper and third dimensions, thus easing the in-coming light onto the physical plane with much less damage, missing parts, and distortion. The combined frequency also carries a greater range of each of the throat chakra's light frequencies into the chakra. It empowers the chakra with the frequencies' previously missing peaks and ridges and, therefore, the fullest possible range and intensity of the in-coming throat chakra frequencies.

By enhancing the light's ability to cross the threshold into the physical plane, the resulting expression of truth benefits from the completeness of the light available. The peaks and ridges of the light frequencies, which are then available to create expressions of the truth, permit a more vibrant and defined vision. The land and sea scapes are more vivid. The mind sees a more complete and expanded truth.

The frequencies of Amazonite are charged with magnetic polarity. They combine with the polarized frequencies of the throat chakra thus offsetting and strengthening the polarity of the chakra. The intensified polarity of the chakra's matrix creates a more powerful attraction for the light coming to the chakra. Both a more complete frequency and a greater range of frequencies then find their way onto the Earth to empower the throat chakra's expression of the truth. Amazonite lights up the vision of the truth.

Amethyst

Calling Card of the Soul

Scientific Properties: (Variety of Quartz)

Amethyst's light frequencies resonate in the third eye chakra at the uppermost levels of the chakra's vibration. Its calming crystalline ray of purple love stills the mind's turbulent, random, and often scattered patterns of thought into a continuous thread. Gradually, the stone helps the mind settle into a place of no-thought.

Normally, the human mind is very active. It shoots from one subject to another and another, and within each subject, it shoots from one thought to another and another. Amethyst calms the monotony, the litany of thoughts, slowing them to nothingness, then makes space in the mind's eye for the essence of love.

Amethyst takes the random jumble of turbulent thoughts within the mind and reorders them. First, it reduces the focus of thinking to a single subject. The stone prevents the mind from arbitrarily shifting from thought to thought and subject to subject. Secondly, it slows the transition between thoughts. By slowing the activity of the mind, one thought leads gently into another similar thought, rather than jumping to an unconnected thought. Amethyst causes each individual thought to follow a linear pattern. A thought begins and ends, without leaving the subject at hand. After the thought comes to completion, the next thought begins and ends.

In the third step, Amethyst loosens the connection between thoughts. Thoughts are not necessarily joined to each other. Thoughts begin and end, but they do not begin again immediately upon the completion of the previous thought. A gap between thoughts occurs. The gap is important. It is a place of no-thought. It is blank, and bestows calm and peace upon the mind. Within the gap is the tranquillity needed to welcome the light frequencies of the soul. The gap is serenity.

Light frequencies coming from the soul are refined, high, and subtle. There is no way that a mind full of turbulence could possibly accommodate the soul's subtle in-coming light. Serenity within the mind is crucial for the transfer of light. Serenity creates the space that a person needs to be at one and in harmony with her soul and the all-encompassing love of the lighted universe that the soul brings.

Amethyst is the invitation to the light of loving essence. It is the "calling card" of the soul.

When light frequencies pass through a crystalline structure, they are altered to receive the crystal's grace. Each frequency that passes through the crystalline structure of clear white quartz receives the light offered by the quartz. Clear white quartz is made up of the total of all light frequencies. Therefore, the core of a light frequency[1] is exposed to all frequencies, from which it builds its own characteristic vibration.

Amethyst is a quartz crystal. It carries clear white quartz along with the purple hues of its own specialization. The clear white quartz brings all light frequencies. The purple hues resonate with the soul. When the light of two or more frequencies are carried by the same crystal, each frequency can pass into the physical forms with which either frequency resonates.

In the case of a quartz piece with Amethyst vibrations, the Amethyst range of purple light frequencies is the means to open the door to the third eye chakra for the totality of frequencies carried by the clear white quartz portion of the stone. Clear white quartz

---

1 The formation of aggregate light frequencies starts with the core Godhead frequency common to all light. As it travels through the universe, including dimensions other than our third dimension, it picks up the presence and influence of many other frequencies. The characteristics of a given light frequency reflect the influences it carries. For the full discussion on the creation of light frequencies, please see, *The Story of Light, Through Heaven's Gate*, chapter four, "Godhead Light", and especially section 4.2, "Core Frequency Enhancement".

possesses the grace to combine with any number of specific frequencies. Frequencies piggyback upon other frequencies. White quartz helps direct the available light flowing through the chakra distribution system. A chakra can attract its own light from the flow. The third eye benefits from the frequencies of the soul coming through the Amethyst and from the full spectrum of the white light coming through the white quartz.

Amethyst uses its purple light ray, which resonates with the third eye, to pull white light, which has piggybacked onto the purple ray, into the third eye. The white light made available through the Amethyst vibration also flows to any other portion of the third eye's essence that can draw light to itself. The vast array of additional available frequencies coming from the clear white quartz, however, does not necessarily resonate intimately with the physical form involved. Each body part or chakra needs its own unique and specialized frequencies. However, there is no need to work explicitly with a specialized range of a body's or chakra's frequencies. The full range of white light includes all frequencies, and therefore, the specific frequency attracted by a particular chakra, evolved or otherwise, is naturally available within the flow. Therefore, the physical form is exposed to all the light it needs for assimilation into Oneness.

Because the physical form is lighted to some degree, it is Oneness to the same degree. To that Oneness, the light of any other frequency is welcome. When the evolution of the Oneness of a physical form or chakra is only just beginning, there is a limited range of frequencies capable of uniting with it. If more sophisticated frequencies, such as Amethyst, are involved in the evolutionary process, the form is already evolved enough to be open to receive high and subtle light.

As the clear white quartz inherent to Amethyst implies, the presence of all light frequencies are part of the process. Their availability facilitates the assimilation of significantly more light. Not only is there a greater number of frequencies immediately available, the order in which they are presented to the physical body or chakra follows in sequence. Frequencies are assimilated in ascending order, with the lower frequency vibrations assimilated first. The evolutionary progress of the form, then, proceeds sequentially according to the order in which light is assimilated from the flow of the white light passing through. While assimilation takes place in an orderly fashion, there is no gap in time. In rapid succession, the light required for form's empowerment enters the physical body or chakra, frequency-by-frequency. The form evolves, as does its ability to accept light. Its resistance to the free-flow of light frequencies diminishes, and the form increasingly strengthens its place as Oneness.

Amethyst ensures that the doorway to the third eye stays open while the light for empowerment flows through. Because of the serenity it brings to still the mind, the flow of in-coming light includes the high and subtle light frequencies of the soul.

Angelite

Bringer of the Higher Truth

Scientific Properties: (Variety of Anhydrite)

The crystal Angelite brings a vibration of grace to those whose Earthly presence has evolved sufficiently to possess an adequate amount of light to meet the requirements of the ascension in this holy time period. Those who acquire Angelite and its vibration are marked for release from their Earthly bonds. They are set to move through all the doorways of divinity, and to return home to the higher realms. The presence of Angelite in one's life heralds the ascension.

Angelite is the truth stone of the angels. While turquoise is the traditional truth stone during a person's stay on Earth, Angelite reveals a person's truth as she merges with her higher-self and the higher dimensions. It is a truth stone, which brings higher frequencies.

The throat chakra expresses a person's truth both internally and externally. The person's inner truth, her I AM presence, is pervasive within the throat chakra. Throughout the ages, the higher-self presented its vibration, and hence its truth, through its connection to the throat chakra, and through the light it delivered. The heart then acted upon the physical body, and the throat in particular, to open them through its love. With love, the truth from the throat chakra moved into the opened essence of the body beyond the throat, giving expression in the external world.

A person's Earthly truth is different than her higher truth. Earthly truth is determined by light frequencies and vibrations that are found exclusively on the physical plane. Every person is constantly living her Earthly truth, whether or not that truth is good or bad, and whether or not that person is connected to spiritual practices. In contrast, a person's higher truth requires the vibrations of the heavens, as well as, those of the Earth. Higher truths come from higher frequencies.

To bring the higher truth from the higher-self down to Earth to join with the physical self, the throat chakra must resonate with light frequencies from the higher dimensions. However, the throat chakra does not normally possess the necessary vibration required to work with the extremely subtle light frequencies from beyond the Earth. To overcome this problem, the vibration of the throat chakra is helped along by the empowering light of Angelite.

Angelite is not limited to working with the body's third dimensional essence, as is Turquoise. However, a person's truth on the physical plane must be established before Angelite can be useful. Angelite re-works the vibration of the throat chakra to assimilate the higher dimensional aspects of the light frequencies of truth[1]. This stone helps the throat chakra to become compatible with its higher truth. In this way, the frequencies of a person's higher truth gently merge with the frequencies of the person's Earthly truth. The person then evolves into her higher truth incrementally.

Angelite does not attract any additional frequencies. Rather, it reconditions the empowered throat chakra to resonate with the higher dimensional aspects of the light frequencies already present within the throat. Angelite exposes the consciousness to light that reflects an expanded and higher truth. The addition of Angelite opens the door for the throat chakra to receive the higher dimensional aspects of the same frequencies.

The throat chakra, as does every chakra and the general bodily form, incorporates a matrix of light receptors. As a person grows in her spirituality, the receptors begin to open, starting with the receptors of lower vibration. Normally, each receptor works exclusively with light frequencies that are already on the physical plane.

---

1   The word 'aspects' is used appropriately in this passage. While the thought may surface that 'higher dimensional light frequencies' could have been used instead of 'aspects', the word, aspects, implies that the light is not complete. To be clear, a portion of the light frequency from the higher realms—an aspect—is involved, but not the full frequency.

Hence, the truth that the throat chakra expresses reflects only the truth of the physical plane. A person is a carpenter, a secretary, or computer programer. In contrast, the effect of the Angelite is to recondition the individual light receptors at the molecular level to work with the higher and multi-dimensional aspects of the same frequency with which it normally resonates. The receptor then reaches up into the higher dimensions to access that portion of the frequency that carries the person's higher truth. The higher dimensional aspects of the light frequencies bring the higher dimensional version of the person's truth onto the Earth plane for expression.

To wear Angelite, especially close to the throat chakra means that a person acquires the frequencies of her truth in an ever expanding way from the vast and enlightened universe. The person gains a sense of the omnipresence of her true being, and expresses that understanding as well. She sees herself as the light-worker and the angelic emissary of the original source of light—the Godhead. She sees the presence and purpose of her being in the third dimension as the end result of this single moment's service to the light in the context of all that is. In effect, she becomes consciously aware of the light that constitutes her truth, as well as, her place as the representative of the larger universe. She understands the contract she has with her soul that brought her here, and what her role and purpose might be, were she to choose to fulfill that role and purpose.

Anhydrite

Herald for the Angelic Ones

Scientific Properties:
> Crystallography: Orthorhombic
> Chemical formula: $CaSO_4$
> Mohs hardness: 3-3.5
> Density: 2.98 g/cm^3
> Colour: colourless, bluish, blue-grey, violet, burgundy-red, white, rose-pink, brownish, reddish, grey, dark grey.

Anhydrite begins in the depths of the ocean where numerous other exquisitely sensuous vibrations are found. Through its pulsing love energy, Anhydrite facilitates the conscious rapport between persons on Earth and spirit beings from far beyond our local solar system. It works to open the person's mind to the presence of inter-dimensional beings of light that intend to serve as spirit guides.

Anhydrite's design has two aspects that contribute to the conscious rapport. Anhydrite, of concern to the commercial mineral industry, consists only of the white, pale blue, or light grey striated crystalline mass. Anhydrite, of concern to the spiritual seeker, tends to be only of the pale blue variety of the striated crystalline mass, but also has encrustations of clear quartz on the shaft sides.

During this recent epoch of new age enlightenment, the Earth's etheric magnetic field is open to the frequencies of light that resonate with the highest vibrations of the conscious body. These are the frequencies picked up by the blue striations of Anhydrite, and which work with the mind. The higher ranges of the pale blue light frequencies of consciousness flow at light-speed along Anhydrite's striated mass. The vibrations of divine white light collect within the encrusted crystals on the stone's shaft sides.

The awakened mind has the power within to sense any variation in the frequencies of light that come into the conscious body. For the mind to be awake in this way requires, first, an etheric magnetic field that is capable of permitting the entry of such higher vibrations of light, and second, an awareness within the person's mind that has adequate sensitivity to the subtle changes among the light frequencies within the conscious body. If a person's vibration can meet these prerequisites, Anhydrite brings the light frequencies that awaken the person to the comings and goings of interdimensional light beings and spirit guides, whenever they present themselves in the vicinity of the person using the stone.

The aware person is intuitively cognizant of the higher ranges of consciousness light frequencies, and is thereby sensitive to any frequencies or vibrations coming from spirit guides. The presence of a spirit guide within a person's auric field makes an impression. Both the impression of the guide's light frequency footprint, and the amount of light that it brings are significant, and happen all at once. The impression is similar to the presence of another person, but without the visual or auditory feedback. The arrival of a spirit guide causes a displacement of the person's light frequencies of consciousness with the guide's own, very much higher, light frequencies. Displacement is equivalent to a low-level cosmic ripple in consciousness.

Intuitive awareness of the presence of spirit guides and their light frequencies is the first part of Anhydrite's contribution to the user of the stone. The second part involves the clear quartz encrustations. Even if the aware individual is capable of sensing the presence of spirit guides and their light, will the individual's third eye also be capable of making sense of why the spirit guide has come, or what its message might be?

The third eye on the physical plane is highly unlikely to be developed sufficiently to take light frequencies, fresh from much higher dimensions, and fit them into third dimensional frames of reference for the mind's intellect. Fifth dimensional wisdom does not fit into third dimensional concepts, symbols, or understanding. The human mind cannot be expected to grasp the meaning of messages from inter-dimensional spirit guides without some adjustment to the physical plane. Because the human mind, consisting of the intuition and the intellect, cannot make the adjustment into higher dimensions, the adjustment is made to the frequencies of light after they arrive on the physical plane.

The higher dimensional light vibration that speeds through the striations of Anhydrite must step down to an acceptable physical vibration. It needs to be translated into a third dimensional format. Translation is the job of the clear quartz crystalline encrustation. It is the decoder. It provides the means by which the light frequencies of spirit guides project their message, meaning, identity, guidance, or communication into third dimensional concepts, ideas, and symbols. Once the light is reconditioned and translated within Anhydrite's encrustations, the intuition and intellect come into the process.

Having the Anhydrite crystal in near proximity at the time that a spirit guide is present is ideal, but not always possible or necessary. The pale blue light frequencies of the stone function to open and empower the intuitive side of the third eye with the light emitted from the spirit guides. Once empowered, the third eye chakra is better equipped for communion with spirit guides, whenever they present themselves. Even without having Anhydrite at-hand, the empowered intuition is aware of ripples in consciousness made by arriving spirit guides. Anhydrite's empowerment of the mind lasts for between 2-3 days and 1-2 months, depending on the vibration of the etheric magnetic field and turbulence in the mind. When a person consistently uses Anhydrite, permanent empowerment takes root.

Anhydrite is a stone of the consciousness, and is therefore best suited to the third eye. However, placing it elsewhere does not lead to any decrease in its potency.

Apatite

Earth's Chakra Healer

Scientific Properites:
(Synonym of: Chlorapatite, Fluorapatite, Hydroxylapatite)

Apatite's peculiar origin is not among the heavenly vibrations coming to the Earth, nor is it one of the Earth's original indigenous stones. Apatite is a creation of the Earth itself. That is, the light of Earth's Oneness has the ability to create[1]. The will of the soul of Earth created the vibration that became Apatite. Apatite, then, is among a select group of stones created by the planet and offered to the physical plane for use on this and any other third dimensional world. Consequently, Apatite works exceptionally well in the third dimension.

Apatite's vibration carries Earthly translucence with a most happy shade of deep green, and offers healing in the classical sense. Place it anywhere on the body and it will accelerate the local mass, which then opens to assimilate the light that is immediately available much more readily. However, beyond its classical healing properties, Apatite diverges most uniquely from other healing crystals.

Apatite delivers a healing vibration specifically to the third dimensional subtle body that is designed to attract and hold subtle light frequencies—the spiritual body. The spiritual body of a person essentially includes the chakras, along with the network of pas-

---

1   Oneness is the presence of God, when God extends outward into creation. It has the power of God to create. Oneness is discussed in various places in volumes one and two of *The Story of Light*. Most notably, it is introduced in volume one, Chapter 1, section 1.2, entitled: "Light + Form = Oneness, and warrants its own chapter in volume two, entitled: "Oneness Light" (Chapter 7).

sageways that connects the chakras (ida, pingala, sushumna). In juxtaposition, the spiritual body of the planet is vested into the land masses that are capable of attracting and holding light. These places are the Earth's light stations, including, for example, Mount Shasta, Banff, Glastonbury, and Sedona. Once the body's mass vibrates at a frequency rate that is fast enough, and if the light available is high enough, light, influenced by Apatite, enters the spiritual body in higher quality and greater quantity, .

The density of the third dimension creates a host of problems that block or retard the assimilation of light into physical forms, and especially into the subtle spiritual bodies. Distortions in the chakra power centres are of particular concern to humanity. Distortions imply imbalances, warps, and slow vibration, and prevent the chakras from properly aligning with the higher self and, thereby, its Light Body. The difficulties of dense vibration can prevent the subtle spiritual bodies from fulfilling their potentials for assimilating light. Apatite's healing works specifically to accelerate the spiritual body, and works especially with the chakras.

The healing offered by Apatite accelerates the mass within each chakra power centre upon which it is placed. It works to bring into the chakra divine light frequencies, which are very high and subtle, and which balance the areas of the chakra having slow vibration with the areas having fast vibration. The balance of vibration evens out the continuity of the chakra's passageways, thereby bringing stability and evenness to the flow of light. The pressure caused by the acceleration of the mass, and the greater flow of more and higher light frequencies, results in the removal of the chakra's distortions. Thereafter, the chakras can accept their normal range of frequencies, and can function as they were intended.

Apatite receives its energy from the light frequencies of its own green vibration, as created by the Earth, and as they become available within the aura. A person's emotional perception of her vibration as being "happy" indicates that Apatite works with the highest frequency ranges. This further indicates that it works in close proximity with the emotional bodies, thus triggering an emotionally driven affinity to the stone. The desire to acquire Apatite tends to be driven by the emotions: "I just got to have it!".

Apophyllite

Balancing Earth's Elemental Energies

Scientific Properties:
Crystallography: Tetragonal
Chemical formula: $KCa_4(Si_8O_{20})(F,OH)-8H_2O$
Mohs hardness: 4.5-5
Density: 2.33 - 2.37 g/cm^3
Colour: transparent, translucent, Colourless, pale green, aquamarine, white, pink, yellow

Apophyllite's crystalline shape is unique and important to the way it works. A properly formed, mature piece has four shaft sides with a blunted, flat terminus. Each of the four corners of the terminus and its two adjacent shaft sides share a triangle structure. Because of the triangles, a properly formed terminus is eight-sided.

Apophyllite's four shaft sides each represent one of the base elements: Earth, Wind, Fire, and Water. The vibrations of each of the elements work together in harmony to bring in the higher Apophyllite frequencies, which are then offered to those fortunate individuals who are attuned to its most joyous loving vibration.

Astrological Influences

Apophyllite's vibration is continuously attuned to the energies of the soul, as those energies flow from the heavens and down through the upper chakras. The light frequencies that enter Apophyllite are arranged according to the base elements of Earth, Wind, Fire, and Water. The vibrational influence of the stone follows the influence of the elements according to the stone's user. That is, the energies of persons on Earth are dominated by one or other of the base elements, as noted in their personal astrological natal charts. The strength and intensity of the light flowing from the soul reflects the dominant element. For example, astrological influences for a person who has four planets in Scorpio will have heavy emphasis on the Water element. The person therefore has a stronger attraction for light frequencies, including soul frequencies, that harmonize with the Water element. Conversely, if the same person has no planets in any of the Fire signs, such as Leo or Aries, her attraction for frequencies having emphasis on the Fire element is minimal.

A person's astrological influences are derived at the exact moment that the light of the soul passes into the physical body of the birthing foetus. The soul's light is imprinted with all of the influences of the heavenly bodies and planets according to their alignments, positions, and gravitational push or pull, as exerted in that single instance of time. The person is then bound to live according to her specific astrological imprint.

An individual's astrological imprint is programmed even before the soul sends its light to Earth. The planets that contribute their characteristics impose their light frequencies onto the frequencies of the soul. Through the soul, the arrangement of the planets influences the person's vibration, which is directly reflected in the blueprint of her etheric body. The planets encode the person's etheric magnetic field[1]. The etherics harmonize best with the base elements that dominate the influencing planets. Because the filters of the etheric body are patterned to accept compatible frequencies of light, and reject incompatible frequencies, planetary influences indirectly determine the light frequencies that a person

1 Understanding Apophyllite, as well as understanding the workings of numerous other crystals, leans heavily on the foundation of knowledge about the etheric magnetic field, or etheric body. The etheric magnetic field is so very important to so many of the insights about the human experience that it was given its own chapter as close to the beginning of the first volume, *The Story of Light, Path to Enlightenment*, as was possible. Please see Chapter 2 of the first volume entitled: "The Etheric Body".

has available to her. Consequently, the planets greatly affect the overall directions of an individual's life path, hence the validity of astrological influences.

The ease, with which in-coming divine light is transmitted through a person's etheric magnetic field, depends upon the harmony it has with the etheric body. Apophyllite's role is to aid harmonization. Light flows from Apophyllite attuned to all four of Earth's base elements. The etheric magnetic field responds best to the light frequencies that reflect the person's own characteristic mix of Earth elements. That is, divine light is in greatest harmony when it carries the Earth elements in proportions that are similar to the individual's own base elements. If, for example, the person's strong elements are Wind and Water, the portion of the divine light that is Wind and Water has the greatest harmony. As in-coming light is subject to rejection by the etherics, and as the etherics stabilize an individual's characteristic range of light frequencies, the elemental influences that are at variance with the etheric body are not likely to penetrate the etheric filter. Without Apophyllite, the person's natural imbalance of elemental energies skews the flow of the in-coming divine light, creating disharmony. The person will have too much Wind and Water elemental energy and not enough Fire and Earth.

Apophyllite's Design

The importance of the shape of Apophyllite relates to the flow of light through it. As mentioned, each of the four shaft sides corresponds to one of the four elemental energies, Earth, Wind, Fire, and Water. A portion of the energies travelling up the shaft sides enters the terminus directly. The remainder encounters one of the triangles located at the corners of Apophyllite's terminus. The triangle deflects a portion of the flow of light frequencies as they move up the shaft side.

Each triangle receives light frequencies from each of the two adjacent shaft sides. Within the triangle, the base element of one shaft side mixes with the base element of the adjacent shaft side. The blend then moves from the triangle onto the terminus. The light that arrives on the terminus includes, therefore, the unmixed elemental energies coming directly from their respective shaft sides, and the mixed energies of two base elements coming from each triangle. On the terminus itself, both the premixed and unmixed frequencies combine into a single aggregate energy. At that point, some of the mixed light becomes available to the person using the stone.

Whenever one elemental energy flow is piggy-backed with an energy flow attuned to another elemental energy, both energies are able to pass through the etherics. Normally, the etheric magnetic field blocks the elemental energy that is out of harmony with the user's astrological designation, and allows the elemental energy in harmony to pass through. By combining elemental energies, Apophyllite creates an aggregate frequency, which is in harmony. It helps a greater portion of the divine light to pass through the etheric magnetic field, and to become available to the person using the stone.

Apophyllite's blunted terminus is a place of pause. The unified light that gathers together on the flat terminus takes on the same form as the light that was originally created in the heavens. Accordingly, it incorporates each element within its mix. Apophyllite, therefore, corrects the person's inherent and natural imbalance. Energies then move through the etheric magnetic field courtesy of their harmony with all of the elemental energies, as opposed to the individual's dominant base element(s).

Correcting the Imbalance

How does Apophyllite correct the imbalance?

The light arriving on the terminus excludes frequencies that are disharmonious with the etheric magnetic field of the person using the stone. Therefore, at the outset, one or more of the base elements may be completely missing—imbalance assured.

On its terminus, Apophyllite first causes the energies present to mix into a unified energy or an aggregate frequency. After that, it divides the aggregate frequency into four separate energies of equal proportion, and assigns one of the four base elements to each. Regardless of the strength or weakness of the elemental energies that arrive on the terminus, each elemental energy leaves the terminus with the same portion and strength of energy as each of the other elements. Upon leaving, Fire equals Water equals Wind equals Earth, even if the only energy to arrive at the terminus was Wind alone.

Apophyllite balances the dominant elements with the weak elements. For example, if an individual is dominated by astrological Fire signs, the stone redistributes the person's total energy into equal and balanced portions among the remaining elements of Water, Earth, and Wind. Apophyllite reconditions the imbalanced elemental energy belonging to the person and reflects equal proportions outward. Although the etheric field initially permits passage of only the harmonious elemental energies, which then dominate the person's vibration, the new balance created by Apophyllite reconfigures the etheric field to allow all four elemental energies to pass unencumbered. The individual, who has perhaps lived life's events through one dominant elemental energy, then experiences her future through an equal influence of each of the base elements.

The great advantage in Apophyllite's balancing of the elemental energies is that an individual is centred in the current reality. Normally, a person is limited to a world-view dictated by their imbalances. She is off-balance. For example, the challenging influences of the Fire sign that create great drive and free spirit are incompatible with the materialism and need for stability that absorbs a person having the strong influences of the Earth element. Fire and Earth energies do not harmonize without strain. However, when a person's four elemental energies are equal, she is closer in vibration to other persons, even if they are influenced by a single elemental energy.

A person, who has had their elemental energies brought into balance by Apophyllite, assumes a central position. The central position is equidistant to each of the other elemental influences, and therefore, provides either the least disharmony, or greatest overall harmony with other persons. The harmony created is imprecise because there is still some distance between the balanced person's centered position and the person whose position is skewed by elemental dominance. Nonetheless, the range or numbers of persons, with which the centered individual shares a common harmony, increases. Further, the central position of the balanced individual embraces each of the other four elemental influences simultaneously, thus allowing the centred individual to have elemental energies in common. The vibration of her balanced and centred elemental energy puts her within range for easier communication with others.

The grace of Apophyllite goes further. The unified and balanced elemental energies can be used by Apophyllite's user through the will. Balanced energy can be wilfully shifted towards the skewed elemental influences of another person. For example, a balanced person can take the viewpoint of a person dominated by the Earth element at will, and thereby, create harmony with that person through the shift of her energies towards the world-view promoted by the Earth element. The shift is a matter of wilfully moving energy from the balanced central position, where all elements are equally disposed, towards the elemental influence in question, Earth in this example. The centred person moves towards the Earth influences, and thereby empathizes with the other person's need, for example, to have the security of a steady income.

In further understanding the nature of Apophyllite, the elemental energies involved come from the planets of our own solar system. Each planetary influence exerts its own specific gravitational force. It provides a basis of attraction for light frequencies, which determine the way the user's lessons occur in life. If an individual is overly constrained by skewed planetary influences, Apophyllite steps in to reconfigure the energies as they arrive within the aura. Accordingly, the magnetic forces that create elemental imbalances are gathered together in the stone, mixed, and then redistributed in equal portions. Apophyllite is continuously attuned to the energies of the soul, and in turn, with the etheric magnetic fields that the solar system itself influences. By gathering and balancing the energies, it removes, or at least minimizes, the dominant influence of the planets and the sun. Apophyllite neutralizes the magnetic astrological distortions of the solar system.

Apophyllite's vibration does not attract light frequencies that are different. Rather, Apophyllite addresses the etheric distortion, which is created at the solar system level, and which causes an imbalance through its polarization of elemental energy. Each of the elemental energies is specific to a particular planetary vibration, all of which are part of the universal Oneness. All vibration is the light and love of universal being. It is the manifest form of the divine formless, and the Shakti of Lord Shiva in the divine form of the light. As a part of the whole, each energy is limited to the influence of its own planetary configuration. If added all together, elemental and planetary influences available on Earth are in balanced harmony. At the level of the aura, these energies are accepted by the Apophyllite in the form in which they come, then united and redistributed more evenly to create balance for the individual using the stone.

Apophyllite's physical configuration has a further feature that needs mention. A quality piece of Apophyllite possesses a blunt terminus at both ends of its four sided shaft. It is double terminated. The energies enter the stone in one terminus and are then passed through their respective side of the shaft, after which they enter the other terminus, where balance is achieved. Light arrives at both terminations, flows in both directions along its respective element's side of the shaft, according to its brand of elemental energy. The light is then balanced on the opposite terminus from which it arrived. Balanced elemental energies flowing in one direction, and skewed elemental energies flowing in the other direction, are mutually exclusive because they are different vibratory frequencies. Each energy flows without interference from energy flowing in the opposite direction. Further, the energies accumulate on each terminus. As energy builds up, the polar charge of person's etheric body takes over to move the available balanced light. It travels through the chakras without emphasis of one or other of the base elements.

Benefit and Impermanence

Apophyllite's encoding of a person's etheric magnetic field lasts for a period of time, after which they become skewed towards whichever elemental influence the person is most exposed. As such, the person might be a Fire oriented person at birth, then balanced with Apophyllite, and then skewed to whichever element they are exposed to next. The tendency towards acquiring the arbitrary influences of the next element of exposure will become a permanent situation, unless further use of Apophyllite is undertaken. Returning to the original configuration of being a Fire oriented person is not possible. To remove one astrological influence is to create a different influence, which is balanced at first. Later and progressively, the influence is based on the exposure to which an individual is subjected. As the new influence ossifies, an alternate astrological influence on a more or less permanent basis is the result.

The change Apophyllite brings to an individual arrives from the lighted universe for the purpose of providing lessons from a different viewpoint. Ideally, the balance of elemental energies needs to be repeated periodically when the stone's user becomes aware of increasing disharmony or limited access with one's contemporaries. By using Apophyllite in one or more crystal layouts, balance is restored and any new influence is neutralized. Ultimately, the significance of a balanced etheric body is that one is less constrained by the limited energies that are created through dominating planetary influences. For some individuals, the very difficult aspects of their astrological charts are neutralized, and they are able to flow through life without the weighty challenges that imbalance creates.

The use of Apophyllite must be done with due respect because the whole approach to life will change. The suggestion is made that its use be strictly guided by the user's intuition or Angelic guides. Once the etheric patterns have been altered by Apophyllite, its periodic use becomes necessary.

In summary, divine source light energy that comes through the solar system is skewed towards influences generated through planetary gravitational forces, which encode the etherics to accept only the dominant elemental energy—Earth, Wind, Fire, and Water. Apophyllite takes the in-coming light energy and redistributes it equally among the four elements thus neutralizing any single planetary emphasis. It creates balance of the four base elemental energies within the individual. Further, a balanced and centered individual may wilfully utilize the light energy of one or other elements to blend their essence with a person who is still under the influences of her inherent, natural, and imbalanced astrological makeup. By creating balance, a person overcomes the problems of disharmony that normally limit their relationships to a fixed viewpoint of the world. Indeed, people become accessible when astrological influences are removed.

Aquamarine

Fast Light to Clear the Throat

Scientific Properties: (a variety of Beryl)
    Crystallography: Hexagonal
    Chemical formula: $Be_3Al_2(Si_6O_{18})$
    Mohs hardness: 7.5-8
    Density: 2.63 - 2.92 g/cm^3
    Colour: vitreous, sub-vitreous, green, blue

Aquamarine resonates exquisitely with the throat chakra. Its vibration works to clear and cleanse the undesirable aspects of a person's will, along with her inability to be expressive. Cleansing refers less to the will to speak verbally, than it does to a cleansing of etheric and auric blockages. Aquamarine helps the throat chakra to overcome the problems that prevent balanced expression.

The will to express oneself to others can be blocked by the traumas a person suffers in life. Trauma takes many forms and arises from many sources. Being told that one is wrong or being suppressed by controlling persons are examples. Traumas can originate with self or others. The ego may also feed into the illusions that block expression. The blocked ability to communicate increases the separation between self and others. These problematic aspects of life on Earth that lead to isolation eventually permeate the desire and will and generate emotional feelings that further inhibit the expression of self to others. Such blockages result in the accumulation of negative energies within the throat chakra centre. Symptoms manifest as muteness, stuttering, or the inability to form words adequately. Symptoms that are anchored in the physical gather strength and have a direct affect on a person's ability to communicate.

Aquamarine does not clear the passageways of the throat chakra to cleanse accumulated negativity. Rather, it offers a soft and gentle vibration that soothes and smooths the emotional traumas, which are the root cause of this category of blockages. Emotional trauma forces the etheric magnetic field to concentrate its energies to repel offending frequencies in an effort to protect the throat chakra. When the etherics concentrate, a blockage results. The tightening of the etheric magnetic field restricts the entry of unwanted frequencies. Unfortunately, many other desirable frequencies are also blocked. Consequently, the empowerment of the chakras stagnates.

To clear the blockage, Aquamarine offers a compensating vibration that stems from compassion. The range of frequencies related to compassion include warmth, trust, kindness, empathy, and many others that raise the person's vibration[1]. The addition of a healthy, positive set of light frequencies within the essence of the throat chakra begins the healing process. Aquamarine's light frequencies help the throat chakra's etheric magnetic field to return to normal by raising the vibration of the throat and by shifting the etherics away from its concentrated defensive posture.

The vibration rate of a throat chakra blockage fully encompasses the lower frequency ranges of the etheric field, and some of the higher ranges as well. Problems are more common with lower frequencies than with higher. Therefore, the reinforced and concentrated etherics are slightly more open to incoming light in the higher ranges.

Aquamarine provides a soothing, calming light having a high and subtle vibration, which is also indigenous to the throat chakra. The stone's frequencies are most exquisite and too high and fast to be resisted by the low vibration of the etheric blockage. They pass into the throat chakra virtually unimpeded by entering through the infinitely fine spaces present in the throat's etheric field. Once

---

1   The foundation discussion on compassion and its relationship to the heart and love can be found in volume one, *The Story of Light, Path to Enlightenment*, section 4.5, "Heart Chakra: Love and Compassion".

inside the throat chakra, Aquamarine's light frequencies combine with the throat's form to become Oneness. Empowerment then begins. The Oneness within the throat creates its own empowerment frequencies, thus lifting its own vibration above the density of the blockage.

The etherics, which reflect the throat's higher vibration, come into balance as a consequence of the empowering light, both internal and external. The fortified and concentrated state of the etherics softens. Etheric concentration dissipates at a progressively faster rate as the quantity of light, entering the throat and created within the throat, increases. Once the etherics have returned to a balanced state, light, normally accepted by the chakra, is attracted rather than being repelled by the etherics.

Early in the process of rebalancing the emotional body of the throat chakra, the user of Aquamarine expresses spontaneous and rather emotionally charged feelings whenever suppressed emotions are released. With continued use of the stone, the user becomes balanced in the way she expresses herself, and the emotional charge of suppressed expression wanes. Once the etheric magnet field comes into balance, further empowerment of the chakra becomes possible. The throat's empowerment continues, not only through the use of Aquamarine, but also through light from external sources. External sources may include light coming from other throat chakra crystals, light from a person's immediate surroundings, or light from the oxygen of the breath.

If a person is in the early stages of their spiritual practice and is a young soul, the quality of light passing through her etherics might be inadequate to make any significant difference to the empowerment of the chakra. The implication is that, while Aquamarine will do its job, the empowerment of the chakra is consistent with the person's current state of vibration according to her spiritual growth.

Atlantisite

A Gentle Step Towards Spirituality

Scientific Properites: (variety of Serpentine, Stichtite)

Atlantisite offers a cheery green vibration of the common garden variety. The variety of green here allows the mind to open without pushing any limits. As a healing stone in the classic sense, Atlantisite accelerates the vibration of the body's form wherever it is placed. What is meant by not pushing the limits is that the stone works within the light frequency ranges of the user's vibration. Its acceleration of the body is therefore subdued.

Atlantisite's green crystalline vibration works its healing magic by gently softening the areas of a person's body mass that are not fully balanced or have distortions in the flow of its light energy. Atlantisite may be called the "naturalizer" because it takes the body's healing process only as far as the body's current state of vibration. It does not alter the body's vibration. It is not a stone for opening or reconditioning the body, or for taking the spiritual path forward.

Once the person's body has achieved a natural, balanced state at the level of its current vibration, the person using Atlantisite can awaken to the light and energy that exists in the immediate vicinity and in the now moment, without pushing the body to higher vibration levels, or causing expansion of form-essence. This is not an evolutionary step, but rather, the opportunity to be all you can be now. Atlantisite's healing casts away the body's imbalances and smoothes the distortions. Light energy flows within the user's body exactly as it should for right now.

The great energy healing work of Atlantisite answers the need to bring a person's vibration into its natural state without the disturbing turbulence of an evolutionary push forward. It is a stone for individuals, who are dabbling with spirituality, and therefore, still carry significant vibrational issues and imbalances, such as the need for clearing karma and learning basic life lessons. By bringing their vibrations into a natural state, the influx of light frequencies received does not go beyond the range that is consistent with the will, and does not go beyond personal choices. Free will is thereby preserved. The spiritual path of the person using Atlantisite proceeds at the person's own pace. Such persons are those whose spiritual evolution is not yet consciously awakened and whose kundalini (base chakra) has not yet opened. If a person is already a spiritual seeker that has willfully stepped onto the spiritual path, that person is beyond the need for the healing that Atlantisite offers. Ideally, a piece of Atlantisite, which has been shaped to have an aesthetic presentation, makes a wonderful gift for someone who is open minded, but has not yet aspired to spiritual life.

Most often, Atlantisite stones also contain inclusions of purple-coloured Stichtite. Stichtite's level of vibration is consistent with the green vibration of Atlantisite and with the same range of the heart chakra's green light frequencies. Stichtite is a worker-bee, drone-level, heart chakra vibration of love that has no direct affiliation with the healing work of Atlantisite. Stichtite and Atlantisite are mutually exclusive, but also mutually compatible. Stichtite steadily contributes to the empowerment of the love in the heart within the lower ranges of the heart's light frequencies.

Atlantisite and its Stichtite inclusions are presented to the world to help the spiritual dabbler muddle forward towards the spiritual path. Their contribution is slow and easy, and well within the expression of the dabbler's will.

Azurite

Making Negativity Disappear

Scientific Properties:

Crystallography: Monoclinic
Chemical formula: $Cu_3(CO_3)_2(OH)_2$
Mohs hardness: 3.5-4
Density: 3.77 g/cm^3
Colour: transparent, translucent, azure blue, blue, light blue, or dark blue

Azurite's non-translucent, deep blue vibration provides a unique vibratory effect on the way life's directions unfold. Within every individual is the need to accentuate her personality's positive and desirable traits, while allowing undesirable traits to dissolve into nothingness. In this way, each of us moves forward along our evolutionary spiritual paths, as we were intended. When an individual moves ahead with enhanced strengths of personality, they indeed evolve. Azurite ensnares negative traits by moving them into their rightful place of darkness, while reflecting the positive light of an individual's strengths outward.

The structure of Azurite is critical to its ability to function. A properly constructed piece of Azurite will be dark cobalt blue, as opposed to lighter blue. It will have well defined nodules protruding from its surface, as opposed to no nodules or a grainy surface. Ideally, the piece should be round in shape. However, roundness is not always possible, and other shapes are acceptable. These are the features of a mature and desirable Azurite crystal. If the dark cobalt blue colour or the well defined nodules are absent, the piece is not a mature stone and will not work as it needs to work. Immature stones should be left in the ground to mature, or at least left on the crystal store shelf for lesser informed buyers. An azurite crystal that has been ground or polished is a serious disappointment.

The functions of Azurite depend upon the principle of density[1] as it applies to the densification of physical form. In brief, lower and slower vibration is denser. High and subtle light frequencies cannot journey to places of significant density. The higher and subtler aspects of a single frequency cannot journey to places of significant density. They remain in higher dimensions or places of higher vibration, having split away from the frequency's lower aspects. The greater the density, the lower will be the vibrations of the light frequencies found within a given form.

When a person uses Azurite, the light frequencies, from within a person's aura, flow into and through the Azurite crystal. All of the light flowing into Azurite, as with any flow of light frequencies, consists of many ranges of frequencies. Each of Azurite's nodules attracts one of those ranges of frequencies. Each nodule contains an epicenter, within which undesirable frequencies are selected and removed from the flow. Hence, the presence of well developed nodules is crucial to its ability to work properly.

The stone's full complement of nodules attracts all of the ranges of frequencies flowing through. Some of the frequencies will be higher vibration, and some will be lower. As well, each individual frequency has within itself a higher positive aspect and a lower negative aspect. Undesirable frequencies are slower and denser than all of the other frequencies. The nodules attract all of the available light within its crystalline structures, then pass it to the deeper regions of the stone.

---

1   The principle of density, which influences the character, action, and presence of light frequencies and physical forms, is discussed directly in a number of places throughout the first two volumes of **The Story of Light**, and indirectly in many more places. Because the principles that govern density, as it affects light and form, are among the primary principles that build the foundation of knowledge for **The Story of Light**, reading the passages that discuss density is recommended. In particular, recommended reading includes chapter one of volume one and chapter eight of volume two. Reading both volumes puts flesh on the bones of the principles of density.

Azurite's primary action is to take light into density. The deeper a frequency goes into Azurite's mass, the greater will be the density to which it is subjected. The highest light frequencies and the highest aspects of individual light frequencies simply cannot journey into greater density or into Azurite. These high and positive frequencies and aspects are sloughed off. They return to the flow of light passing back out of the stone and into the etheric field of the aura. The body's natural energy currents pick up this very clean and positive light and make it available to those parts of the body for which it was originally intended.

The light frequencies of lower vibration and the lower aspects of individual frequencies continue to journey farther into the stone—and into greater density. Soon enough, the remaining positive frequencies and aspects of frequencies, encounter levels of density that they, too, cannot tolerate. These are also sloughed off and return to the person's aura. The negative aspects of the incoming light that remain are absorbed deep into the stone, where they undergo even further densification. The slowest and densest frequencies and aspects of frequencies continue into the depths en route to the core of the Azurite crystal. The higher and less dense frequencies and aspects continue to be sloughed off.

The journey to the core of the Azurite crystal brings the incoming light frequencies into greater and greater density. The stone continuously draws the negative aspect of light deeper and deeper, while separating out the positive aspect. Only the purest of negative vibration, void of the positive polarity, arrives at the stone's core zero point. At the core, the negativity becomes unto itself. It assumes its truth. The truth of negativity is nothing. Negativity merges wholly with the absolute nothingness at the core of the stone. It becomes nothing—and it disappears! Azurite makes negativity disappear, and is one of the very few stones that actually works with negativity.

The slower frequencies, which Azurite draws to itself, are the weakened vibrations of the aura. The stone purifies the weaker vibrations by purging its negativity. The light that remains is clean, but retains its original characteristics. The light also contributes to the specific empowerment function at its intended destination in the physical body. Relieved of its negativity, it accelerates to a higher frequency rate, thus brightening its vibration. Its new brightness is now a strength, where formerly there was a weakness.

Although Azurite is generally considered to be a third eye stone, it can be placed anywhere within the aura. Because it draws the slower vibrations of light to itself, it is best placed wherever the user wants to increase the strengths of the weakened aspects of the aura. If placed on a chakra, the weaknesses of that chakra densify into nothingness. The coexisting positive aspects of light are released and then reunite with the chakra. The chakra is thereby cleansed, purified, and strengthened.

The use of Azurite on the third eye chakra has the effect of cleaning up the light frequencies that contribute to a person's conscious world view. When the mind works with the light of consciousness that has been purged of negativity, the thought-forms that arise will be most positive. Because of its affect on a person's improved consciousness, Azurite is readily noticed, and perhaps, too quickly rendered as an exclusively third eye stone.

The most significant benefit offered by Azurite is the ability to strengthen the overall aura. The presence of excessive amounts of slow and dense, negative aura vibrations leads to holes in the etheric body's protective shield. Light frequencies, which are inconsistent with a person's vibration, may potentially invade through such holes. Inappropriate light frequencies can cause the destabilization of third dimensional form. Wherever Azurite removes the negative light, and frees and releases the coexisting positive light, it strengthens the aura and, thereby, removes the potential for vulnerability. If undesirable spirit entities prey upon those with weak and vulnerable auras, they quickly find that the body of a person using Azurite, into which they intend to invade and take up residence, is unavailable.

Banded Jasper

Making Truth Acceptable

Scientific Properites: (variety of Chalcedony)

Banded Jasper is formed with a central core surrounded by several bands of alternating light and dark brown crystalline substance. Its frequencies are most delicate and, therefore need protection from disruptive external energies, which could cause erratic dispersal and significant distortions of those frequencies. The banded construct of the stone both protects the stone's energies and creates the channel pathways, which direct their flow.

Jasper's light frequencies resonate with the throat chakra, but are not indigenous to it. Its frequencies facilitate the energies of truth, which are the responsibility of the throat chakra, by helping the chakra to open to divine light. As divine light arrives in the proximity of an individual's throat chakra, its conversion to truth on the physical plane is often distorted by humanity's illusions. How should a person present his truth to avoid the illusions of others? Conversely, how should others interpret a person's presentation of his truth?

Beyond individual perceptions, truth is what it is. Truth can come to a person with gentle, soft, and comforting feelings; or it can be abrupt, raw, and stark. Which presentation is preferable? An individual easily sees the importance of his own truth within its original conceptual framework, but will anyone else? The truth, projected in a raw and uncensored way, is clear to those who are advanced enough to sense the truth as it is. The adept person sees and accepts the truth within in its unmolded and beautiful form. However, for the less adept person, truth needs to be shaped and re-created with beauty and appeal. The expression of the truth must resonant much closer in its vibration, to those who are less advanced in their spirituality, to be acceptable. The uncut rock of truth, per se, needs to be presented as a gem to be appreciated.

Banded Jasper modifies the vibration of the light frequencies of truth. The light of the crystal adds softness and peace, and the smoothness of rounded edges to the energies of the truth that project from the throat chakra. It enhances truth and makes it more acceptable to those less able to see truth in its numerous forms. In effect, the out-bound expressions of the throat chakra are processed by Jasper. The throat's light frequencies are first absorbed into the stone, where they are pruned, culled, molded, and polished. Thereafter, the light passes out from the throat chakra to the external world in a more beautified form thus expanding the range of persons that are capable of accepting it.

The bands, as stated before, are part of a design that channels the throat chakra's extension of the light frequencies of truth. Besides directing the flow of light, the banding contributes to the reshaping of the truth by grinding and polishing its rough edges. The banding is simply a more expedient way to run the chakra energies through the stone thus ensuring a most definitive experience of light sculpting.

To say that a person could benefit from using Banded Jasper is itself a truth. Having this stone makes the expressions of words, body language, and communications in whatever form, from emails to phone conversations to a singing telegram, easier for others to accept no matter how adept or narrow the other person may be.

Bloodstone

Healing with a Sledgehammer

Scientific Properites: (variety of Chalcedony)

Bloodstone is an ancient healing crystal. It has the power to open those passageways of the body that have become blocked by the decay of diseased vibrations. Where tension has plagued the physical body's arteries or created constrictions, Bloodstone has the ability to remove the most stubborn of negative influences.

The vibration of light created within Bloodstone courses its way to and from its crystalline structure along the body's etheric magnetic pathways. It does its healing work within the physical body's etheric magnetic field. If the etheric channels that guide the flow of the stone's vibration are open, the flow is continuous. If the channel pathways are confused, blocked, or otherwise distorted, the problem shows up as anomalies in the etheric field patterns.

The flow of Bloodstone's light energies is restricted only by the most acute blockages. Upon encountering a blockage, Bloodstone's energies get caught in the distorted patterns of the etheric field, where they accumulate. The blockage prevents any further flow. Once an adequate amount of light energy has been trapped, it pounds away at the blockage. It shakes it up and rattles it loose. Bloodstone is not a high vibration and resonates best with the second chakra. When its low and slow vibratory pulses of healing light energy go to work, they do so as a sledge-hammer might.

Bloodstone pounds through the density that stops its flow, but does not enhance the vibration of the physical form, which carries the blockage. Rather, its healing work takes place within the innermost layers of the etheric magnetic field, closest to the physical body. Bloodstone works with the etherics, but not the physical body.

The intensity that builds as a result of the accumulation creates the power to break up the dense vibrations that caused the blockage. Analogous to the stone's level of activity, Bloodstone may be thought of as the cleanser that flushes out the effluent of sewer drain pipes. Once the stone's slow and intense vibration has rattled the etheric magnetic field adequately, the flow of Bloodstone's light frequencies resumes. The free flow of the body's own indigenous light frequencies also resumes. Further, the amount of light flowing within the channels of the physical body increases, especially at the localized site of the newly cleared blockage. As the anomalous energies clear away, so too, do the physical body's symptoms, which may have already manifested as a physical disease. Particular symptoms, related to blockage and energy accumulation, might best be understood as a stiffening of the physical body's movements, especially at the joints, but also includes muscle fatigue and paralysis.

Placement of the stone is best at the site of the blockage, especially if symptoms are apparent. While preference may be to place Bloodstone at the site of the diseased vibration or blockage, in a crystal layout it is best placed on the second chakra. Direct placement on the symptomatic location is the most effective and most concentrated, but only at that location. When placed on the second chakra, Bloodstone's healing vibration maintains the etheric flow throughout the physical body.

Blue Lace Agate

The Voice, Undenied and On-time

Scientific Properites: (variety of Chalcedony)

Blue Lace Agate offers a most joyous and happy set of light frequencies for the empowerment and encouragement of the expression of love. The clearly soft and warming hues of sky-like blue are a treasure for those who want to offer the expressions of their loving hearts without the undesirable blockages of suppressed feelings. Blue Lace Agate, however, is not a stone designed to break through the density that inhibits expression. Rather, it is a gentle way to mesh the inner heart's expression with external worldly vibrations in a way that does not create the conflict or confrontation that might accompany other ways of expressing the true heart.

Blue Lace Agate resonates at the high, but not the highest, end of the throat chakra's vibrational range. Its light, which is drawn from the golden rainbow beam of light frequencies entering the aura through the crown chakra, offers a warm and quiet, unobtrusive glow to one's speech. The innermost feelings are given their expression unfettered by the problems of a hostile opposing situation. This does not preclude the presence of differing viewpoints. Rather, Blue Lace Agate permits the quiet ease needed to create the environment, situation, or atmosphere within which a person is then able to offer his deepest feelings.

The Blue Lace Agate's soothing vibration invokes a patient and conscious inner knowingness for the best timing to express one's deepest truth. The person wishing to vent his truth cannot always find the right moment or place consciously or mindfully. He may be facing internal resistance and external hostility. Blue Lace Agate helps to select the appropriate moment and an acceptable place for his emotions to be expressed outwardly. He does not need to rely on his own sense of this "divine" timing. Under the in-

74

fluence of Blue Lace Agate, the expression happens spontaneously. It occurs at the exact moment that the vibratory pulse of the emotion to be expressed connects with the appropriate environment. When the external environment vibrates at the exact frequency rate that permits the pulse to be given harmonious expression, the person's truth finds its voice.

If the person expressing the emotion is accepted by the person, to which the expression is directed, there is little problem in the exchange. Blue Lace Agate promotes harmony for the expression. Through the attraction of the upper frequencies of blue light, Blue Lace Agate creates the necessary space for the harmonious exchange between two people of the most intimate of the heart's truths.

The person, who is receiving the expression, may not, however, be capable of handling clear messages of truth from the uninhibited emotions and heart. The emotional distance between the speaker and listener may be great. Harmony may not always be possible. Blue Lace Agate can handle only so much disharmony. To understand the limits of the stone, the user needs to understand that its task is to expand the environment within which greater acceptance can take place. When Blue Lace Agate is strong enough to bridge the distance, expression happens with as much harmony as is possible. Where hostility continues to lurk, the user needs to recognize an eventual limit. The distance may be irreconcilable.

Blue Lace Agate functions largely to attract the frequencies of its soft blue hues, as opposed to creating its own light. Light accumulates within the stone. When someone holds the stone, his physical body magnetically draws the stone's light frequencies within. If placed in the proximity of the throat chakra, the light activates the higher ranges of the chakra's light frequencies directly. If placed elsewhere, the body's etheric field will redistribute the stone's light, eventually bringing it to the throat. Through the empowered throat chakra, the emotions of the highest order are given expression.

Boji® Stones

Healing and Balancing with Earth's Devas

The Boji®[1] stone is a unique and interesting extension of the energies of the Earth. Its relatively recent emergence as a healing crystal comes under the protective custodianship of Karen Gillespie and Kellie Jo Conn, who brought them to light a little over two decades ago. The many insights offered by Karen and Kellie, and the claims they make, are verified as truth by the angelic ones, the Councilate of the Ascended-Light, who inspired this book.

The Boji® stone is a priceless and very old contributor to the health of light beings on Earth. Its name[2] is a vibration that causes a certain amount of excited energy. This stone is to be used by those who have the ability to ascertain the dualistic nature of overly unbalanced light energy.

The Boji® stone works with its user to re-balance the vibrations within the chakras. If the energy emissions of the chakra, upon which a Boji® stone is placed, are not cleansed by its own light frequencies, as flow through the crown to the chakra, the Boji® stone steps in to accelerate the vibration of the chakra. Thereafter, a greater amount of light enters to effect healing. The light in-question is the light of the Earth, and not of heavenly origin, and so, it is within the black light range of frequencies—Earth's indigenous light. The balancing takes place when the impure light that is causing the imbalance is displaced by the light brought forth by the Boji® stone. The cleansing follows the grounding of the

---

1   The use of the registered trade name Boji® in this book has been kindly permitted by Karen Gillespie and Kellie Jo Conn, GG (the crystal deva). Karen and Kellie are the caretakers of the Boji® Stones and the Earth devas within by divine appointment. Please see the following websites www.Boji®stones.com and www.avaloncrystals.com for more information about genuine Boji® stones.

2   The story behind the origin of the name, "Boji®", is found at www.Boji®stones.com/Boji®-stones/information.html.

Earth's light within the chakra.

Because the Boji® stone is from the original substance of the Earth at the time of the planet's most humble beginnings, as is claimed by its custodians and reaffirmed here, a patron of the Boji® stone might sense that the life of the Earth, the deva, that is present in the Boji® has a character of its own. The deva within each Boji® is an extension of the spirit of the Earth. This is because the life within the stone, which the deva of the Boji® carries with it, has evolved during its long presence on Earth and evolved as an Earthly being. It will reflect the inherent character of the Earth with its numerous manifold expressions of how life is: funny, humorous, serious, sedate, happy, sad, and so on. The stone's expression—extension of the life of the Earth—emitted at any one time, usually, but not always, corresponds to the opposing duality registered in the Boji® by the person holding it. If the person is depressed, the stone is likely to, but may not always, reflect joy to cause a balancing of the person's general spirit.

When focusing on the chakras, the Boji® acts to efficiently ground Earthly light into the midst of the tainted unbalanced energies within the chakra upon which it is placed. Whenever the Boji®'s deva detects a person who is attuned to the Earth and the ways of light, its offerings may be coloured by a variety of the extensions of the Earth's character in a spontaneous, usually joyful way. There is no way to predict how the deva will come across to any particular person, thus making the Boji® a most unique and delightful stone full of surprises.

The negative-positive energy flows, using male-female energies, ensure greater efficiency in moving light through unbalanced chakra centres. Some Boji® stones carry male energy, and some female. They are not difficult to distinguish energetically or by appearance. Male stones are fewer in number, weigh more, have a crystalline surface, and present an outgoing male energy. Female stones are usually found surrounding the male stone at the centre and have a smooth surface.

There is no general rule as to how the stone might be placed around the body. Simply use the male and female stones at opposite sides of the chakra centre that needs balancing or healing so that light is brought into and taken out of the centre. Being specific about which stone goes above or below is not required—simply opposite sides.

The use of the polarity principle, of male-female opposition, has greater effect than a single Boji®. However, if a person uses only a single Boji® stone, male or female, the results are only marginally less effective in regards to the movement of light to displace a chakra's tainted light. As well, placing the stone directly upon an unbalanced chakra is of greater effect than simply carrying it in one's pocket.

The Boji® stone is perhaps the oldest healing stone on Earth, and also one of the most effective.

Calcite

Scientific Properties: (from the Calcite group)
Crystallography: Trigonal
Chemical formula: $CaCO_3$
Mohs hardness: 3
Density: 2.7 g/cm³
Colour: transparent, translucent, white, yellow, red, orange, blue, green, brown, grey

Calcite-Optical

Gatekeeper to the Heavens

Calcite was given birth in the new age to facilitate the opening of the Stellar Gateway chakra. It is composed of singular units of crystal that are the same in both shape and arrangement of molecular structure. Each unit is identical down to the most infinite levels of essence. A unit within a Calcite crystal has six sides, each of which is a parallelogram. One side of each parallelogram resonates with the light of the upper heavens; the other side resonates with the Earth. The merging of the frequencies of heaven and Earth occurs within the unit constructs of Calcite's essence thus raising the frequency that becomes available for use on the physical plane. As above, so below. The vibration, which results from the union of the two sides, heaven and Earth, provides the person using the Calcite with the highest frequency with which she is still able to resonate.

The use of Calcite reaches a zenith during the current epoch as the work of the Angelic Hosts raises the light vibration of the planet. As Calcite is fully engaged with the current changes, its greatest task involves working with the light coming from distant Angelic beings. At the point of the human being's Stellar Gateway chakra, which extends from a few inches above the crown chakra, Calcite moves divine light down from the upper dimensions. At the same time, it moves the frequencies of the third dimension up. The Stellar Gateway chakra is where the union of the vibrations of heaven and Earth takes place facilitated by Calcite. The gateway chakra is the open door to the love that the Angelic Hosts bring to this plane.

By comparison to Calcite, the crystal, Selenite, serves as the pathway by which a person's highest angelic presence and light frequencies are gathered together and made ready to be received within the physical body. Calcite performs the complimentary task of bridging the frequencies of heaven and Earth to create a combined vibration. The newly created vibration offers the gift of the stars. It is heavenly light, which has the quality of being usable on Earth. Calcite helps the soul and the multi-dimensional Light Body to cross from the heavens into the depths of the physical body. When a person's vibration is high enough to resonate with her angelic higher-self, the combined use of Selenite and Calcite provides the opening for the arrival of the Light Body.

Using Selenite and Calcite is the most effective means to invoke the Light Body offered by the crystal world. However, they are not the only crystals that can do the job, nor are they the only means. Fluorite will also work if the physical body has been well prepared.

Human beings on Earth are graced with free will and divine light. Once the divine Light Body has been invoked, the physical body becomes Oneness in common with the lighted universe and carries the promise of the new age. According to the promise, the vibrations of the physical body and its Oneness are intended to move into and out of all dimensional spaces as directed by the will of the soul.

The newly combined light frequencies of heaven and Earth, which come together within Calcite, are distinctly Earth-oriented, but move both up and down between dimensions. Calcite is one of the facilitators that helps to send the light frequencies of the enlightened third dimensional body into the heavenly realms. It removes the barrier to the extension of light from Earth to the heavens, thus allowing the soul to consciously experience physical sensation and density at will. The soul's acquisition of the combined frequencies carried by Calcite, along with the Earthly experiences they bring, gives the soul the ability to project directly onto the physical plane.

The inhabitants of Earth are unaware of their souls' initial use of their physical bodies to acquire conscious experiences because the soul projects its energies into the physical body through Calcite. Calcite does not allow consciousness to pass through, therefore, awareness of what the soul is doing is not possible. Consciousness cannot pass through Calcite to the heavens for good reason. Calcite is the keeper of the Stellar Gateway. Energies flowing to the heavens must be compatible with the very high and subtle vibrations of the higher dimensions. Earthly consciousness, coming straight from the mind of persons still caught in the karmic imbalances of the physical plane, could potentially bring quite negative vibrations into the heavenly realms. Calcite is the fail-safe gatekeeper that ensures that consciousness that is not anchored in the physical plane[1] does not pass into the higher realms.

Calcite is the way through the Stellar Gateway. The point

---

1   The human mind, while in meditation, shares a compatibility with the vibrations of the heavens and can transcend its reach into the higher dimensions. The human consciousness touches upon the divine light of the heavens to receive enlightened realizations not available on Earth. This type of extension is a temporary surge of conscious energy that is firmly anchored on the physical plane and returns after a short time. Conscious energy from the mind retains its vibration as a physical construct and is not sufficiently similar in vibration to the heavens to remain there. When the soul acquires the consciousness, or more accurately, the conscious experiences of the incarnation on Earth, it receives conscious energy that carries a vibration that is both too high to remain as part of the human mind's inventory of light, and detached from the person from whom the conscious energy originated.

is—the gate swings both ways. On the one hand, the person acquires the use of the soul's vibratory frequencies. On the other hand, the soul acquires third dimensional vibrations that offer conscious experiences. The enhanced soul is then able to project onto the physical plane, at will, directly into selected situations to gather the lessons it needs to progress on its evolutionary path. It does so without the need to go through the incarnate cycle of birth and death, and without the tedium of life, which is dictated by the polarity needed to attract life's chosen lessons.

In the current state of Earth's affairs, minuscule amounts of soul-force energies enter a person's physical body, according to what the person's path of light and her devotion allow. The process of acquiring the soul essence is greatly enhanced by using Calcite. The doorway is opened to the soul, who steps into Earthly life to become a greater factor in the harmony that the incarnate individual enjoys. To a greater degree, as a person walks through time and space on Earth with Calcite in-hand, she becomes soul-guided.

In this age of enlightenment, as the union of heaven and Earth draws closer, persons using Calcite are changing their vibrations at the body's molecular levels to accommodate the in-coming light, and thereafter, the Light Body. Calcite is not complex. The exchange and union of physical and heavenly vibration is what takes place within the unit structures of the stone. The implications of Calcite's contribution to human evolution, however, are not simple and are yet to be fully realized.

Calcite-Green

Helping the Heavenly Light Flow Faster

Green Calcite carries the healing properties of a classic healing crystal. Healing, however, does not fully describe its role. The grace brought forth by Green Calcite is the expansion of form. Expansion refers to the opening of the physical body's form to allow light to move through it with much greater ease. Expansion is not a matter of recreating the form at a higher vibration rate than already exists. Rather, form is accelerated in the classic healing sense. Acceleration raises its frequency rate, thereby allowing it to accept a greater amount (but not necessarily a higher vibration) of light. The frequencies that are acceptable to the newly accelerated form are the same ones that previously moved through the form, but now they move through faster.

The frequencies coming into Green Calcite are similar to those coming into Optical Calcite. They are both from the heavenly planes and from the Earth plane. Because of the green vibration inherent to the stone, the frequencies originate from the healing aspects of both the heavenly heart and Earthly heart. Green Calcite facilitates the opening of denser areas of vibration, wherever blockages in the flow of light exist. This does not say that Green Calcite is a classical healer in the way that green stones work to clear blockages and heal physical form. Indeed not! Green Calcite opens the channel pathways between the higher self at the level of the soul and the person's heart on Earth. In the heart is the seat of the Godhead—the expression of the Christ Consciousness on Earth. Green Calcite opens the passageways to speed the flow of the energies of the heavens as they move into the Earthly heart, and to speed the flow of the energies of the Earthly heart as they transcend into the heavens of the soul.

The light frequencies involved in the work of Green Calcite are already of the highest order. These are the frequencies of the Christ Consciousness. These are the frequencies of love from the Guru's expression of the divine Shakti. They are the love frequencies of the heart of God moving in accord with the will of God from their place in the heavens onto the Earth. These are the frequencies for which Green Calcite was intended. Green Calcite opens and prepares the physical form for the acceptance of this most exquisite divine light of love.

Physical form does not come already prepared for the assimilation of the very high and subtle frequencies moving through Green Calcite. The physical body makes the necessary adjustment with the use of the stone. There is little opportunity for the direct invocation of the specific range of divine light frequencies into the body without Green Calcite. The stone facilitates the accelerated movement of the light, as well as, the preparation of the physical body.

To use Green Calcite, placing it over the heart is optimal, but not a fixed requirement. The chakra distribution system (including ida, pingala, and sushumna) will carry the light that the stone brings to all parts of the body as a matter of course no matter where the stone is placed. The expansion of the physical body's form begins in the heart. Green Calcite quickly takes the expansion process into every part of the physical body, thus accelerating the assimilation of God's love vibration throughout.

The frequencies that are transmuted from Earth into the heavens ensure that the love and conscious experiences of the person using Green Calcite enter the heavens. The vibrational maturity of the person's spiritual evolution is exactly what the physical plane has achieved and, therefore, exactly what it has to offer. By gauging the quality of the love offered, the Angels calculate the progress of the Earth's evolution. If evolution is lagging behind the divine schedule, and if help is needed, the Earth can be helped along. The quality of the Earth's love vibration determines what that help might be.

The quality of the light moving in the opposite direction—from the heavens to Earth—is determined by the quality of light that the physical form can assimilate. The exact range of frequencies is determined precisely by the mutual movement of light up and down the spiral vortexes connecting the Earth with the heavens. When the heaven-bound spiral and the Earth-bound spiral pass by each other, their states of vibration must be in perfect balance. To create balance, the light moving from the heavens is adjusted to harmonize perfectly with the light rising from the Earthly person's heart.

Earth-bound light is the divine light of love from the heart of God. The adjustment this light makes to be in balance with heaven-bound light involves reducing the in-coming range of divine light frequencies to that of a similar vibratory quality and quantity to the out-going light. Light frequencies flowing through Green Calcite constitute a specific range of frequencies that resonates with the Earthly love frequencies and creates balance. Divine consciousness light frequencies that are beyond the vibratory limits of the participating person will not harmonize with the light flowing through Green Calcite on its way to the heavens. Therefore, only the range of frequencies that creates balance and can be assimilated by the person are sent from the heavens.

The use and acquisition of the light offered through Calcite is a true blessing of salvation. It offers nothing less than the love of God perfectly calculated to be the perfect quality and the perfect amount. Green Calcite brings a change in vibration that is gentle, but most profound.

Calcite-Cobaltoan

Balancing the Heavenly Vortex with Love

Cobaltoan Calcite brings to the third dimension a very precious and intense loving pink vibration. From the viewpoint of the heavens, it is looked upon with fond adoration, for indeed, it offers a very special light. As with all Calcite crystals of whatever colour or shape, the frequencies of both heaven and Earth are given a space-in-common where they can mix. The two vibrations unite to create a common vibration, which is available both to the individual on Earth and to the will of the soul. Calcite links heaven and Earth.

The deep pink hue of the Cobaltoan variety of Calcite is an

intense heart chakra vibration, which resonates at a level slightly above the mid-range of the heart's frequencies. The Cobaltoan Calcite vibration then is very near the core of the heart. While Rose Quartz resonates at the center of the heart chakra, Cobaltoan Calcite has a slightly higher frequency. In a crystal layout, it is best placed slightly above the heart chakra center.

From its place of grace within the heart chakra, Cobaltoan Calcite works with the heart's innermost Earthly light. It also works with the heavenly frequencies of the soul. The stone's ability to mix the light of the heart and the soul is the gift that makes the presence of the soul available to the upper core level of the person's heart.

Cobaltoan Calcite's pink hue is intense. It can easily draw light energies through the upper chakras and into the heart. The intensity has significance because it permits the range of the soul's frequencies, which correspond to the pink hue, to resonate with the stone below the vibration of the upper chakras at the heart. The frequencies of the soul are not usually capable of descending below the crown or third eye without some third dimensional conditioning. Such conditioning usually removes most of the higher and more subtle frequencies before they reach the heart. Cobaltoan Calcite helps to overcome much of this problem.

Cobaltoan Calcite may be used in combination with Selenite in a crystal layout. While Selenite makes the full range of light from the higher-self available, Cobaltoan Calcite strongly attracts the pink frequencies for accumulation within the aura. Additionally, while Cobaltoan Calcite makes the soul's light available to its user on Earth, it also makes the deep pink frequencies of love from the user's heart chakra available to the soul. The pink light frequencies of love transcend the third dimension through the stone.

The information about Cobaltoan Calcite herein came about because a friend wanted to add it to her medicine wheel and wanted to understand how it worked. By placing the stone on the wheel, an exchange occurs between the frequencies from the soul and the frequencies from the heart chakra. To understand the process, first visualize the flow of light along a twisting and bending spiral vortex coming and going to and from the Earth and the heavens. The polar magnetic differentials reap havoc with the balance of the vortex spiral, as the two sets of frequencies flow in opposite directions. The vacillating polar charges carried by the flowing frequencies creates instability within the vortex that can potentially sever the connection with the heavens.

The exchange between the soul and the physical heart creates an intensity of love within the medicine wheel's vortex that facilitates balance. Balance is maintained through the love vibration coming from the core of the heart of the person using the medicine wheel (or meditating on the higher-self). Love is truly the middle way. Where its vibration is predominant, the journey will take the middle path in perfect balance. Under the influence of love, the Shaman (or person in meditation) holds steady in her journey within the spiralling vortex. Without love, the Shaman's journey is likely to fall off the vortex' vacillating frequency range, or strain to ride within it. The analogy is that of the radio tuner knob being used to find the strongest point of the transmitted signal. By using the Cobaltoan Calcite, tuning in to the vortex frequency is accomplished through the intense love vibration offered by the stone. There is little conscious effort involved. Placing Cobaltoan Calcite on the medicine wheel (or holding it in meditation) permits greater ease of journeying within the vortex of the wheel.

In addition, Cobaltoan Calcite creates a common resonant vibration consisting of the upper core light frequencies of the heart chakra of the person using the stone and the corresponding higher-self-level frequencies. Through the common light vibration and the balance afforded to the vortex, both the person and her soul are capable of maintaining their common vibration through the twisting turbulence of the vortex spiral.

Calcite links heaven and Earth. With Cobaltoan Calcite, the link is secured through love.

Carnelian

The Storehouse for Beauty Vibrations

Scientific Properties: (A variety of Chalcedony, Quartz)

Carnelian has been resident on Earth since the start of our current millennium. It is a most beautifying vibration of Earthly sweetness that has matured into the dignified stone that it so truly is. Praise to this second chakra crystal for its service in sustaining the beauty of the Earth!

Carnelian attracts particular light frequencies that resonate with Earthly form. The light is acquired, then stored within the stone. It is released when and where the physical environment is hospitable to the cultivation of the frequencies of divine beauty coming from the heavens. Carnelian is said to possess the knowledge of the past, meaning that it stores light vibrations for future release.

The frequencies residing within Carnelian are subtle and offer a most gracious vibration of beauty. Beauty, here, is the positive aspect of light within a range of frequencies that works to enhance vitality and the openness of vibration to receive love from whatever source love comes from. The stone becomes a safe haven for storage, and further, orients the vibration of heavenly beauty to the physical plane. In the process of their preparation, the frequencies at the periphery of the beauty vibration that are incompatible with Earthly density are released, either because they are too high, or because they are impurities. Carnelian makes ready a cleansed and enhanced frequency of heavenly beauty at the appropriate vibration level.

Carnelian's subtle aspects of divine beauty involve the key vibration, or central flower, on the stage of love. To release the light frequencies stored within, the stone needs to be placed into its own unique environment of love in anticipation of the arrival of the central flower to that environment. The central flower is the user of the stone. Carnelian's unique environment is where the central flower or person can grow and be in harmony and comfort. The environment is usually the person's home sanctuary or sacred space within the home. The sacred space is a place of serenity free of turbulence, rough vibrations, and negativity. Carnelian then contributes its vibration of beauty.

Once the person—the key vibration, the central flower—is positioned within the local ethers of the sanctuary, Carnelian releases (or imposes) its vibratory frequencies of beauty upon that sanctuary. The environment is thereby prepared. Into it comes the love of the person's own vibration, which then merges with the divine beauty released from the Carnelian. The light released elevates the vibration of the welcoming sanctuary with harmony that is suitable to the person. Carnelian's effect may be likened to house cleaning and vacuuming in anticipation of an honoured guest. It releases the heavenly frequencies it carries to beautify the surroundings within which the key of love enters. Carnelian is the red carpet for love's sweet substance.

Celestite

Accelerated Empowerment

Scientific Properties: (synonym of Celestine)
 Crystallography: Orthorhombic
 Chemical formula: $SrSO_4$
 Mohs hardness: 3-3.5
 Density: 3.96 - 3.98 g/cm^3
 Colour: transparent, translucent, light blue

As the name implies, Celestite carries a divinely high and reverent vibration. Its heavenly light frequencies work to open the matrix of the thousand petal lotus of the crown chakra, and to help the crown accept light as well.

With each new light frequency that it acquires, the crown chakra opens gradually matrix-by-matrix, and light receptor-by-light receptor. At the beginning of its empowerment, the chakra is open to receive light, but its matrices and its light receptors are not yet active. The very lowest light receptor opens first. It receives the unique light frequency with which it resonates and becomes active. Activation of the lowest light receptor is followed by the very next higher receptor in perfect sequence[1]. The next receptor opens, receives its unique light frequency, and becomes active in the same way. Always in sequence, the next higher receptor opens, and the cycle repeats until all receptors are open and active.

The process of opening matrix-by-matrix and light receptor-by-light receptor is the standard for all chakras, but can be painfully

---

1   The opening of the chakra light receptors in order from lowest to highest vibrations, along with the assimilation of the relevant light frequencies in order from lowest to highest is an important principle that is discussed in *The Story of Light, Path to Enlightenment* (volume 1) in the seventh section of Chapter 3, entitled, "Chakra Empowerment".

slow. Numerous difficulties can impede progress[2]. Celestite works to remove impediments. By connecting the opened light receptors and matrices with the unopened light receptors and matrices, Celestite helps the activation process within the crown to bypass the usual one-by-one scenario. In the presence of Celestite, the opened receptor shares its light with the unopened receptor. Because both receptors are almost the same vibration, light passes easily between them. They temporarily unite, and the inactive receptor activates. The empowering light vibration of the Celestite crystal greatly accelerates the opening of the crown chakra's receptors. Celestite re-configures each individual matrix within the crown into a functional unit without the normal delay that comes with progressive light acquisition.

Celestite might be called the unity stone because it unites vibrations without discriminating between which vibrations it unites. It can open the receptors and matrix of any chakra in the same way as it opens the receptors in the crown chakra. After exposure to Celestite's divine light frequencies, both the crown and the other chakras come to possess fully functioning matrices. Quite quickly, Celestite empowers the respective chakras with the light frequencies, which are intended for empowerment, and which have managed to become available within the aura after passing through the filter of the body's etheric magnetic field.

Celestite's vibration comes from the realm of the higher-self and brings its influence. Celestite's light frequencies work with the person's chakras and channel pathways in an unobtrusive, gentle,

---

2   The difficulties surrounding the assimilation of light is the core problem that impedes the fulfilment of our mission to bring light to Earth. This problem is discussed in a number of places throughout both volumes of ***The Story of Light***. A few of the salient passages can be found in volume one, Chapter 1.5, "The Descent into Density", Chapter 1.8, "Problems Encountered in Anchoring Light", and Chapter 3.2, "The Physical Body". In volume two, Chapter 14.7, "Problems with Consciousness Frequencies", offers a numbered list of specific problems that plague the use of light.

and divine manner. They are the caress of God. Third dimensional light receptors and matrices line the walls of the chakras and chakra channel pathways. By empowering them with the light of their own higher-selves, Celestite establishes a connection between the form on Earth and its presence in the heavens. With the harmonious connectedness between higher and lower selves, the light of the higher-self flows to the individual on Earth without impediment.

When the light from the crown passes into the chakra channel pathways for distribution, it moves more quickly because Celestite reprograms the body's receptors to work with higher dimensional light, which is naturally faster. As the light is taken in, moved along the channel pathways, and absorbed into the chakra, the receptors receive a significantly expanded range of light frequencies. The availability of the very much higher light frequencies of the higher-self moves the individual's vibration forward by evolutionary leaps and bounds.

Does Celestite remove the need for progressive light acquisition? Although skipping the frequency-by-frequency process might seem to be a questionable practice because of the dangers of acquiring an excessive and overwhelming amount of light too quickly, the stone does not resonate with everyone. It is reserved for persons whose spiritual path is well established. The vibration of the spiritual devotee is high enough to work with Celestite. In addition, each frequency that is absorbed into a light receptor is modified by its passage through matrices that have been reconditioned by Celestite. The receptors and matrices accept their own unique frequencies, but only the higher aspects of those frequencies. Celestite offers enlightenment from the top down. It ensures that the reworked parts of the matrices and its receptors will only accept high and positive pure light frequencies or parts of frequencies, devoid of negativity and with no damaging characteristics. Thereafter, the body's chakra matrices maintain a very high level of light vibration.

Light frequencies possess both high and low vibration rates.

Light receptors and matrices also possess both high and low vibration rates. Because the lower vibration matrices are open before a person is eligible to use Celestite, only the higher vibrational portions of the matrices come under Celestite's influence. Celestite only opens the higher ranges of the body's matrices and only to the higher octaves of each frequency. The result is the acquisition of the most celestial aspects of light.

Cerussite

Not Quite on Earth Yet

Scientific Properties: (part of the Aragonite group)
Crystallography: Orthorhombic
Chemical formula: $PbCO_3$
Mohs hardness: 3-3.5
Colour: transparent, translucent, colourless, white,
gray, blue, or green; colourless in transmitted light

A crystal usually offers us, the spirits, who receive the channelled information about the crystal, its will, first to work with
light, and second to participate in the offering of light to the Earth.
In the case of Cerussite, the light it offers cannot cross into the
third dimension. The fragments of its physical formation, which
are on the reddish base of the piece, which was used to conduct
the channeled information, do not reflect the truth of Cerussite
adequately for us, the channel spirits, to offer a reasonable explanation.

In order that we obtain the knowledge of a crystal's use of
the divine light, that crystal will have had to descend onto the
physical plane with at least the core frequency[1] of its essence. In
the case of Cerussite, the core frequency has yet to descend. We
offer that the disorganized patterns of white striated material that
constitute this piece are merely the residual marks of the attempt
to draw Cerussite's light energies onto the Earth. These residues in
manifest form were initially impregnated with Cerussite's core light
frequency. However, the residual formations here, and in other
examples of Cerussite, were unable to anchor and hold Cerussite's
vibration.

---

1   The discussion on "core frequencies" is available in ***The Story of
Light, Through Heaven's Gate*** (volume 2), in section two of Chapter
4, entitled: "Core Frequency Enhancement".

In the piece used to do the channel, the base, which served as the landing platform for Cerussite's frequencies, was of a very unwelcoming character. Its rough and dark reddish substance was neutral in its influence, but necessary for the first attempts to bring Cerussite into physical density. This base was not conducive to Cerussite's establishment on the physical plane. Because there was no true Cerussite vibration retained by the physical base form, there is no information about its contribution to the Earth's light.

As to the base form, the attempt to draw light onto the planet resulted in the deposit of the extension of primitive aspects of an essence-form into which the Cerussite vibration was able to cross the threshold of the third dimension. However, it was unable to remain on the third dimension. At this point, Cerussite is being reconditioned at its creative source in the heavens with the vibrations needed to bring it into physical form. For now, Cerussite is unable to contribute to the Earth's light.

Chalcedony, Brown

Herald of Future Vibrations

Scientific Properties: (variety of Quartz)

Upon observing a specimen of Brown Chalcedony, one will notice that it has a number of distinct layers, the first of which is a slate foundation with malachite inclusions. This slate structure possesses a very consistent vibrational frequency, and it forms the base for the second layer which grows upon it. The second layer is quartz crystal. With the clean slate and malachite foundation to anchor and hold the initial vibration, the quartz layer is also quite clean and pure, as well as, quite even in its thickness. The slate foundation emits an etheric magnetic field that ensures that a very even amount of light gets through to its physical form, hence the evenness of the second quartz layer. The quartz, too, puts out an even and consistent etheric magnetic field for the purpose of attracting a third layer, which is Brown Chalcedony.

To say that Chalcedony is brown is somewhat misleading. Rather, the third layer, which grows upon the quartz layer, is similar to a Citrine vibration because it expands the space for even more vibration to join the existing layers. The brown substance gets its colour from the presence of iron. The iron serves as a purely magnetic force to attract the uppermost layer of Chalcedony. Because the first two layers of the slate and the quartz are so even in their thickness and strength, the third iron-filled layer on the top surface of the quartz is also consistent in quality and thickness over its breadth.

The magnetic field of attraction resulting from all three layers of foundation is markedly even. Therefore, the whitish material that grows on the foundation and juts out into tiny peaks is relatively even across the surface.

The third layer of foundation, the whitish material, is a hybrid of quartz that is exceptionally clean and high in its vibration. It is not a Selenite-type material, but a most pure form of common silica quartz. This layer brings in a highly charged range of frequencies that are at the upper end of the Earth's natural third dimensional vibration. The whitish layer of Chalcedony, then, is an extremely high, but strictly third dimensional Earthly quartz vibration that sets up a further foundation for a crystalline light frequency that has yet to make itself available. Brown Chalcedony is a rock of future ages. The final vibration that is destined to become part of the Chalcedony is not due to arrive on Earth for another 400-600 years.

Working with Brown Chalcedony may easily produce outcomes that are beneficial to the user. Benefits, however, are incidental, stemming from the quartz component with a marginal contribution from the Malachite component. The benefits, are the same benefits that accrue from using any other piece of clean, clear quartz. Brown Chalcedony, therefore, is of very little direct or necessary consequence to persons or vibrations in this period of time. Possession of Brown Chalcedony, when directed by the Earth's angelic caretakers and by higher purpose, goes to individuals who are themselves caretakers of the stone. Chalcedony crystals are still in the process of growing foundations for a vibration that is as yet unavailable. Appropriate responsibility for caretaking of a Brown Chalcedony entails keeping it in a secure and undisturbed place and ensuring that its next owner does the same.

Chrysocolla

The Woman's Voice

Scientific Properties:
> Crystallography: Orthorhombic
> Chemical formula:
> $Cu_{2-x}Al_x(H_{2-x}Si_2O_5)(OH)_4 \cdot nH_2O < x < 1$
> Mohs hardness: 2.5-3.5
> Density: 1.93 - 2.4 g/cm^3
> Colour: translucent, opaque, green, bluish green,
> blue, blackish blue, or brown

Chrysocolla is the woman's voice. It gives expression to the loving ways of the divine light, as is the feminine side of any frequency of expression.

Truth is the vibration expressed by the throat chakra. Truth is the essence of our existence as multi-dimensional beings in the heavens. Truth is that part of the higher-self that projects outward from the higher dimensions to become the incarnate person on Earth, male or female. Conversely, as each person on Earth grows into an enlightened individual, her yearning to leave the Earth and return to the heavens to rejoin her higher-self follows the fulfillment of her truth. Whether the direction of the energy of life is towards the Earth or towards the heavens, truth is the core of all that is.

Upon coming to Earth, each being assumes its truth in its incarnate form. The divine light energy of the human higher-self, as it exists in the heavens, divides into its aspects of male and female to enter the realm of Earth's duality. We become human beings, existing as individuals in sexually polar opposition. The male-female split is necessary. It is the innovation that draws truth into the physical plane. The complete and whole creation of the truth of our higher-self is simply too high and subtle to descend into the overwhelming density on Earth without the innovation of separate magnetically charged aspects[1].

Polar opposites apply not merely to the sexes, but to every light frequency attempting to descend onto the physical plane. Many of the light frequencies that carry the finer qualities of light cannot cross from the higher planes into the third dimension without great difficulty, and many frequencies cannot cross under any circumstance. The light frequencies of truth, as do many other frequencies, split into polar opposites to find their way to Earth. The throat chakra, then, works with a person's frequencies of truth, and with each of the separate polarized aspects of her truth as well. Further, the throat chakra works to reunite the polarized opposites into whole and complete frequencies, and then to express that truth.

Truth encompasses all levels of one's being. Its presence on the physical plane can be whole and complete. However, truth is more likely to begin its journey on Earth in the most minute of quantities as polarized portions of the whole. The I AM god-presence of a person on Earth arises through truth whenever the person's light and form unite into Oneness. Even the great grace of the Godhead, in its light aspect and its form aspect, comes to Earth both charged with polarity and in its separated aspects. Therefore, when the throat chakra does its work, the truth that it expresses dwells in duality and is rarely unified. Further, the strength and substance that can make truth effective to the point of realization within the physical context takes a significant amount of time to manifest.

Chrysocolla steps in to help the throat chakra. Its influence

---

1   Please see the complete discussion about the innovation for splitting light frequencies to bring them to Earth in volume one, *The Story of Light, Path to Enlightenment*, chapter one, section 1.9, "Innovating Physical Duality".

is feminine[2], but not necessarily negatively charged. Its feminine vibration attaches itself to the throat chakra, then strengthens the polar magnetic field that already exists within the chakra's matrices. Whether negative or positive, the strengthened chakra attracts the vibrations of truth that resonate and are consistent with the vibration of the person using Chrysocolla. If the throat chakra is negatively charged due to the negative aspects of the frequencies therein, Chrysocolla strengthens the attraction for positively charged aspects. Conversely, Chrysocolla enhances the positively charged throat to attract the negative aspects of the light.

Chrysocolla's influence comes with qualifiers, and can be quite distinctive. There are hundreds of chakra light receptors and matrices, but Chrysocolla works only with those receptors and matrices that are already opened. The stone continues to work with more and more receptors as each opens in its turn. Further, Chrysocolla enhances only select aspects of the vibrations of the many truths within the throat. It shapes the expression of the truth with particular characteristics, which originate with the higher-self. The higher-self sends numerous frequencies in a variety of ranges that constitute the I AM presence of an individual. The qualities of these frequencies determine a person's innate human characteristics, and determine the characteristics of the expressions that one projects to the external world.

Chrysocolla and the truth are best expressed through the involvement of the throat chakra. However, truth, as previously indicated, is the core of all that is. Chrysocolla, then, is best placed on the throat chakra where it is most effective, but can be placed elsewhere as well. Chrysocolla will enhance the magnetic field of the body to attract and repel the light of truth wherever it is placed.

---

2   The essence of a feminine vibration in the context of enhancing the chakras means that light is either attracted, if desirable, or repelled, if undesirable. The masculine vibration added to enhance a chakra instills the qualities of extension and withdrawal.

Citrine

Creation's Creator

Scientific Properties: (variety of Quartz)

Citrine crystals bring wondrous splendour to the relationship between the divine universal creation in the heavens and the physical plane on Earth. Offering Citrine a home brings its owner the golden treasures of abundance that the universe yearns to share with all incarnate beings. Citrine is the gift of magnetic love for those who wish to cherish its vibration.

Citrine's golden hue draws to itself the most exquisite light of physical form. Gold, of all the colour bands available to Earth, relates closest to the essence of abundance on the physical plane. The golden light ray does not herald the coming of the soul as does the sacred purple light. It is not involved with love as are the pink light vibrations. It does not ground light as do the black light frequencies. Citrine's vibration facilitates the appearance and realization of manifest object at the physical level as originally intended by the light frequencies that were sent from divine source. Citrine is the stone of creativity.

As all things are a vibratory frequency of one type or another, the many frequencies on Earth constitute a vast array of physical manifestation. The many colour bands of vibration slow down and condense into a variety of physical objects as their unique frequencies descend from the heavens into form having Earthly density. There is no limit to the qualities of the resulting manifestations. Each object on Earth originates as a higher dimensional light frequency, which then assumes the density of its third dimensional format. If the process is reversed by accelerating the molecular essence of these objects, their forms return to the higher dimensions in their original state of non-dense, subtle, high, and pure vibration.

The descent of light frequencies from the heavens into the extreme density of the third dimension often distorts and removes the finer qualities of their original vibrations. The third dimension cannot accommodate the highest and most subtle frequencies belonging to most physically manifested objects. As well, individual light frequencies split apart. The frequencies' lower aspects descend to Earth, and its higher aspects remain in the heavens. However, in order for the original vibration to establish itself on Earth in its original state, both the finer qualities of its vibration that were left in the heavens, as well as, the dense mass that descended to Earth, need to unite.

The higher refined frequencies of the object are not lost when the remainder of its mass descends into the extreme density of the physical plane, but they cannot enter the physical plane either. Instead, they enter a grand pool of similar vibration that becomes the light energy reservoir for all disconnected dense objects that condense into manifest form. This reservoir, or reserve of the object's energies, resides outside of the density of Earth in a slightly higher dimensional vibration.

When an object that has manifested on the physical plane vibrates closer to its original frequency rate, the magnetic attraction for its missing higher light frequencies increases. The attracted frequencies, however, remain unable to enter their intended physical form because the density of the form is still too great. As an alternative, they are assigned a place within a separate, but coexisting mass. The coexisting mass is a medium, which both resonates with the physical object and accommodates the missing frequencies. Through the medium, the object and its higher light frequencies are indirectly joined together. Because of the union, the larger abundance of the creative universe is imbibed in the object at hand. The presence of the higher light frequencies allows the dense object to take on the greater life-force of its whole being, and to do so on the third dimension. The result is not so much an inclusion of light, as it is an inclusion of the essence or life-force. The connection is unrelated to the Light Body or the consciousness. Rather, there is simply a reunion of the manifest form with its life-force, void of the consciousness.

The individual's role, in working with Citrine, is that of being the medium. The individual's involvement causes the acceleration of the Earthly object. However, the object does not vibrate any faster at the physical level. Rather, the higher frequencies of the object's essence, which are held in reserve outside of the third dimension, become available to the third dimension through the individual acting as the medium. Because the object's higher frequencies are not completely or literally united with the object, the object maintains its current form and vibration rate. Union occurs between the object and the medium, which carries the life-force frequencies or essence of the object.

The complete and whole energy vibration becomes embodied in the union of the object and the medium. However, the united and completed vibration cannot present itself as a single unit structure. Rather, union of the object and the medium is achieved through near physical proximity. The combination—of the vibrations of the object as dense mass, plus the object's light frequencies held in reserve by the mediating essence—is sufficient to allow the original vibration to be whole, and to fulfil a greater part of its physical potential.

Whenever a person contemplates a particular Earthly object and then attracts the object's higher frequencies into her essence, the two separated aspects of the original vibration unite by simple possession and the proximity gained through ownership.

The golden glowing Citrine is quartz and often has clear quartz in its presentation. Its golden inclusions move the golden ray through its structure and concentrate the ray's energies. The light that Citrine brings is available primarily to the third chakra at the navel[1], which is the power center of creativity in the human

---

1   The discussion herein focuses on the benefits of Citrine. For a more complete understanding of the how the navel chakra is involved

being. Once the navel chakra has been opened and activated, its ability to assimilate the golden ray is substantial. The golden ray, while not exclusive to the navel chakra, presents a most high vibration with which to energize the dormant powers within. By infusing the golden light, the navel chakra is empowered.

The mind can play a part. The light, needed to fulfill any of the contemplative mind's directives involving the physical plane, is attracted to the navel chakra. That is, the creative visualization or contemplative focus upon an object of desire, as generated by the mind, activates the navel chakra to draw the object's energies in reserve from outside the third dimension into itself. Using Citrine by having it within the aura enhances the powers of the navel chakra through the stone's direct acquisition of light. The strength to draw the object's reserve essence into the physical body of the stone's owner is increased by the ability of Citrine to draw in the golden ray.

The reserve life-force of the visualized object of desire is absorbed and assimilated into the essence of the person who created the desire. Simultaneously, a state of polarity arises between the dense mass of the third dimensional object and the newly acquired reserve life-force energy of that object. The two aspects of the object (physical and reserve) are attracted magnetically to each other. The original form of the vibration becomes whole, as it was prior to the separation that occurred upon entry to the physical plane.

The model of creativity described above is straight forward. A third dimensional object is attracted to the person who is able to acquire the reserve essence of that object through creative visualization techniques, which are enhanced by the vibration of Citrine, which empowers the creative navel chakra with the light of the golden ray. While it seems straight forward, individuals tend to possess mental blockages to their creative mind's potential thus

---

in the process of creativity, see **The Story of Light, Path to Enlightenment**, (volume one), Chapter 4, section 4.4, entitled: "Navel Chakra: Form Expansion".

dampening the result.

The implicit examples to this point focus on solid mass objects. The creative powers, however, are not limited in this way. The acquisition of theatre tickets, for example, employs the creative model much more subtly. Theatre tickets are not the focus of the contemplative mind. Rather, the person in the mediating role creates a visualization of the experience of the theatre. She sees herself in attendance at the theatre, sitting in her seat, and watching the play as it happens. The exercise involves placing the creative imagination directly into the place and time of the performance and actually sensing the feelings and thoughts that would be relevant to that occasion. By creating the event within the visualization, the person draws into herself the object's life-force energy in reserve. The theatre tickets are then attracted to provide the means by which the actual event of watching the play manifests. Thereby, as qualified by the limitations of the third dimension, the union of the physical event in time and space with the reserve energies of the experience from the higher planes creates a wholeness of the total vibration. The acquisition of the reserve frequencies leads to the fulfilment of the contemplation when the person takes her seat to watch the play at the theatre.

Citrine enhances the union of reserve essence and object by the greater empowerment of the navel chakra. The chakra is effective in acquiring an object's reserve essence, which in turn attracts the object of desire. The only limits on the person's desire are those imposed by the dimensional constraints of the physical plane. Whether solid object or perceived concept, whatever one directs her attention towards becomes available as the realized creation. A person can 'think up' whatever she wants, and then create it in her mind's eye for transmission into the navel chakra's center of creative power. Therein, the essence in reserve, not yet united with its original vibration at the third dimension, is assimilated in sufficient quantities to attract the object of desire to the person, be that a car, an evening at the theatre, a new pair of sunglasses, or a large bank account.

Citrine empowers the creative force, which attracts the higher essence of the object of contemplation, which in turn attracts the object in the physical plane.

Citrine quartz channels the golden ray, and the golden ray empowers the creative potential by bringing the light of the highest vibration. Because Citrine's empowerment is of the highest order, the only mediating essence capable of attracting the Earthly object is also of the highest quality. The high quality of the medium thereby restricts the objects attracted to those desires, which reflect the equally high truth of abundance. High vibrational empowerment cannot attract objects or life-force frequencies that are less than the truth of abundance. The presence of abundance is the grace from the Godhead.

To further understand the creative process, an awareness of the mediums used as the means to acquisition is needed. Money is a prime example of a medium for life-force energy. Where objects of desire are drawn to a person, manifestation usually comes about through some specific medium. With money, a person simply buys the object of desire.

When the creative process provides the necessary medium by which to attract the desired object, it is advisable to use the medium for the intended purpose. For example, if the thirty dollar bonus in your paycheque is used to purchase theatre tickets, the medium of money serves its intended purpose. Money facilitates the alignment between the manifest concept (watching the play) and the reserve energies. To use the money for its intended purpose allows the process to unfold appropriately.

Appropriate use of the money for the intended purpose keeps the person in alignment with the flow of further abundance. However, using the money for something else blocks the attraction of the two polarities of the original vibration for each other. Were the blockages to become excessive through hoarding and greed, for example, the medium becomes stale and sours the creative life-force itself. It's like keeping rotten meat in the fridge. Pretty soon all the food is going bad. If a person is to be offered further abundance, she needs to consciously recognize the gifts she is given and use them appropriately.

The keepers of the creative force in the heavenly realms understand well that not all persons on Earth are so consciously aware of what constitutes the means to the object of desire. The divine universe offers great compassion in cases of the misappropriation of the life-force energies, and no penalty is forthcoming. However, whenever a person consciously or unconsciously uses the mediums offered by the creative powers to draw forth the objects for which they were intended, the creative powers are increased accordingly. A person might feel their way along and do the right thing or get lucky by spending the bonus money in the correct manner. Either way, the creative power that attracts life-force energies in reserve increases along with the abundance of third dimensional manifestations.

A person is wise to adequately cultivate her ability to sense how the creative power works to bring about the fulfillment of her true desires. Add in Citrine and the quality of the manifest objects of desire will reflect the grace of divinity. The grace of divinity is Earthly love—in material form and in abundant quantity.

Danburite

The Neutralizer

Scientific Properties:
> Crystallography: Orthorhombic
> Chemical formula: $CaB_2(SiO_4)_2$
> Mohs hardness: 7-7.5
> Density: 2.93-3.02 g/cm^3
> Colour: usually transparent-colourless, also pale yellow, yellowish-brown, or pink.

Danburite is the stone of inequity, of all eternity, of peace and harmony, and of the equilibration of that which has imbalance.

The striations on the shaft sides of a natural piece of Danburite move light frequencies extremely fast. Danburite is clear in colour, as is Quartz, therefore, it works with the white light, hence it works with all light frequencies. While it can work with all light, it works primarily with the frequencies that are in close proximity, and that have taken on imbalance, and therefore, a polar charge.

Light frequencies that have a polar charge can attract frequencies having the opposing polarity. Danburite comes with no particular polar charge of its own, but quickly detects the presence of energy that is flowing and polarized. Because it is well striated and carries no initial charge, it serves as a free catalyst for an even greater flow. Light quickly moves into and through the stone. The initial attraction for the first set of charged frequencies coming into the stone arises from its catalysing action as light flows freely into its open space. The attraction does not arise from any polar attraction. Even so, the most highly polarized frequencies play a part in the process. Without exception, the most polarized light frequencies enter the stone ahead of less polarized frequencies.

The magnetic polar charge of the light flowing into Danburite's free and open space empowers the stone, which then acquires its own polar charge. If the in-coming light is positive, so, too, will be Danburite. The charged in-coming light creates a magnetic field within the stone, and thereby sets up the attraction for a second set of light frequencies having the opposing polarity. The light entering Danburite is from two different sources—the source that polarizes Danburite, and the source that is attracted by the polarized Danburite. Each source carries the polar charge that is opposite to the other source. The two energies cancel each other out, thus effecting balance—hence, the 'neutralizer'.

The primary source of both types of light frequencies that contribute to Danburite's neutralizing action is the stone's immediate surroundings. The secondary source is the higher dimensions and the vast universe. Danburite serves as a vessel to accelerate the flow of the first set of charged frequencies. Once charged, the stone quickly attracts the second set from whatever light is immediately available to offset the stone's polar charge. If this second set of frequencies brings the stone and its light into balance, Danburite loses its charge, and thereby, its attraction for more light.

If the necessary balancing frequencies are not readily available, the stone's attraction expands its scope. The attraction first radiates beyond the aura into wider and wider distances in the physical plane. If the balancing frequencies are still unavailable, the stone's attraction for light reaches beyond the physical plane into the immediate upper dimensions, and progressively to higher and higher dimensions. Once the light needed has been attracted and balance is satisfied, Danburite again loses its polarity and attraction.

The outcome of balance does not always take place completely upon the first attempt. At the start, the light initially attracted to Danburite flows quickly into the stone and out again. The light's polar charge is significantly reduced on this first pass. The charged light mixes with the light of the opposing polarity, thus gradually reducing the polar imbalance, but not all of it. Light that remains charged is returned to the local environment, only to be attracted again to Danburite. The type of attraction reverts to the initial mode of attraction. That is, the first set of charged light frequencies is brought into the stone not through polarity, but through the promise of a free and open space through which the polarized light can flow and accelerate. The whole process of creating an attraction for the frequencies of opposing polarity within the stone repeats. The polarized light polarizes Danburite, and together the light and stone attract the light of the opposite polarity. The first set of polarized frequencies combine with the second set of opposite frequencies. The result leads to a neutral charge and balance.

What benefits does balance bring? Reduction of turbulence and negativity are umbrella benefits that can be applied to numerous human activities. Danburite can balance the difference in viewpoint between two arguing individuals. It can bring a room full of conflict to a point of reconciliation, given that there is enough Danburite to go around.

An individual in a situation of contemplation can more easily acquire the realizations leading to solutions and insights. The imbalanced gravitational field of the contemplation attracts light, whose polar charge initiates the balancing process within Danburite. By attracting the opposing polarity, the mind receives the missing frequencies of the other side of the contemplation. The mind, then, sees a more complete picture in a state of balance, from which the realizations of the potential, the solution, and the answer spring forth.

Danburite's beneficial balancing action can also be applied in meditation. Danburite brings balance to the energetic of the mind, creating serenity and centredness. The spiritual devotee overcomes the turbulence of the mind one frequency at a time, in rapid order. Another way to benefit from using Danburite involves environments that are significantly negative. Negative vibration is inherently polarized and, therefore, easily attracted to Danburite, where its charge is eventually neutralized.

Danburite begins its contribution to enlightenment in a state of inequity, with clear polarization of the energies present in its

vicinity. With the balance that comes from Danburite's acceleration of the flow of light, situations of difficulty, including difficult
relationships, disagreements, opinionated conflicts, and misunder-
standings come into progressively greater peace and harmony.
Danburite restores the equilibration of that which has imbalance.

Descloizite

Dinosaur Enlightenment

Scientific Properties:

Crystallography: Orthorhombic
Chemical formula: $Pb(Zn,Cu)(VO_4)(OH)$
Mohs hardness: 3-3.5
Density: 6.2 g/cm^3
Colour: Brownish red, red-orange, reddish brown
to blackish brown, nearly black

Descloizite is an ancient Earth stone. Its contribution involves lower light vibrations and dimly-lit light-beings on Earth.

Beings that are drawn to use Descloizite have a lower vibrational frequency rate than is average for Earth. With regard to human beings, when persons at the lower ends of the human spectrum are exposed to Descloizite, their vibrations move upward to a level better able to resonate with other human beings, who are vibrating at an average rate.

The stone causes the acceleration of the magnetic polarization of physical form. By accelerating and, thereby, increasing the magnetic attraction of the molecular structures of lower organisms, a greater infusion of light results, thus initiating a move upward on the evolutionary scale. Presenting Descloizite in this way is not a challenge or judgment to beings, including human beings, drawn to the stone. Earth holds a wide range of frequencies relevant to its inhabitants. While use among the lower Earth entities is the intention, more advanced species with normal rates of vibration benefit as well. The benefit needs be understood as occurring within the lower ranges of light, and especially within the range of black light frequencies.

The specific parts of an organism's molecular structure that are enhanced by Descloizite are limited to areas of its physical form that resonate with dark light frequencies. Descloizite's accelerating action creates the space available for the entry of the low and dense dark frequencies. At the lower levels of density, light is scarce, and has only a limited role to play. Descloizite has no light of its own to contribute. It serves merely to increase the vibration of low density physical mass.

The buzz, or perhaps more accurately the drone, of molecular-level activity is consciously detectable to most higher light beings, but would be comparable to watching a turtle run. Indeed, a turtle running is a notable event. Descloizite's affect of helping a relatively unlit entity to work with some amount of light is also a notable event.

Descloizite might be best positioned when placed beside the skeletal remains of the dinosaurs, as part of the exhibitions found in the museums of the world. Dinosaurs ate Descloizite, along with their usual diet of tree stumps. As the stone passed through the digestive tract, these prehistoric creatures experienced an acceleration of their bodily mass, thus allowing greater amounts of Earth's lowest black light frequencies to enter their bodies.

The accumulation of light during Earth's infancy was a painfully slow process that necessitated the presence of minerals that could work with the lowest levels of light. Descloizite was a primary light gathering stone during the prehistoric period.

Dioptase

Ascension Triage Healing

Scientific Properties:
Crystallography: Trigonal
Chemical formula: $CuSiO_3 \cdot H_2O$
Mohs hardness: 5
Density: 3.28-3.35 g/cm^3
Colour: Transparent, Dark blue green, emerald green

Dioptase is a rare and enchanting stone. It brings the darker green rays of healing into our new age. Specifically, Dioptase works with the lower range of frequencies of the evolved soul. Evolved souls are graced with an abundance of Oneness, and are, therefore, among the souls, which are destined for ascension.

Although the frequencies of graced souls are quite high, if they are in need of Dioptase, their incarnations on Earth have suffered significant traumatic dislocations within their etheric bodies. The light intended to empower such persons encounters blockages and distortions that interfere with spiritual development. Because the soul and its light are evolved and high, the usual healing stones of ancient times are ineffective. Peridot, Green Adventurine, or Bloodstone frequencies are much too low. On the other hand, Green Tourmaline frequencies are too high. While the vibration of Green Tourmaline is likely to be effective, the level of healing work involved is beneath its advanced abilities. Dioptase, on the other hand, resonates between these two sets of frequencies, perfectly positioned to do the required healing.

Dioptase works with the person who suffers from distortions in the emotional and etheric bodies, and to a lesser extent, in the physical and conscious bodies. Dioptase is a classical healer in the sense that it accelerates the bodily form, which then allows more light to enter. The Dioptase crystal's frequency range is most specific. It allows the body to accept soul frequencies, which are intended for a person, who is spiritually awakened or nearly awakened, and who is very much in line for the ascension. Dioptase does not work with persons who are not in line for the ascension. Vibration needs to be within range.

Dioptase is not specific to a particular chakra or part of the body, and is best placed at any point along the midline to work with the chakra light distribution system (ida, pingala, sushumna). Its healing light energies move throughout the person's energy pathways. Bodily form in its healthy state does not alter or impede the flow of Dioptase's light frequencies. Tissues with distortions or blockages, however, present anomalies to which Dioptase's light energies naturally gravitate. The slower vibratory rate of the unhealthy mass attracts Dioptase for healing. The attraction does not arise from a polar charge within the body, but rather from the alteration or retardation of the flow of light.

Wherever Dioptase frequencies encounter slower bodily mass, which impedes their flow, they initiate the agitation of the mass at the molecular level, thus creating an increase in its frequency rate. The agitation action is caused by the collision between the Dioptase frequencies and the molecules of the slower mass. The Dioptase energies possess significant strength of momentum, and therefore, cannot be stopped by the distortions in the bodily form. Rather, they encounter difficulty passing through. The flow of Dioptase frequencies rebounds from the slower mass back into itself. The flow then compounds as Dioptase rebounds again, back into the slower mass. The build up of Dioptase energies rebounding off of the blockage and off of the continuing flow of its own frequencies causes movement within the slower mass and a build up of Dioptase's strength and intensity. The resulting increase in the number of collisions, which come from all angles, accelerates the vibration of the blockage's molecular structures. Once accelerated adequately, the blockage or distortion clears, allowing the Dioptase frequencies to pass through.

With no remaining impediment to the flow of light, the higher and subtler empowerment frequencies of the new age, now available on Earth, can enter to nurture and raise the vibration of the person's physical form in preparation for the ascension.

Elestial

Mix-Master of the Crystal World

Scientific Properties: (Variety of Quartz)

The first to be noticed, and most striking quality, about the Elestial crystal is its unique shape. Basically, Elestial is a six-sided clear quartz crystal with varying amounts of radiation. Most often, it comes with terminations at both ends of the crystal, making it double terminated. Its uniqueness derives from the configuration of its facets. Each facet is tiered with several parallel sub-facets.

The sub-facets are integral to the way it works. Each tiered sub-facet is a level of knowledge—a plateau of spiritual attainment. The quality of attainment is personal for each individual who uses an Elestial. The level of attainment corresponds to the highest light frequencies with which the user can resonate.

The Elestial is divinely radiated. It, therefore, has a smoky appearance and presents with radiated wisps of darkened crystal. Divine radiation[1] means that the light of the Godhead resides within. Because of the presence of the Godhead, the smoky Elestial can lead an individual through the attainment of an infinite number of plateaus of divine wisdom.

Light in a variety of frequencies comes to the Elestial. These are random, diverse, and non-homogenous light frequencies that collect together within the stone. The result is a unified frequency consisting of the aggregation of all available frequencies. The aggregation of light takes place within the Elestial in the same way as that of any six-sided clear quartz crystal. The frequency that

---

1   IMPORTANT CAUTION: As with Smoky Quartz, the artificial radiation of an Elestial crystal is possible. The same important caution about the dangers of artificial radiation applies to both crystals. Please see Smoky Quartz for details.

comes together within the Elestial is directed outward through the termination.

The Elestial pushes the combined vibration of the six dominant ranges of frequencies outward through the termination in the same way as the six-sided clear quartz crystal. There are, however, significant differences. Firstly, the Elestial's termination is quite different. Each of the Elestial termination's facets incorporates sub-facets. Secondly, the Elestial works with multiple layers of frequencies, and not simply the dominant six. The umbrella layer of the Elestial's aggregated overall light frequency consists, firstly, of the six primary ranges of frequencies. In turn, each of the six primary frequency ranges consists of a number of sub-ranges of frequencies. Each sub-range corresponds to one of the sub-facets. Finally, the individual light frequency itself consists of multiple layers of partial light frequencies. Elestial crystals work with them all.

The sub-facets are integral to the processing of the diversity of light flowing through the Elestial crystal. Each of the six primary facets works with its own dominant range of light frequencies. Each sub-facet works with its own sub-range of frequencies within its respective dominant range. The sub-facet processes one of the many layers within each frequency range or individual light frequency.

The sub-facet exposes the depths of the light. For the purposes of creating an example, if each primary facet has seven (7) sub-facets, the Elestial works with 42 individual ranges of light frequencies. That is, the six primary frequency ranges of the six primary facets are subdivided by the seven sub-ranges of the seven sub-facets to yield 42 individual ranges of frequencies (6 facets x 7 sub-facets = 42 frequency ranges).

The complexity of the light that finds its way into an Elestial is significant. The presence of a double termination further doubles the complexity because light moves in both directions into a second set of sub-facets on the second termination. The number of frequency ranges in the example then doubles to 84. According to this arbitrary example—worth repeating—the elestial receives the light it is exposed to, then divides that light into six primary ranges of frequencies at the facet level, and a further seven sub-ranges of frequencies at the sub-facet level for a total of 42 individual ranges of light frequencies. The number of ranges and sub-ranges are doubled again by the second termination with its six primary facets and seven sub-facets.

The light that enters an Elestial must first be available. The stone depends on the user's own set of light frequencies to provide most of the frequencies it processes. This usually means that the light from the person's charkas is used. Each of the strongest of the user's six primary frequencies, one per primary facet, enters the Elestial. Exposing the many layers of depth within the ranges of frequencies flowing into the Elestial, as the sub-facets do their work, emphasizes the complexity of the light.

The largest facets are reserved for the highest of the chakra energies. Consequently, the largest of the six primary facets carries the light from the crown chakra. The facets to either side of the largest facet carry the light from the two other upper chakras. That is, the light of the throat chakra resonates with the primary facet on one side, and the light of the third eye chakra resonates with the primary facet on the other side. The light frequencies entering the Elestial from the base chakra resonate with the primary facet that is diametrically opposite to the primary facet of the crown chakra. The other lower chakras, the pelvic and navel chakras, resonate with the facets located on either side of the primary facet that resonates with the base chakra. The light from the heart chakra couples with the facet of either the throat chakra, the navel chakra, or both.

Because the crown and base chakras are in opposing positions within the structure of the Elestial, the implication is that heaven and Earth are also in opposing positions in the Elestial. The heavens resonate with the crown, and the Earth resonates with the base. This further complicates the light entering the Elestial, because the light frequencies of the crown and base, and of heaven and earth, are not merely broken down into their parts by the primary facets and sub-facets, but are also in polar opposition to each other.

Opposing polarities are made even more complex when the opposite shaft and facet sides are factored into the balance. The facet edge, which lies between two primary facets, is precisely neutral in polarity to both of the adjacent facets. The facets that are diagonally opposite also exist in equal balance. For the purposes of this example, each of the primary facets are labelled A, B, C, D, E, and F, respectively going around the crystal. As such, side A is in equal balance with its diagonal opposite side C, and so too, will be sides A and E, B and D, B and F, C and E, and D and F. The polarity of the primary facets of the stone are diagonally and diametrically opposite, and equal, thus giving the Elestial symmetry, balance, and harmony.

The effect of polarity goes beyond the facets. Because of Elestial's double terminated structure, the polarity of the termination on one end exerts an opposing polarity upon the termination at the other end. At any one moment, light shoots out from one of the terminations. Each termination draws the negative and positive polarized frequencies to itself. Half of the time, each of the terminations draws positive light, the other half of the time, each draws negatively charged light. At a cyclical rate that is too fast to be measured, light leaving the Elestial's terminations alternates between its negative and positive forms continuously. This push-pull of light is identical to the way light moves out of the Herkimer Diamond. Please see Herkimer Diamond for additional explanation.

The Elestial has the ability to superimpose light upon light. Layers of light vibrations come in from each of the charkas at various depths side-by-side with the light from the divine Godhead coming through the stone's radiated matrix. All of these frequencies become a glorious mixture of light that constitutes the sum total of the light of the person using the Elestial. Each of the six primary frequencies that correspond to the six shaft sides and six facets, each of the secondary frequencies that correspond to the multitude of sub-facets, and the Godhead light that corresponds to the divinely radiated darkened areas, join together within the stone. The Elestial mixes the light together. It then projects the mixture outward, as does any other crystalline point, into the user's aura.

The ultimate product of the Elestial vibrates exactly as the state of the user's vibration dictates. If the stone's user is deficient in some frequency, the output of the Elestial reflects the deficiency. If a person who has only just begun her spiritual journey uses the Elestial, the light available is more limited than the light available to a person who is spiritually adept. The deciding factor is the quality of each user's vibration.

The sum total of a person's range of light vibration is a most exquisite collection of frequencies. Because of the presence of Godhead frequencies, the light itself is a step-up from the limited quality possible from the combined light frequencies of the stone's quartz component alone. With Godhead present, the Elestial's light frequencies constitute Oneness and are united. They consist of the person's main ranges of frequencies, plus the seal of divinity through the Godhead's contribution—hence Oneness. With Oneness, all of the creative properties of the Godhead are potentially possible. The individual light frequencies within the Elestial exist without separation from each other. They are part of the Oneness.

The use of an Elestial crystal offers further benefits. Besides the presence of the Godhead's light, the mixing of a person's own light frequencies has its own distinct advantage. Each frequency within the mix corresponds to some part within the person's body. Because the body part in-question resonates naturally with its own light frequency, each of the other frequencies in the aggregated mix of Oneness assumes surrogate resonance. The indigenous frequency returns to the body part of its origin taking all of the other frequencies with it. Each of the other frequencies also returns to its respective original body part, also taking all of the other frequencies with it—both Earthly and divine. Therefore, all of the Elestial's light frequencies are available to all parts of the body for the benefits that light brings—balance, healing, empowerment, and more.

The availability of all of the Elestial's light frequencies to all of the body's parts gives the Elestial's user the ability to incorporate the light of each body part and chakra into each of the other body parts and chakras. Once empowered with the full radiant spectrum of light that the person already possesses, plus the added light from the divine source, the body and charkas are most capable of making their full potential effective. The light, created by the Elestial through its mixing process, moves into and out of the body's parts easily, simply by the attraction and repulsion of the person's own etheric magnetic field. This light is familiar and aligned with all body parts and carries the Oneness of divinity.

The Elestial is best placed on the body's midline at either the heart or the solar plexus. In this position, its light is given off where it can quickly enter into the circuits of the body's chakra distribution system (ida, pingala, sushumna). Although this placement is ideal, placing it within the aura is all that is required. Its light does not conform to any one chakra, and so, the chakra distribution system and the body's etheric magnetic field automatically carry it to the other chakras and throughout the body. What naturally follows is empowerment, healing, balancing, and harmonizing—whatever light will do.

Epidote

New Age Shuffler

Scientific Properties:
> Crystallography: Monoclinic
> Chemical formula:
> ${Ca_2}{Al_2Fe_3+}(Si_2O_7)(SiO_4)O(OH)$
> Mohs hardness: 6
> Density: 3.38-3.49 g/cm^3
> Colour: Transparent, Opaque, Yellowish-green, green, brownish-green, black

The striated, green, healing shafts of Epidote move light from the heavenly realms onto the Earth. Epidote is among the newly emerging crystals that are here to serve the new age. Its vibration works to raise the body's lower chakras into a much higher vibration. Epidote is a classical healer that accelerates the base chakra in particular, and to a lesser extent the pelvic and navel chakras.

The usual empowerment for the base and lower chakras comes primarily from frequencies that are available from within the etheric magnetic field—the aura. This is Earth's light. However, the base chakra does not always achieve sufficient empowerment to fully participate in this age of enlightenment, with the ascension immediately ahead. The reason is that individuals consciously and wilfully draw exclusively higher frequencies into their bodies to empower only their upper chakras. Their hope is that the upper chakras will satisfy the desire to be aware of higher dimensional energies and improve their ability to commune with the higher realms. Communing with the heavens is noble, but creates an imbalance. These individuals tend to neglect the base chakra. Their focus on the spiritual growth of the upper chakras ignores the base and lower chakras, which then lag behind. Without the participation of the lower chakras, the body's overall vibration is inadequate to qualify for the ascension.

Epidote's dark green healing frequency is dark enough that it resonates with a person's physical body in the lower vibration ranges. Epidote also works with the higher light frequencies of the ascension. It works with the frequencies that prepare the physical body to receive the Light Body—but in the lower frequency ranges. Specifically, it reconditions the base chakra. Once the base chakra[1] is reprogrammed to work with the new ascension frequencies, it works as the base chakra was intended. That is, it performs its function of placing the person in the environment appropriate to the person's vibration. In this case, the Epidote-empowered base chakra directs the person into environments that are conducive to achieving the ascension.

Epidote indeed empowers the base chakra with light that cannot resonate with mundane or lower vibrational spaces. The empowered persons using Epidote will find that their choices of activities change. They will increasingly reject useless preoccupations, and gravitate to functions, persons, and spaces that have higher light frequencies and vibrations. The higher light frequencies, both from a person's higher vibrational associations and from Epidote, work to prepare the body to function at a higher spiritual level. The higher frequencies also displace unwanted negative energy from the physical body and prepare it for Light Body invocation. Epidote empowers the base chakra to move the individual into environments that lead to higher spiritual outcomes.

Call epidote the "new-age shuffler". It empowers the base chakra to help an individual to shuffle along into higher spiritual places and into an accelerated path to the ascension.

---

1   The background discussion of the function of the empowered base chakra can be found in *The Story of Light, Path to Enlightenment* (volume one) in Chapter 4, section 2, entitled, "Base Chakra: Environmental Compatibility". The discussion of the base chakra related to its protective function can be found in volume one, Chapter 3.3 and 3.4, entitled "Inventing the First Chakra" and "The Seed-Light", respectively.

Fire Agate

The Soul's Enforcer

Scientific Properties: (variety of Quartz)

Fire Agate is a stone of much grace and carries with it the vibrations of light that pierce through the bonds of mental illusion. The mind creates its own reality and, in doing so, causes mischief in its endeavour to control the light of consciousness in the ways that it wants. The mind interferes with the arrival of higher light frequencies, and seeks to empower itself through light, which it attempts to manipulate with the integrity of self-centredness.

What does this mindful problem look like? The mind directs the contemplative focus. According to the attraction created by the contemplation, light enters the conscious body where it is then stored. Light stored in the conscious body is later released to follow the mind's directives, and is thereby brought to bear on the focus of the contemplation[1]. At times, the light offered from the soul triggers the mind's contemplations. When the soul seeks to communicate with the mind, the person moves into direct alignment. The means to enhance the connection between the mind and the soul is through the person's consciousness and is, therefore, the propriety of the mind. The person's overall vibration determines the extent to which the mind can connect with the soul. The vibration of the conscious body determines which soul frequencies are acceptable either directly, indirectly, or not at all.

The mind is capable of communicating with the soul. If the

---

1   The reader may want to delve into the discussion of the workings of the consciousness, mind, thought-forms, conscious body, and the light of consciousness further. As background, this discussion will round out the reader's foundation of knowledge about the consciousness. Please see *The Story of Light, Through Heaven's Gate*, Chapter 14, entitled: "Consciousness".

general state of the individual's vibration is calm and serene, the mind does not interfere, and the light of the soul and higher-self moves into the person's consciousness easily and harmoniously. If the mind is compelled to contend with turbulent movements of light because of an irrational, ungrounded, and delusional state within the individual, the mind is preempted from linking-up with the energies of the soul. The mind interferes with the soul-connection because of the problems it experiences in dealing with the turbulence. Turbulence might include scattered light, imbalanced reception, imbalanced light frequencies, illusions, dominating foci, and assorted other difficulties. Turbulence is the antithesis of calm and serene. Whatever light the soul sends enters the conscious body of the mind where it is lost to the turbulence.

Meditating on a regular basis to achieve the desired serenity and tranquillity, needed by the soul to send its light, is highly desirable. The role of Fire Agate, however, is not to create serenity. Rather, Fire Agate accelerates the frequencies sent by the soul. Fast moving light can better pierce through the mind's turbulence. The light from the higher-self blasts through the blockages within the troubled mind. Fire Agate helps the soul to enforce its communion with the consciousness of the person using the stone.

The means by which the light is accelerated past the blockages arises from the way in which light is routed within the stone. The iridescence of Fire Agate implies that its construction consists of a maze of caverns and passageways through which light must pass. As light meanders through the maze, it passes by numerous receptors located on the walls of the stone's passageways. The light is attracted into the receptors, which amplify its speed. Fire Agate is a light accelerator.

Fire Agate's light receptors speed and gather the light passing through. The stone combines frequencies sent by the higher-self with frequencies, which are both present within the conscious body, and which have similar resonance. The newly combined light includes frequencies and sets of frequencies that have a presence in both the soul and the person's conscious body. The stone then directs the combined light frequencies into the mind's conscious body. As the combined frequencies are both coming and going from both the higher-self and the conscious body, the mind's contemplative focus increasingly attunes with the higher-self. Dissynchronous light frequencies cannot cause the problems of interference because they are outside of the vibration range of both the higher-self and the conscious body. The combined light of the soul and the conscious body displaces the turbulence within the mind, and the problem resolves. Serenity and calm prevail, and the contemplation proceeds unhindered.

The energies of the higher-self are offered to the person on Earth in a random fashion. Fire Agate's role of directing light, therefore, does not relate to particular frequencies or sets of frequencies. It remains non-specific. Rather, the frequencies of light move into the conscious body according to the way the soul sees fit to offer its energies and in the quantity and frequency range of the soul's choosing. As the flow of light contains random frequencies which cannot be scrutinized at a conscious level, Fire Agate is best placed at the crown chakra for the reason that light better enters the chakra light distribution system through the crown.

Fire Agate accelerates and combines the light of the higher-self with the identical frequency found in the conscious body of the mind, thus establishing a very powerful link between the soul and its incarnation. Fire Agate's primary purpose is to create the soul-to-person link in the face of the problem of a mind plagued with turbulence and vibrational disturbances, which normally prevent such a link.

Fluorite

Oneness is Oneness is Oneness

Scientific Properties:
> Crystallography: Isometric
> Chemical formula: $CaFi_2$
> Mohs hardness: 4
> Density: 3.175 - 3.56 g/cm^3
> Colour: Transparent, Vitreous, Dull, Purple, lilac, golden-yellow, green, colourless, blue, pink, champagne, brown

Fluorite!

This most precious of the new age stones provides the Earth with a very exquisite form of love from the high octaves of the heavens. The vibration of Fluorite's love creates a space into which the Heavenly Hosts can descend to take up temporary residence during this sacred moment of the birthing of the Earth Star into the fullness of its Light Body. Fluorite's unique vibration facilitates the ease of energy exchange between the angelic ones and the user of the stone.

The divine light energies, for which Fluorite is the conduit, journey through the third eye as they descend from the Crown chakra. Placement of the stone at the third eye presents no problem and is preferred over placement at the crown. Because the Heavenly Hosts can take up residence within the stone itself, third eye involvement has comparatively more to offer to the human consciousness than the crown.

Fluorite is not indigenous to Earth. It comes in this recent age in a quartz-like format having similar workability to quartz, even though its hardness rating is less (Fluorite's hardness is 4 Mohs. Quartz hardness (SiO_2) is 7 Mohs.). Because of the way that Fluorite vibrates, both the conscious human being and the Angelic Hosts are afforded the opportunity of meeting within its etheric hallways and temples.

The human conscious mind generally operates at a frequency rate consistent with the physical plane and, at times, at a rate above the physical. Human consciousness readily resonates with Fluorite because the stone accommodates the vibration of physical consciousness. In the same stone, but above the physical plane's third dimensional awareness, Fluorite carries another distinct vibratory frequency—the sixth dimension[1]. Fluorite's sixth dimensional vibration is not manifest on the third dimension, and therefore, is not detectable with third dimensional methods. While the stone appears to be a solid rock, the higher vibrations of the sixth dimension give Fluorite unique characteristics, which will be revealed shortly.

Both Earthly and heavenly frequencies coexist within Fluorite. It is a product of the New Age. As above, so below. The creation of this new stone follows a long time period during which the angelic caretakers of the planet waited in anticipation for the

---

1 What is a dimension? Any numbered dimension, sixth, fifth, twentieth, etc., is defined within the framework of third dimensional perception. Definitions of higher dimensions are third dimensional concepts. To be blunt, the fifth dimension is a third dimensional concept. Does the sixth, eighth, or eleventh dimension exist? If they do, they cannot possibly be fully, or even properly, understood using third dimensional symbolism or view points. The reference to the sixth dimension made in this section is also a third dimensional concept. Because human beings need to use reference points to communicate, the third dimensional concept of the sixth dimension is valid to discuss within the framework of this Earthly discourse. The primary concepts that support using the 'sixth' dimension herein include the following: the sixth and higher dimensions are free of negativity, the sixth dimension has a vibration that is high enough to readily accommodate spirit beings from higher planes, and the sixth dimension is all-encompassing Oneness. Below the sixth dimension, negativity is a problem for spirit beings, vibration is not high enough, and Oneness is not all-encompassing as there are gaps in the Oneness vibration.

successful merging of the two vibrations of the third dimensional physical plane and the sixth dimensional heavenly planes. The presence of Oneness makes this possible. Fluorite holds the vibrations of both third dimensional Oneness and sixth dimensional Oneness at the same time.

Before such a stone could be created, the means by which third dimensional form acquired light needed to be understood and experienced. The arrival of Fluorite on Earth became possible only after the long apprenticeship of pioneering light-work of those who attained enlightenment on Earth and thereafter pursued the knowledge of how to do so.

The enlightened state is 'of the light' and a part of the Oneness. Conversely, the unenlightened state is not of the light and a part of the darkness. The Earthly third dimension, is neither fully of the light and Oneness[2], nor fully of the darkness without light. Some physical forms on Earth, both persons and objects, hold Oneness, and some have no Oneness. Further, most objects and persons consist partly of Oneness and its counterpart, the unlighted form. Oneness is integral to achieving enlightenment and to the valuable contribution that Fluorite makes to the enlightenment process.

If a person attains the high vibration needed to receive the Light Body and thus becomes enlightened, he merges with the Oneness of his higher self. The skill to go beyond enlightenment to contribute to the enlightenment process of the mass substance of the physical plane is *the* task for human mastery. Through the enduring work of Earth's light-workers, the planet has received much of the light of its Light Body, but not all. Human beings have helped the Earth by participating in the bringing of light into selected locations on the globe. These places have become Earth's

2   "Oneness" is a specific concept that may need a more in-depth explanation for many readers. The discussion about Oneness can be found sprinkled throughout volumes one and two of *The Story of Light,* with definitive discussions found in section 1.2 of volume one, and Chapter 7, "Oneness Light" of volume two.

spiritual power centres. They include the light vortexes found in Banff, Sedona, Lhasa, Glastonbury, Mount Shasta, and numerous other places.

In the same way that light was invoked into Earthly substance, the vibration of Fluorite was birthed onto the physical plane thus placing Fluorite's enlightened Oneness into a basically quartz structure. The vast majority of crystals and other forms on Earth manifest when light enters into form to create Oneness. Form and light come to Earth separately and unite sometime later. Fluorite, in stark contrast, arrives on Earth as Oneness. There is no need for the light and form of Fluorite to unite, because they are united prior to arrival within the physical plane. Fluorite is fully complete and unified as Oneness before it moves onto the Earth plane.

The value of the Oneness of Fluorite, which resonates in both third and sixth dimensions, plays a very significant role in the enlightenment process. Both the Oneness of the Angelic Hosts and the Oneness of the person using the stone can enter into the Oneness of the stone. Oneness is Oneness is Oneness, and can merge with any other Oneness. Simply holding the stone is all that a person needs to wilfully merge with the stone's third dimensional Oneness. Possessing the Light Body is not a prerequisite.

Fluorite's sixth dimensional aspect of Oneness makes the participation of the Angelic Hosts possible. The Angelic Ones are very high inter-dimensional beings. They need a place to come that is free of even the most subtle of negative vibrations. The third dimension is rife with negativity, and while the fourth and fifth dimensions are higher in vibration than the third, they still carry more negativity than the presence of the messengers of God can tolerate. Fluorite's sixth dimensional vibration of Oneness is the haven required by the Angelic Ones to participate.

What possibilities might be expected from the profound union of third and sixth dimensional vibrations of Oneness? What potential lies behind their mergence?

The sharing of divine Oneness is sheer grace. In order to

enhance the communion of the energies of the soul with the third dimension, Fluorite serves to bring Earthly and heavenly vibrations closer to each other. Over time, the merging of lighted persons with the Angelic Hosts will take place en masse. The moment for the upward acceleration of Earth's vibrational octave will be ushered in through frequencies that have been stepped up or stepped down, and thereby, contribute to a process of mutual adjustment. This is not to say that Fluorite is the means to bring forth the Light Body of Earth. Rather, it is the stone that helps with the adjustment of vibration, during which period light frequencies are exchanged. Following the adjustment and light exchange, the person on Earth becomes capable of resonating with higher dimensions, and the Heavenly Hosts acquire a place from which they can offer themselves in service to the Earth.

By placing Fluorite within the aura, the benefit received is the acceleration of one's personal vibration to a higher level while remaining within the bounds of third dimensional time and space. To begin, the Oneness of the person using Fluorite resonates with the third dimensional Oneness within the stone. The third dimensional Oneness within the stone resonates with the sixth dimensional Oneness, also within the stone. Simultaneously, the Oneness of the participating angelic beings resonates with the sixth dimensional Oneness of the stone. The Oneness of the angels inherently resonates with the vast Oneness of the heavens. Hence, through Fluorite's Oneness, a person on Earth can resonate with the vast Oneness of the heavens.

On the Earthly side of the equation, when an individual lends himself to the great shared divine Oneness through the use of Fluorite, he begins to attune to light frequencies from the far reaches of the divine universe. On the heavenly side of the equation, for the Angelic Ones, the sharing of light within the Oneness of the Fluorite enhances their comprehension of actual experiences of the physical plane and permits their exchange of divine wisdom.

The veils of Earthly illusion, ignorance, and karma that block spiritual evolution are not lifted automatically with the use of Fluorite. Rather, the shared Oneness within Fluorite facilitates the raising of a person's vibration through the subsequent influx of light frequencies from the higher dimensions. Fluorite can be used to great advantage by an individual who is not yet enlightened by the invocation of his Light Body. The stone helps to step-up the incarnate physical vibration to the point that the Light Body can enter. Fluorite is often the precursor to enlightenment.

The ability of the individual on Earth and the Angelic Hosts to join together in the Oneness within Fluorite's essence causes the bridging of all separations. The previously unlighted person is thus brought closer to the light of all creation, and at times, in a conscious way. Moving into and out of the stone with one's lighted Oneness, however, is not synonymous with having an awareness of the experience. While some users are aware, the ability to return from the heavens to third dimensional consciousness with the conscious experience intact is not available to everyone using Fluorite. Higher dimensional frequencies of consciousness are most often too subtle to make the journey into the density of the physical plane and the Earthly third eye chakra. Fluorite provides an adjustment to the accelerated vibrations of the higher octaves, but awareness is a factor of the development of the third eye. The capacity to be aware of the angels who have taken up residence in the stone increases with its use.

As the state of Oneness is eternally emersed in the realms of unified time and all space—beyond time and space—all events are manifest in the point of conscious awareness. Within the Oneness, the conscious awareness is opened to the ability to see past experiences and future possibilities. When one attunes to the Oneness of the Fluorite and transcends the time-space continuum, untold infinite potentials of experience become available. This potential, however, is reserved for those whose vibration has made the upward adjustment. Along the way, there is a spiritual awakening in increasingly significant steps.

Fluorite has many colour variations including purple, lilac, golden-yellow, green, colourless, blue, pink, champagne, and brown. Within the human community, primary groupings of individuals create the need to offer different colours. An individual may resonate with the vibration of one colour better than another. Different coloured Fluorite crystals skew their vibratory influences to correspondingly different ranges of frequencies. By using the appropriate colour, the less attuned individual receives light frequencies that resonate somewhat closer to their own. The colour of choice facilitates the initial movement of the individual's essence into the Oneness in the stone. Once attuned, however, the colour patterns are of no concern because Oneness is what permeates the lighted substance of the stone. Oneness is Oneness and resonates with all other Oneness irrespective of colour. Fluorite is Oneness. Any Fluorite in any colour will do!

Fluorite can also be used to contact specific persons or beings in one's life, including beings that are both incarnate and discarnate. To initiate contact, a person makes a specific request for contact. The person, who is being called, may or may not be aware of the call, depending on his conscious abilities. The discarnate being in the heavens is always aware, but may or may not be inclined to answer the request. In either case, contact is possible and much easier with the use of Fluorite.

Fluorite is a profound addition to the inventory of crystals that bring promise to the new age. Through its Oneness, the person on Earth has a direct link to the innumerable divine light frequencies throughout the grand universe.

Fuchsite

Millennium Reconditioner

Scientific Properties: (Variety of Muscovite)
Crystallography: Monoclinic (Cr is Trivalent)
Chemical formula: $K(Al,Cr)_3Si_3O_{10}(OH)_2$
Mohs hardness: 2.5
Density: 2.77-2.88 g/cm^3
Colour: Green (with shiny Chromium surface)

Fuchsite manifests onto the Earth quickly. It is part of the mica family of minerals. Its bright to emerald green, smooth, and shiny surface are unique. Although Fuchsite is a classic healer because it accelerates vibration, thus allowing more light to enter bodily form, the frequencies it brings are not common to most human bodies. Fuchsite is among the many new and different crystals that are surfacing as a herald to the cataclysmic changes during this new age.

The mica content on the surface of Fuchsite smoothes the flow of light both into and out of its form. In effect, the light is realigned by mica's etheric magnetic field to match the form. The mica helps to harmonize the etheric body, not by conducting light, but by ensuring that the frequencies exchanged between the stone and a recipient host's body are appropriate. Vibrations that are tainted, out of harmony, misaligned, or outside of the range of frequencies that resonate with Fuchsite's user are filtered out by the user's enhanced etheric magnetic field, following the field's empowerment from Fuchsite. Mica is known for its insulating qualities. It selectively isolates undesirable light frequencies from desirable light frequencies, thus capturing the range that nourishes bodily form and eliminating the rest.

Fuchsite is not specific to any one area of the body, although, because of its green colour, it is basically a heart frequency. Once light frequencies enter the stone, they become available to the general bodily form wherever they are wanted. Fuchsite's energies are designed to correct imbalances that do not allow light to flow properly due to areas of density within the physical body. The light frequencies of the current millennium are much higher than they have been in the past. More crucially, blockages are much higher in vibration as well. Blockages, with such higher vibration, are not truly blockages. They do not stop or retard the flow of light. Rather, vibration all around the anomaly is higher, and light moves at a steady, yet faster pace. Fuchsite helps the body's slower areas of vibration to accelerate, and thereby reconditions them to work with the higher ranges of frequencies present.

Fuchsite is destined to be one of the foremost healing stones going forward. The roughness of its primary vibration is a very fresh healing vibration that is softer than the Earth's traditional premier healer, which is Green Adventurine. The frequencies that Fuchsite works with are significantly higher than frequencies aligned with Adventurine. Fuchsite's frequencies need to be higher because they offer healing at higher levels of vibration. Fuchsite has come to replace Green Adventurine, which will be leaving the Earth. It needs to find a new home on a physical world that has a similar vibration.

Fuchsite is an all-purpose, new age, healing stone that is only just beginning to fulfill its role of reconditioning bodily form to work with increasingly higher light frequencies.

Garnet, Green

Healer of Light's Distortions

Scientific Properties: (Garnet)
Crystallography: Cubic rhombic
Chemical formula:
$(Ca^{2+}, Mg^{2+}, Fe^{2+})_3 (Al^{3+}, Fe^{3+}, Cr^{3+})_2 (Si\ O_4)_3$
Mohs hardness: 6.5 - 7.5
Density: 3.1-4.3 g/cm^3
Colour: green, (Garnet also includes orange, yellow, red, blue, purple, brown, black, pink and colorless varieties)

Green Garnet adds frequencies of higher light vibration to the frequencies of the heart chakra to balance shortfalls in the heart's vibration.

To begin to explain Green Garnet's touching sweet vibration, Earth's distant past was not a time with a great abundance of light. Because of the lack of light, numerous crystals took on multiple roles that were quite different from their sister stones. That is, crystals carried most distinct and separate roles, while still maintaining a common role.

Red Garnet, which is discussed in this volume, brings a dark shade of red light to the lower frequencies of the second chakra. Because Red Garnet balances anger by adding its own light to the second chakra's mix, its role is specific to the second chakra only. Similar to the Red Garnet, Green Garnet shares the role of drawing light into regions where the light has been tainted by the problem of negativity. In the case of the green variety, Garnet's light frequencies are primarily, but not exclusively, within the range of the lower light frequencies of the heart chakra.

The problem of negative polarized light is common within

the charkas simply because of the problems that third dimensional density creates. The empowerment of the chakra, however, depends upon this same tainted light. When the light of empowerment is tainted, so too is the chakra. Green Garnet works to bring balancing light frequencies to the heart chakra to overcome the problems caused by vibrational distortions.

Heart chakra distortions mean that love is not whole and complete. The love offered has some aspect of its true vibration missing. For example, love's missing aspect might be respect, it might be warmth, or it might be a host of other love-related vibrations. It is love with a trailer—an attached proviso. In essence, the love is conditional.

To overcome the 'conditions', the love expressed from the heart chakra needs the additional frequencies of respect and warmth, or whatever other light is missing. If the love offered by the heart is not whole and complete, it is not balanced. Adding the light frequencies of respect and warmth generate the necessary balance. This additional light incorporates the 'conditions' of respect and warmth, which then attach to the heart's incomplete love vibration. Once sufficient additional light has been added and the love is complete, there is no need for further additional light to fulfill the condition. However, when the heart's love is distorted, its light frequencies need to be propped up through fulfillment of the conditions—respect or warmth. The added frequencies to fulfill the condition also work to alleviate the strain placed on the conscious body, which works strenuously to supply these frequencies to balance the heart chakra's polarized light.

For Green Garnet to work, placing it at the heart is best, but it can be placed elsewhere as well. It can be used wherever the body carries negative polarized light frequencies that inhibit growth and empowerment. When used in places in the body outside of the heart, the light frequencies involved correspond to that body part. Infected throat chakra light frequencies mean that the light of truth is tainted. Infected navel chakra light frequencies mean that the light of form expansion[1], or creativity, is tainted. Green Garnet brings the additional light frequencies needed to offset the tainted frequencies coming from those aspects of the body or heart, which are not in balance. When the heart chakra's love vibration needs to be made whole and workable, because of the missing conditions of respect and warmth, Green Garnet provides the additional light of respect and warmth that brings balance to the heart's love. It fulfills the conditions attached, and makes them unnecessary.

In juxtaposition, the operation of Green Garnet might also be viewed as the introduction of a faster light frequency into the chakra area, where a slower frequency previously created a blockage. The imbalanced, distorted, or otherwise tainted light frequency that carries a negative polar charge is the slower frequency, while Green Garnet brings a faster light frequency to balance the overall frequency rate and polarity. Once this correction is instituted, the frequencies of the heart chakra or other affected parts of the body are freed to fulfill their true potential by empowering the blockage from within. Thereafter, love comes complete with respect and warmth, along with all of the other conditions that make love whole and complete. Similarly, truth comes with honesty and integrity, along with all of the other conditions that make truth whole and complete.

As does the Red Garnet with the pelvic chakra, Green Garnet adds light frequencies to the mix within the heart chakra to dilute and eventually displace the negative aspects of the light energies that are creating problems.

---

1   The navel chakra is known to be the chakra of abundance, but what exactly is abundance in terms of the flow of light? For more information, first see the discussion on the navel chakra in volume one, *The Story of Light, Path to Enlightenment*, section 4.4, entitled: "Navel Chakra: Form Expansion", then see "Citrine" in this volume.

Garnet, Red

Anger Resolution

Scientific Properties: (See Green Garnet)

Red Garnet is an old Earth stone. It attracts light from the frequencies available within the auric field of the person using the stone. Red Garnet brings a dark red vibration to the lower levels of the second (pelvic) chakra and at times, to the first (base) chakra. In addition, it possesses some grounding qualities. Of the light made available by Red Garnet, a portion is grounded into the Oneness of the soul-seed or kundalini in the base chakra. Garnet's primary function is to calm the difficult red light frequencies, which tend to be converted to anger.

Base Chakra Confusion: Red versus Black

Some confusion arises from attributing the colour red to the base chakra. Throughout *The Story of Light* series, the base chakra is ascribed the colour black and the pelvic chakra is red. However, numerous other sources of new age writings ascribe the colour red to the base chakra and omit the black light frequency entirely.

Why the difference? In volume one of *The Story of Light*, the black light frequency is described as being Earth's indigenous light frequency[1]. The reasoning is that, in the very beginning, at a time when light was absent from Earth, only the lowest and slowest of all frequencies could descend into the density of the physical plane. This was the black light frequency. Therefore, Earth's journey to enlightenment begins with the assimilation of black light. The

---

1   See *The Story of Light, Path to Enlightenment*, Chapter 1, section 1.3, entitled, "Black: the Light of Earth", for the discussion on Earth's indigenous light frequency as it was in the beginning.

natural consequence is that, first, the Earth resonates with black light. Second, all grounding is within the black frequency range. And, third, to best harmonize with the Earth, the base chakra has traditionally resonated with the black light frequency range. Additional reading regarding Smoky Quartz and the base chakra will add clarity to this line of thought[2].

Why then do other literary sources ascribe the colour red to the base chakra? First, the reader must discern the origins of the source. Is the source of writing from among the souls who incarnated onto the Earth at the beginning of time? Or, is the source of writing from among souls who incarnated in this current millennium? The soul's origin makes a difference.

The original arrivals on Earth began at the lowest levels of Earth's dense vibration and at the beginning of time. The recent arrivals began in the new age, with no exposure to the extreme density that dominated Earth's beginnings. Earth's vibration in the new age is almost ready for the ascension, and is, therefore, significantly higher than at any previous time, and especially higher than at the beginning. Many new age authors, who make reference to the base chakra, are recent arrivals from far away planets and star systems. The Pleiades and Sirius star systems have made themselves known, but these are not the only ones. The recent arrivals bring a fresh perspective and a message that is unique to their own home world. They are here to help Earth through its process of ascension, but equally importantly, they are here to learn what Earth has to offer—namely, to learn about life in a physical world.

The source of confusion comes from the application of perceptions that are limited to the new age. The vibration of the incarnate body of the original arrivals on Earth began at a much lower frequency rate than the vibration of the incarnate body of the recent arrivals. The base chakra of the original arrival has resonated

---

2   See Smoky Quartz in this volume; and see *The Story of Light, Path to Enlightenmnet*, Chapter 4, section 4.2, entitled: "Base Chakra: Environmental Compatibility".

traditionally and primarily with black light frequencies, but the base chakra of the recent arrival resonates at a frequency rate that is a full octave higher. The recent arrival's base chakra does not reach down into the lower range of the grounding black light frequencies. It, therefore, resides within the red light frequency range with limited understanding of the lower black light.

In their quest to help Earth through written publication, the recent arrivals write from the perspective their own vibrations. This perspective reflects familiarity with the higher vibrations that presently dominate the current new age, but not familiarity with the traditional lower vibrations that are still very much present on Earth. Black light, then, is not indigenous to the recent arrival.

To the soul that has been on Earth since the beginning, the base chakra carries black light frequencies, resonates readily with the Earth, and responds to love and the divine vibration of Smoky Quartz for its opening. In contrast, the soul of the recent arrival sees the base chakra at a higher vibration level, which is within the red range of light frequencies. The need to open the base chakra is integral to the original arrivals' spiritual journey, but may not even be mentioned by the recent arrival, except in an empowerment context, which assumes that the base chakra is already open.

Using the perspective of the original arrivals on Earth, and discounting the perspective of the recent arrival, Garnet is within the red light frequency range, and resonates primarily with the pelvic chakra.

Penetrating Red Light

The red light frequency range warrants further comment. The colour red is relatively low on the vibrational scale. It is above the black frequency range, but below the orange or golden ranges. Its most notable quality is its strength of flow. Red light can penetrate form easily. For example, laser beams derive from the red light of the Ruby and are used to cut through metal. While not all parts of the red light frequency range contribute to the cutting power of the laser beam, red light can be used to pierce through the densest of physical forms. Red light's strength is not only found in its penetrating power, it can also dominate other frequency ranges. Both sex and anger are driving energies that come from the red range of frequencies, and both are difficult to dislodge once embedded into a person's emotional state. Red light's strengthens of penetrating force and dominance can become problems.

Discerning Anger

Anger is not always an unwanted emotion. A distinction needs to be made between mundane anger and divinely-inspired anger. Mundane anger is a range of red light frequencies that are full of negativity. Ego plays a major role in the promotion of mundane anger. If, however, the red light of anger is not negative, if it is pure and in balance, the anger is not mundane, but an expression of divinity. At times, the divine universe uses anger to advance its purposes. Divinely-inspired anger does not work against the progress of the evolving soul. As with anything else that is divine, it brings love. Divine love, expressed through what may seem to be undesirable anger, facilitates the learning of life's lessons, which are intended to benefit the soul. Divine anger is not to be judged. Rather, those involved with lessons imposed by divine anger are wise to look for the underlying *divine* lesson.

Red Garnet's Contribution

Anger is usually a problem, but not always. Its immediate effect is to create separation between the person projecting the anger and her victim. The force driving anger is the red light, which displaces any other light frequency. Red light makes anger a strong emotion. The light of reason cannot sustain a place in the face of the light of anger. In short order, the angry person becomes consumed. Separation sets in. Reason becomes impossible. Because the angry person's mind is so full of the piercing, dominating, and penetrating red light frequency, change is difficult. Anger continues with no sign of abatement.

If the second chakra is imbalanced and not providing a means for the expression of divinity, the more accentuated flare ups of the potent red light frequencies of anger need to be tempered. Red Garnet provides the solution to the difficulty posed by anger's intransigence.

In essence, anger amounts to a vibration of light, nothing more. Its light exists at a specific vibrational frequency rate, which is within the lower ranges of the second chakra. The solution to the problem of anger is to introduce a frequency within the red light range that will resonate with the red light frequencies of anger without fueling its effect. Red Garnet's frequencies affect the impure aspects of the red light of anger by offering light at approximately the same vibration rate. Combining the red light of anger with the red light without anger, coming from the Red Garnet, dilutes the light that is driving the person's angry emotions. Combining the two sets of frequencies also generates balance and neutralizes the frequencies of anger. Red Garnet creates a neutral space within which the red light of anger can be contained. Because the space provides a calmed environment of peace, the more potent aspects of anger are tempered. Thereafter, the red light of anger dissipates.

Although the balance, created by adding frequencies that have no anger, is empowering to the person experiencing the anger, it is not empowering to the second chakra. When impure, negatively charged, red light dominates the empowerment of the second chakra, anger is the result. Infusing light into the chakra, however, does not always purify the frequencies of anger. The two red light frequencies offset each other, but tend not to affect the second chakra. The chakra, still empowered with the red light of anger, continues to radiate anger outward. However, the effect of the added frequency of red light undercuts anger's dominance and makes possible the influx of other frequencies, which in turn, eventually displace the frequencies of anger.

Red Garnet dilutes the potency of the impure red light of anger with its own red light frequencies. Thereafter, anger is tempered by the imposition of a vibration of calmed balance. Red Garnet blunts the sharp edge of mundane anger.

Green Aventurine

Looking forward to Retirement

Scientific Properties: (variety of Quartz)

Green Aventurine is an unobtrusive, rather quiet green stone. It brings with it the loving healing of Earthly light, as it has ever since the time when Earth first played host to incarnate beings. It is a very old stone of great value. It works to heal in the most difficult of circumstances.

As an Earth stone, Green Aventurine works with the light available from within the Earth's etheric magnetic field, and further, within the etheric field of the person using the stone. It attunes with frequencies ranging from the dark green to lighter green shades. At times, variations of red light frequencies may be mixed into the stone in the same way as other crystalline vibrations mix into other stones.

Healing follows the presence of light. Green Aventurine is a classic healing stone. It works by accelerating the molecular mass upon which it is placed. Whenever the mass of the human body's form is accelerated, space opens for more and higher frequencies of light to enter. Green Aventurine facilitates the influx of light; hence, it facilitates healing. It may be placed anywhere on the body where healing energies are needed to overcome areas of density and blockage. Placement is crucial to the quality of the stone's healing. Placed within the aura, Green Adventurine will be of benefit. Placed at the specific area of concern, whether on a chakra centre or body part, has the greatest effect.

A number of qualities may be erroneously attributed to Green Aventurine. That is, the stone accelerates mass, which then receives an increased quantity of light. The error arises from incorrectly associating the effects of the light with the stone. From person to person, there is little consistency in the consequences of the incoming light, but, in every instance, mass is accelerated in the vicinity of the stone and healing results. As the stone's placement is valid for any part of the body, the needed healing occurs. The healing effect, however, often leads to the false assumption that Green Aventurine is specific to one or another type of healing, and that its healing affect applies to a specific part of the body.

Green Aventurine is quite generic. It works wherever placed to accelerate mass. The light that follows the opening of mass is consistent with a broad range of frequencies that come with any of the quartz crystals. Healing can be the result of any of the frequencies present, thus causing a reaction on the part of the form that is unique only to the vibration of that particular form. There is no specialization of either the light involved or the bodily form upon which the light works. The light goes in and healing happens for whatever body part and with whatever light frequency is used.

Green Aventurine is most effective when the healing requires that pockets of slow and dense vibration be accelerated. As healing involves mass whose vibration has been slowed to the point of illness and disease, the stone is right-at-home with the usual long list of human ailments. As an all-purpose healer, it is unparalleled in its work with disease.

Green Aventurine works with the slower and lower frequencies of the Earth's light. However, the Earth is entering a new era of enlightenment wherein the quantity and quality of light readily available is better than ever before. In this time of epic changes, Green Aventurine's usefulness has long passed the point of its zenith. Earth's vibration is accelerating beyond the stone's primary range of light frequencies. Therefore, Green Aventurine will be returning home to its place in the larger universe in the heavens at the end of this millennium. Once home, it is scheduled to be rejuvenated and made ready to again descend into the third dimension as a healing stone in another place and on a different planet.

Hawk's Eye

See the Larger Picture with all the details

Scientific Properties:
Hawk's Eye consists of Limonite, Quartz, Riebeckite

Hawk's Eye has the dark blue colour of deep consciousness. It comes with a shimmer or iridescence that foretells of the presence of cavernous formations deep within. The stone's design consists of a matrix of caverns or passageways lined with an iridescence throughout. The shiny iridescence reflects light from the tiny cavern walls into its core. The wise old sage might say that the various caverns within the stone carry their own set of reading glasses. As the light penetrates, the different parts of the stone read specific frequencies from within the flow of light passing through.

In the areas of the passageways, the shimmer is the reflection given off by the tiny light receptors that line the cavern walls. The receptors, which may number in the hundreds or even thousands, process the entire spectrum of light that enters and flows through the stone. Each receptor is unique. It is encoded to pick out the single light frequency, with which it resonates, and reflects the rest. The individual light receptor amplifies the light frequency it picks up, then passes the amplified version on, and up the hierarchy of receptors.

Communication between individual light receptors follows the flow of light frequencies that are moving through the matrix of Hawk's Eye's molecular structure. The process is similar to a chain-reaction. Through amplification of its unique frequency, each light receptor accelerates the adjacent receptors and molecular structures. Together, the amplified frequencies contribute to an aggregated impression of the energy held within all of the receptors. What remains is to read and make sense of the impression.

The stone's unified mass as a whole resonates as a single unit.

The mass vibrates synchronously with each individual light receptor simultaneously, thus creating a single unified light frequency. This unified frequency vibrates at the median or average point of all the frequencies combined. In effect, the light frequencies in total are read and then transferred into a single vibration.

Within the umbrella vibration is the united vibration of all amplified frequencies that have been read individually, read as a group, read as a sub-group, and read as one. The frequencies of each receptor remain separate with their own identities, and are held intact. The light processed by Hawk's Eye may be understood as the totality of all of the readings of the amplified light frequencies combined, as they pulse through the stone. The combination is the single highest vibration of the frequencies present. It provides an overall picture of all of the light frequencies contributing to the mind's awareness within the realm of consciousness. This is the umbrella vision offered through the wisdom of Hawk's Eye.

The amplified version of a single light frequency generates its own portion of the overall picture. The most remote areas deep within the stone absorb light rays at frequency rates, which are infinitely subtle and far too weak and delicate to be perceived by the human mind. The light receptors enhance the signal strength of these light frequencies and bring their vibrations within range of the human conscious awareness. Through amplification, the nature of the vision is made available to the observer. Reading the aggregated frequency provides the overall picture, and reading the individual frequency provides the details.

The contribution to anyone using Hawk's Eye is the vision of the highest overall light of Oneness, as well as, the most infinitely subtle aspects of a single unique frequency passing through the stone. As an analogy to describe Hawk's Eye, one might look upon an Earthly scene from the vantage point of the soaring hawk. The eye of the hawk is sharp and able to distinguish minute detail in addition to seeing the broad scope of the entire scene below, including each of the sub-scenes within the larger landscape.

Hawk's Eye is a "seer's" stone, and therefore, is best placed on the third eye. For effective use, once so placed, the user then needs to move the mind into the contemplative state. Contemplation creates the magnetic field that attracts the light frequencies needed to fulfill the mind's query. The light attracted from the storehouse of the conscious body passes through Hawk's Eye. By the stone's amplification and aggregation of the individual frequencies into sub-groups and groups, the stone figuratively lights up the countryside, so to speak. Thereafter, the overall vision and details of the spiritual landscape, which is the subject of the contemplation, enter the awareness. Once the infinitely small details are clear to the mind, the user becomes capable of very significant discoveries in the realms of the wisdom of the light.

Hawk's Eye is a vision stone that makes the subtle frequencies of divine light visible to the awareness of the naked third eye. It is the microscope and the view from the mountain top of the essence of light.

Hematite

Nature's Ground Rod

Scientific Properties:
Crystallography: Trigonal
Chemical formula: Fe_2o_3
Mohs hardness: 5-6
Density: 5.26 g/cm^3
Colour: Black and shiny

Hematite has a distinctive black and shiny surface. It is the simplest of all crystals in the way that it works with light. Hematite's black aspect grounds the lowest of all of Earth's frequencies—black light, and its mirror-like, shiny surface reflects off all other frequencies—simple as that! Within the range of black light, Hematite works almost exclusively with the lowest and slowest black light frequency.

When Earth first entered the third dimension, it had no light of any description. Earth's form manifested into the void of space totally unlighted. The very first light frequency to assimilate into Earth's mass was the lowest black light frequency that could both enter into the physical plane and still carry the core frequency[1] of the Godhead. It was the lowest frequency possible.

At the very beginning of time, Hematite helped bring the

---

1   Reference to the 'core' frequency arises from the construct of basic light frequencies. The core frequency is the original frequency arising from the Godhead, and the frequency, upon which all other light vibrations of influence adhere. The aggregate is a light frequency that is divine and marked by the characteristics of all other frequencies present. Core light frequencies are discussed at length in *The Story of Light, Through Heaven's Gate*, volume one, section 4.1, entitled: "The Initiation of Form: Core Frequencies".

very first black light frequencies to the unlighted Earth. Similarly, it works to bring the very first (black) light frequencies to other unlighted forms, including parts of the human body that have no light. Hematite works with any form or any body part. As such, Hematite initiates form's journey into Oneness, however primitive that Oneness might be. The significance is that Hematite can help jump-start the process to enlightenment of any person, who cannot otherwise assimilate light. This quality is especially significant for the person that has no understanding of spirituality. Hematite is the place to start.

Hematite is one of the primary stones used in the crystalline layout to invoke the Light Body. It is the best of all the grounding stones to help bring the Light Body into the physical body. Because it works with only the lowest of the black light frequencies, its grounding action means that the person's Light Body descends to the very lowest of places within his physical body. Hematite helps to ensure that the Light Body gets all the way into the physical body, and not merely part way.

A second important quality that makes Hematite the best stone for Light Body invocation is that its vibration is the lowest and slowest of vibrations. Because its vibration is lower and slower than the vibration of the person receiving the Light Body, the Light Body descends to its place within the physical body without being drawn into vibrations that are lower than the physical body. The Light Body gets all the way into the physical body without passing through to denser vibration.

A third important quality is that, because Hematite works only with the lowest black frequency, it can hold the Light Body in position in the physical body without assimilating the physical body. Invoking the Light Body would hardly be divine if it entered the physical body, only to be pulled into a vibration of mass that was not part of the person receiving the Light Body. As the invocation process requires, the Light Body does not enter into Hematite's mass.

Many black crystals have excellent grounding qualities. What separates Hematite from the others is its ability to ground light into the very core of the mass upon which it is placed.

Herkimer Diamond

Purest, Cleanest, Crystal Light

Scientific Properties: (Variety of Quartz)

The double terminated Herkimer Diamond delivers flowing waves of magnetic light, which originates from the centre of the stone itself. The Herkimer creates light out of the nothingness at its centre, then moves it in both directions to both terminations to be expressed to the external world.

Light from the Herkimer Diamond is created by the magnetic pull generated by the stone's two terminations acting upon the space of nothingness at the centre of the stone. In the stone's creative centre, the potential exists for magnetic polarity that alternates from negative to positive, and from one termination to the other. The polarity changes occur in synchrony with the negative and positive polarity shifts of the terminations themselves. The polarity of each terminus pulls light, created within the stone's Oneness, away from the centre of the stone.

The nothingness at the centre of the Herkimer Diamond, and the creation of light out of that nothingness, arise directly out of the Earth's duality acting on the creative potential of the stone's Oneness. Herkimer Diamond creates light from its Oneness[1]. Negative and positive charges are the opposing polarities within duality. In the same way, duality governs both the darkness and its opposite, which is light. By nature, vibration is a pulse arising

---

1   Oneness is the expression of God in creation outside of the Godhead. As God, Oneness has all of the creative powers of God. Herkimer Diamond uses its Oneness at the centre of the stone to create light. For the foundation discussion, please see *The Story of Light, Path to Enlightenment*, section 1.2, entitled: "Light + Form = Oneness", and *The Story of Light, Through Heaven's Gate*, Chapter 7, entitled: "Oneness Light".

from the duality of yin and yang. The vibration found at the centre of the Herkimer also oscillates between yin and yang or negative and positive.

The Herkimer's two termination points draw both the light (positive charge) and the nothingness of the darkness (negative charge) from the stone's creative centre to one end and then to the other end. When one of the terminations draws the darkness, the other draws the light. This creates a constant flow of light and dark to each terminus. The creative potential of the Oneness at the centre of the stone yields both light and dark and in a rapidly pulsating fashion. The speed of the cyclical vibration is infinite and unmeasurable. In short, the Herkimer creates light by magic.

The alternating dark and light flowing from each terminus provides light half the time in each direction. Light is emitted from the stone 100% of the time, with 50% coming from each end in an alternating cycle. The duration of each individual emission is of little consequence beyond making the distinction between the light and the dark of Earth's duality. The darkness is of no harm as it is nothingness; and the light created is quite pure.

The light of the Herkimer is absolutely pure at the mathematical centre of the stone where it originates. Herkimer's light suffers only a very few extremely minute distortions as it passes from the stone's centre through the stone's inclusions and impurities, and then out through the terminus. Herkimer Diamond creates some of the cleanest, purest light frequencies available to the physical plane. Placing a Herkimer on any part of the human body, or on any chakra, will allow light of exceptional quality to permeate the area in which it is placed.

The Herkimer Diamond passes light from one terminus to the other in the same way as the flow of polarized light moves along the chakra distribution system (ida, pingala, sushumna). In the chakra distribution system, light is shunted along the passageways via the polarity differentials encountered at each position within the passageway[2]. The polarized light frequency is attracted or repelled by the change in polarity within each of the distribution system's sub-units, thereby giving it directional flow. In the Herkimer Diamond, each terminus creates an attraction for the positive polarity of the pulse generated from the stone's creative core. The Herkimer causes the newly created light from within the stone to pass outward in both directions. Placed between two chakras, it ensures that both chakras are nourished with the stone's exceptionally clean light, as well as, whatever amount of external light from the local environment happens to be passing in the direction to which the terminations are aligned.

The light from the Herkimer Diamond must be distinguished from external light that passes through. The polarity of the oscillating pulses generates a magnetic attraction, which also draws light from the immediate external environment into the stone. Once this external light passes into the stone, it is processed to bring it into harmony, and then passes back out into the environment.

The external frequencies entering the stone are routed into the stone's oscillating flow of polarized light in synchrony with the pulse of light and dark energies. The in-coming frequency's negative aspect separates from its bond with the positive aspect and each joins with the flow of its own polarity. The positive aspects of the incoming frequencies of light are drawn to each termination, separately from the negative aspects. This separation renders the dark and negative aspect unto its truth of nothingness[3], while giving directional flow to the positive aspect, according to how the terminations are pointed. When negative energy harmonizes with the darkness of the stone's pulse, it becomes nothingness.

---

2   Please see the discussion of the flow of light from receptors in the crown chakra, to the light distribution channels, and then to the chakras and bodily form for assimilation, found in *The Story of Light, Path to Enlightenment*, section 4.8, entitled: "Crown Chakra: Thousand Petal Lotus".

3   Negative energy standing alone is a negation of existence; it is nothing.

The harmless darkness or nothingness disappears, while the positive aspect of the light moves outward from the terminations to be offered to the body and the Earth where it does its work of bringing love and light. In effect, the Herkimer acts as a light purifier.

There is no change in the amount or quality of the positively charged frequencies coming from external sources. The dynamic of the stone's pulse means that half the light drawn moves one way and half moves the other. It also means that negativity is removed from the light passing through the stone, thus making its purity comparable to the light created within the stone's Oneness.

In addition to the creation of its own light and the purification of external light, the Herkimer Diamond deflects negatively polarized light. This is again due to the continuously pulsing polar charges moving between the terminations. The impurities of any light passing by the stone are met with the energies of the opposing polarity, which is positive. The positive aspect fills the space of the Herkimer Diamond, while the negative aspect assumes its truth and disappears. A frequency that is not overly negative enters the stone to be purified. However, there is simply no room, or polarity, to accommodate light frequencies that are primarily negatively charged. If a frequency is distorted and tainted, and carries too much negativity, it cannot enter the stone, and simply bounces off.

The Herkimer Diamond is a rare gift of Earthly light and love. Anyone so fortunate to possess such a wondrous stone will indeed experience cleansed and pure light. While monetary value is a mundane fixation reflecting perceived value, this "diamond" is priceless in the service of bringing light into spaces of darkness. It is truly a magical stone that creates light from nothingness. The light given off by the Herkimer Diamond is the cleanest on Earth.

Howlite

Feminine Enhancer

Scientific Properties:
Crystallography: Monoclinic
Chemical formula: $Ca_2B_5SiO_9(OH)_5$
Mohs hardness: 3.5-6.5
Density: 2.53 - 2.59 g/cm^3
Colour: White with Silvery inclusions

Howlite's white colour and silvery streaks blend together most eloquently. They bring forth the gracious influences of the feminine vibration wherever Howlite is placed. The solid consistency of the white colour is the mark of a vibration of purity. The silvery-coloured inclusions, while not metallic, conduct the Howlite vibration in and out of the stone. The inclusions allow Howlite's vibration to mix with the light frequencies present in the stone's immediate environment.

Howlite offers no vibration or light frequency of its own. It is best used in conjunction with other stones or, more accurately, with other vibrations, which includes, in particular, the human body and its chakras. The white substance of the stone provides a feminine influence, which resonates with the light of the dominant vibration or light frequency present in the auric field or conscious body. The dominant frequency may be understood as the frequency in nearest proximity to Howlite, and having the strongest intensity. Howlite lends its influence to the dominant frequency, and simultaneously, but to a lesser extent, to other slightly less dominant frequencies as well.

The basics of the feminine mystique need to be explored. The purely feminine influence is one of attraction-rejection, rather than extension-withdrawal, which is the masculine influence. A polarized magnetic field is set up to generate the attraction. The feminine polarized light frequency attracts to itself its opposing counterpart, which is the masculine polarized light frequency. The feminine influence is one-half of the energy of any particular manifestation of Oneness, and is equal in measure to the masculine influence.

The attraction set up by Howlite's feminine influence is strictly magnetic, and the format it takes conforms precisely to the polar opposite of the vibration that it is influencing. For example, the feminine influence helps set up an attraction to enhance the clarity of a person's world view. Howlite's feminine polarity infiltrates the mind through the feminine vibrations of beauty, gentility, calm, reservedness, and accommodation for all vibrations that reflect the vibration of the mind and its world view. The feminine influence then uses these traits, among many others, to empower and accentuate the mind's etheric magnetic field, which in turn attracts the light frequencies needed to fulfill the mind's world view. Further, the feminine influence ensures that the correct light frequencies to support the person's world view are accepted, while frequencies that do not conform are rejected.

Feminine polarity is labelled negative. Negative polarity, however, is merely one of the two sides of a magnetic energy. The word 'Yin', from the Chinese language, can be substituted. Yin is the feminine vibration without semantic connotations. Yin, or negative, is simply the opposite pole and carries with it no undesirable qualities. Howlite accentuates the yin-negative-feminine polar influence of the dominant light frequency in nearest proximity. The enhanced feminine influence strengthens the dominant frequency's attraction for nearby light frequencies having the opposing polar charge.

Enhancement of the feminine pole also accentuates the purity of light. The single, specific, dominant light frequency that is under the feminine influence courtesy of Howlite's attachment, attracts its opposite or masculine pole, while all other polarized frequencies are rejected. By working strictly with its own vibration, and repelling vibrations that are not of its own vibration, the frequency's feminine influence filters out disharmonious, undesirable vibrations. It, thereby, serves to purify the quality of the light falling under its influence. Purification of vibration by attraction-rejection is indeed feminine.

Because Howlite does not resonate with any specific polarized frequencies of its own, it does not resonate with any chakra or particular bodily essence either. Howlite harmonizes with the dominant light frequency, to which it is exposed, and adds strength to the frequency's attraction for its opposite polar aspect. With Howlite, only the feminine polar attraction is at work.

To use Howlite, place it wherever it is needed to accentuate the attraction—the feminine aspect—of the light or form to which it is exposed. If placed upon a chakra, the heart for example, it sets up the negative (feminine) polar field, which attracts the light frequencies for the heart's empowerment in the positive (masculine) pole. The attraction, however, does not preclude the coming of light in either the feminine or masculine polar charge. Feminine denotes attraction. The attraction simply brings the chakra's empowerment light frequencies in the opposite polarity.

As the in-coming light frequency arrives at the chakra, its negatively charged pole aligns away from the negatively charged heart chakra in the same way as a magnet[1]. This causes the incoming light to flow in a uniform and consistent manner. Because the light attracted already conforms to the vibration of the heart chakra's dominant frequency, the attraction is not due to Howlite, but rather due to the chakra's light frequency. Although Howlite facilitates the alignment of a negatively charged polar attraction by enhancing the attraction through its feminine influence, the incoming light arrives with both polarities in harmony. The desirable effect achieved is that light arrives in greater quantity, as the addi-

---

1   Place two bar magnets with their ends closest to each other. If the ends are opposing polarities, they will come together quickly. If the ends are the same polarity, they will resist coming together.

tional attraction implies, and as the uniform flow allows.

Howlite realigns the polarity of the light already within the body to create an enhanced attraction that further strengthens the flow of the light coming into the chakra. There is no specific influence attributed to Howlite's own frequencies apart from the light already present, wherever the stone is placed. The bottom line is that Howlite enhances the ability of the user to attract light.

Iolite

The Crystal Compass

Scientific Properties: (synonym of Cordierite)

Crystallography: Orthorhombic
Chemical formula: $(Mg,Fe)_2Al_3(AlSi_5O_{18})$
Mohs hardness: 7-7.5
Density: 2.6 - 2.66 g/cm^3
Colour: transparent, translucent
Iolite: blue-violet
(*Cordierite:* Grey, blue, greenish, yellowish brown; colourless to very light blue in transmitted light.)

Iolite brings a sweet loving glow to the consciousness of the mind. It offers its user the soft and gentle light frequencies of enhanced consciousness.

Light frequencies that affect the consciousness of a person's mind empower the will. The will, however, might stray into realms, which do not reflect the truth of the person's path. The empowerment of the mind that leads to higher states of consciousness does not automatically mean that the spiritual devotee is capable of making willful choices that lead to greater enlightenment.

As a person works to acquire light along her spiritual path, and works towards enlightenment through the invocation of the Light Body[1], she must be willing to steadfastly make choices to be at One with the truth of her path. As the spiritual path is full of deceptions and deviations, and creates choices that test a person's will to bring light within, she is faced with numerous obstacles and potentials that lead to the pitfalls of darkness.

---

1   For the in-depth discussion of the Light Body, soul, and higher self, along with the processes involved, please see *The Story of Light, Path to Enlightenment*, Chapter 5, entitled: "Enlightenment".

To address the concern about darkness, and to add the light of consciousness to a person's choices, Iolite offers itself in service to the Earth. As a principle of the divine universe, choices follow the will, and so, wherever the will leads, the universe offers its light and love accordingly[2]. If light is the choice, Iolite becomes a welcome facilitator for the illumination of a person's choices by adding light to the consciousness of her mind. As a strict prerequisite for the effective use of Iolite, an individual is required to dedicate her will in service to the light. Being something other than willing and focused in spiritual practice leaves doubt as to a person's intent in the exercise of the will.

The individual lacking spiritual devotion cannot proceed in life without some hidden resistance in the will. The person, who is not committed to spirituality, emits an etheric magnetic field that does not resonate with the path of the light. The etheric configuration sets up a blockage, which shields light from the mind's consciousness. Because the light, which is blocked and cannot enter the person's mind, is the energy of the will, the effective use of the Iolite diminishes.

Iolite is a blue translucent crystal. Its frequencies vibrate within a narrow band of the light of consciousness. Its blue light resonates only with the conscious will, and only when the focus of the mind is lifted in contemplation. Iolite's vibration is among the higher frequencies of the seeing mind of the third eye. It links the mind's consciousness with the mind's intuitive awareness. Because Iolite is within a narrow and high band of consciousness frequencies, the contemplative energies generated by the human will are

---

2   The universe does not offer its love and light to persons on Earth unconditionally. The key word is 'accordingly'. If choices are made with the intent and integrity of proceeding towards enlightenment, the divine universal energies are available accordingly without restriction. If, however, choices will lead to negative outcomes, divine energies are provided equally accordingly. That is, the intention to work to a negative outcome leads to the truth of negativity, which is nothing. Divinity, therefore, offers nothing—no love and no light.

needed first to activate the third eye chakra. The third eye opens to the in-coming Iolite frequencies at the point of choice initiated by the will. Because of the universal principle not to interfere in a person's sacred free choice, the role Iolite plays is specific. Iolite illuminates the energies motivating the choices.

The spiritual path, upon which the devotee walks, consists of vibrations of form and light, as is every other manifestation of God's creation. Similar to any path on Earth, the spiritual path is visible to the naked (third) eye for a certain distance ahead. In the brilliance of a sunny day, the way ahead is easy to see. All of the features, including smooth surfaces, potholes, puddles, and trees across the path are quite apparent. During the darkest hour of the night, however, the path is almost impossible to see. Inevitably, paths, including spiritual paths, come to forks in the road. The option to go left or right prompts the traveller to make a willful choice. Depending on the light available to illuminate the two forks, the traveller may see which way to go clearly or not see at all. Adding illumination to the way forward helps to make a better choice.

Iolite is the spiritual traveller's flashlight. It is like using an automobile's high beams to see down the road at night. At the crossroads of choice, Iolite illuminates what is ahead, thus allowing the mind to contemplate the implications of each choice.

The light frequencies used by Iolite to illuminate the path originate within the aura of the person using the stone. They are the individual's own light. Therefore, the choices, the motivating energies, and the outcomes of the choices, all come from within the person and resonate perfectly. Iolite brings the narrow frequency bands of the light, related to the choices, from the individual's auric field first, and then brings the compatible portion of this light into the etheric magnetic field patterns created by the contemplation of the mind. The light is then routed by the etherics into the intuition, and later into the intellect, thus leading to conscious awareness. Because the mind has more light to work with when it looks upon the choices ahead, it sees a brighter landscape. The mind sees the path ahead, but more importantly, it sees the fork-in-the-road, as well as, some distance along each of the paths leading beyond the fork. Iolite does not involve judgments of what lies ahead, nor does it create any light beyond that, which is needed to highlight the paths to be decided upon.

As Iolite's light frequencies come from vibrations that resonate with the mind and its consciousness, they are the frequencies of contemplative awareness. Iolite does not cause an expansion of the consciousness as does Lapis. Rather, it brings a soft hue of conscious blue light to illuminate the landscape of one's contemplations. The enhanced vision that results sets up the individual to make the choice best suited to the will. Again, Iolite is not available to those not wilfully committed to the path of light with only rare exceptions. Through the will to serve the light as expressed positively in the etherics, the result is the attraction of Iolite's illuminating band of consciousness enhancing light frequencies.

Although Iolite is useful when placed anywhere within the aura, it is a third eye stone. Ideally, the user places it on the third eye when doing a contemplative meditation to focus on the apparent choices. Because the person's natural light distribution system involving the chakras and bodily form bring light to all parts of the body, Iolite can be worn as a pendant or in one's pocket with comparable effect. If Lapis is used with Iolite, the illumination of the choices expands and provides exquisite empowerment to the intuition of the third eye.

Kunzite

Love's Flow Stone

Scientific Properties: (variety of Spodumene)
Crystallography: Monoclinic
Chemical formula: $LiAlSi_2O_6$
Mohs hardness: 6.5-7
Density: 3.1 - 3.2 g/cm^3
Colour: transparent, translucent
  Kunzite: colourless to pale pink
  (Spodumene: Colourless, yellow, light green, emerald-green, pink to violet, purple, white, grey.)

In the heart trinity, Kunzite is the vibration between Rose Quartz and Tourmaline. Rose Quartz draws divine love into the heart chakra. Tourmaline shapes that love into a recognizable vibration of exquisite angelic love. Kunzite is the bridging stone that initiates the flow of the heart's love vibration into the external world.

Polarity is necessary to move a light frequency from one place to another. Kunzite aligns its light vibrations with the light vibrations of the heart chakra. The stone's polar charge then draws the light frequencies of the heart outward, making them available to the space immediately surrounding to the heart. If the Kunzite crystal has striations, its polarity gives the attracted light frequencies a clear directional flow. If it has no striations, the flow of light tends to radiate without direction. Because the light frequencies of the heart are directed or radiated outward, the vibration of the space immediately surrounding the heart rises.

At the same time as Kunzite generates a flow of the heart's love outward, it cleanses the light in its own way. Outbound love empties the heart chakra, leaving a vacuum. The vacuum automatically refills as more of the light of love enters. The universal principle is that love begets love. The vibration of the heart chakra that has just been emptied of its love is still very much within the love vibration. Therefore, the vacuum in the heart can only be refilled with vibration that is aligned and in resonance—more love. Kunzite's indirect, secondary role, then, is to accelerate the flow of love into the heart chakra. Its cleansing action takes place because only the frequencies of love that are pure enough to resonate with the vibration of the empty heart can enter its space.

When the first stone of the heart trinity, Rose Quartz, is placed beside Kunzite on the body, love is readily available. The opened and emptied heart chakra quickly draws upon the reserve of love held within the matrix of Rose Quartz. The heart chakra is then refilled and empowered.

By placing Kunzite on the heart chakra, either in a crystal layout or by wearing it as a pendant, the heart's love vibration moves from its place deep within the caverns of the heart out to the external world in a raw or semi-raw form. Raw love comes without the companionship of compassion, which brings a person into love's embrace through its warmth, kindness, respect, acceptance, and more. Compassion, in its many forms, makes harmonizing with love a natural process[1]. Raw love has no such refinements and may not be recognizable, or even acceptable, to many persons.

If the third member of the heart trinity, Tourmaline, is placed at the heart, it processes the raw love vibration after Kunzite draws it from the heart. Tourmaline adds its own love to the heart's love. The new vibration is then both angelic[2] and consistent with the user's vibration. The person's vibration and the vibration of the immediate locale determine which colour of the Tourmaline crystal

---

1   The interaction between love and compassion and the reason that makes compassion so important to the palatability of love is discussed in *The Story of Light, Path to Enlightenment*, section 4.5, entitled: "Heart Chakra: Love and Compassion".

2   To understand the angelic influence on Tourmaline, please see the section in this volume on Tourmaline.

comes to process the love being expressed.

Tourmaline's vibration aligns with the chakra, body part, venue, and love vibration with which it resonates according to which colour is best suited. Black Tourmaline helps love find its way into otherwise negative environments. Aqua Tourmaline takes the love brought forth by Kunzite and helps the mind's intellect and intuition open to higher vibrations and to greater conscious awareness of love. Pink Tourmaline processes the heart's love only in an environment that is conducive to love itself. It adds the exquisitely high love vibration of refined angelic love to the heart chakra's love vibration. Green Tourmaline reconditions the heart chakra, using the classic healing model, thus preparing the heart for the coming of the frequencies of the Light Body.

Without Tourmaline to channel and recondition the light of love coming from the heart through Kunzite, the polarity of the stone moves the love out of the stone and into the body's etheric field without any refinement. The love frequencies are simply expelled, but they are not lost. Rather, the chakra distribution system (ida, pingala, and sushumna) picks them up and redistributes them to the rest of the body. The love received by the various body parts is the heart chakra's love, which is quite empowering, but it comes without the angelic presence that Tourmaline brings.

Ideally, Kunzite is best placed at the heart, but is also useful when placed upon other chakras or body parts—wherever love is desired. In a normal situation, the love of the heart chakra flows throughout the body. Although Kunzite, when positioned on the heart, uses its polarity to draw love from the heart, that same polarity can be used to draw love from the flow of love elsewhere in the chakra system and body. Kunzite draws love from the flow and directs or radiates it into the chakra or body part upon which it is placed. The local area of its placement then fills with love.

Other stones used in combination with Kunzite, but not already mentioned, are also beneficial. For example, Malachite, placed near Kunzite, in a crystal layout uses its Earthy grounding qualities to direct the flow of love frequencies downward to the lower vibrations of the body and chakras, and adds its cleansing effect to the flow of the light. Positioning Hematite beside Kunzite grounds the love available from Kunzite wherever they are placed on the body. Hematite grounds the lowest and slowest of love's frequencies, which is the black light aspect of love. Hematite can be used also to initiate the enlightenment of bodily parts that have never been exposed to light before.

Kunzite starts the flow of love outward from the heart. Other crystals, used in combination, make their own contributions to how love works within the body.

Kyanite

Faster than the Speed of Light

Scientific Properties:
> Crystallography: Triclinic
> Chemical formula: $Al_2(SiO_4)O$
> Mohs hardness: 5.5-7
> Density: 3.53 - 3.67 g/cm^3
> Colour: transparent, translucent
>> Blue, white, light gray, green, rarely yellow, orange, pink

Precious Kyanite is among the power stones[1] of the new age. It prepares the mind for the infusion of celestial light flowing—with love—from the Soul-Star (causal chakra) and Stellar Gateway chakras of the newly implemented eleven-chakra system[2]. When placed within a person's etheric magnetic field in a crystal layout, Kyanite attracts the frequencies of the soul found in the local environment. It moves light into the Soul-Star chakra, which is located at the back of the skull.

Flowing along the striations of Kyanite, light energy is trans-

---

1   The four power stones facilitate the invocation of the Light Body. Besides Kyanite, the power stones include Selenite, Optical Calcite, and Hematite. They work with the physical and higher-self to invoke the Light Body. For more background on the process of Light Body invocation, please see *The Story of Light, Path to Enlightenment*, Chapter 5, entitled: "Enlightenment".

2   The chakras began as an experiment with the purpose of bringing light to the human body. During successive time periods, the systems of chakras have evolved from a single chakra, to the three-chakra system, to the seven-chakra system, and now, to the eleven-chakra system. Please see the section in this volume entitled: "The Eleven-Chakra System".

muted from the upper chakras, especially the Stellar Gateway chakra, into useable form for the physical plane. These light frequencies create a stilling effect as the rush of the soul's light is directed into the orbit of the mind. Each of the stone's striations contributes to the acceleration of the incoming light beam of the Stellar Gateway and helps move it through. In the process, light is pushed forward at great speed past the threshold of the third dimensional barrier and into the physical plane. The speed of the transfer prevents the light from being hindered by the blockages created within the etheric magnetic field of the mind. The mind's etheric field blocks slower frequencies. The etherics also block the numerous, but undesirable, higher light frequencies that are foreign to a person's vibration. When light frequencies are accelerated within the striations of Kyanite, they cross the etherics without delay. Kyanite, then, is a light accelerator.

Most soul-level light frequencies are blocked by the etherics, and so, individuals have little opportunity to experience the light of the higher-self. By altering the etherics through meditation, by balancing the etherics, or by using soul-oriented crystals such as Prehnite, the individual acquires higher vibrations of light. Kyanite makes its contribution by taking the soul's higher frequencies, which are not otherwise permitted to enter the aura, and accelerating them within its structures. Boosting the flow rate of the soul's higher frequencies creates a vibration, which resonates above the level of the most refined aspects of the body's etheric field. The accelerated light is then free to cross what would otherwise be a barrier.

The mind's acceptance of light frequencies from Kyanite is dependant upon which frequencies are being offered. Kyanite accelerates any soul-level light in its vicinity, but the only frequencies accepted by the mind must be from the person's own soul. Because of this prerequisite, the use of Kyanite is not harmful even if the dominating soul frequency belongs to an intruding, ill-intentioned source. The mind is simply unable to resonate with an undesirable alien vibration, therefore, the vibration's presence is of no consequence.

By using the empowering crystal, Selenite, in conjunction with the Galactic Centre chakra, the light of the soul and higher-self is attracted within the space of the user's auric field. The light from Selenite comes in the form of the specific frequencies of the star-lineages of the higher-self—the frequencies of the higher-self from every dimensional level. The person using Selenite is naturally attuned to the light of her higher-self. By placing Kyanite nearby, Kyanite accelerates the newly arrived frequencies past the etheric barriers to become available to the mind and consciousness.

The select frequencies of the soul and higher-self take on a very much higher vibration as they pass through Kyanite. Their accelerated rate of vibration transcends the potential for harmfulness. When a frequency is accelerated by Kyanite, it becomes incapable of carrying negativity. Further, after reaching the speeds of the accelerated level, only that portion of a light frequency that is fully attuned to the person, who is using Kyanite, is capable of resonating in harmony with the person's essence. While all other frequencies are also accommodated within Kyanite, as soon as they reach the point of acceleration, the stone effectively vibrates the existing negativity out from the flow of the light. Negativity is removed because it cannot reach the higher vibrations created with Kyanite's help. Negativity is incompatible with the high and accelerated soul frequencies, and therefore, drops away. Without negativity, the soul frequency assumes a pure state, which is at One and in harmony with the person receiving it. Purity precludes any negativity. Therefore, Kyanite's acceleration of the soul's frequency makes it the purest light possible.

When the soul's light enters the mind, the individual's consciousness becomes enveloped with the purest of frequencies. The etheric magnetic field continues to allow the denser forms of light to enter the mind, but the newly available light, as accelerated by Kyanite, dominates. The dominant light frequencies displace the lesser frequencies with the light of the soul, thus providing the mind with a most profoundly enlightening experience. The change in the level of vibration experienced by the mind is usually quite significant.

The presence of the soul's light, even though it is specific to the individual, is a vibration, which the mind is not familiar with. Therefore, in the initial uses of Kyanite, the mental processes of the mind go through a period of adjustment. As the new frequencies displace the old, the person's life-path moves into harmonious attunement with the soul and higher-self. The person's ability to attune to the light of the higher planes also increases with Kyanite's use.

When Kyanite is used for the first time in the crystal layout intended to invocate the Light Body, it causes the soul's light frequencies to dominate the mind, thus forcing the mind to attune to the soul. The mind responds with some strain, but, as the use of Kyanite increases, so too does the mind's attunement. The mind, dominated by the accelerated light frequencies of the soul, is cleared of the usual mental chatter, which might interfere with the invocation of the Light Body. Kyanite greatly facilitates the Light Body's invocation, especially among those persons whose evolutionary process and spiritual discipline is somewhat lagging behind. By dominating the mind, the mind's usual blockages to the light are held in check.

The use of Kyanite in the absence of Selenite involves the same process, whereby the soul's frequencies are accelerated past the etheric magnetic field. The ability to provide significant amounts of soul-level light, however, is severely curtailed. Kyanite is the accelerator of soul frequencies. It is not the bringer.

Continued regular use of Kyanite increases familiarity of the mind with its own soul's vibration. The higher and more subtle frequencies available to the mind open the way, thus empowering the person to move her conscious awareness upward into the heavenly realms of the beyond. The potential for a multitude of new experiences of the higher dimensions arises from the use of Kyanite. Angelic light, entering from the beyond through the Stellar Gateway chakra, passes through the Soul-Star chakra bringing the highest of divinity's frequencies to be stepped down into the Oneness of the third dimension. The divine light in its third dimensional form presents itself to the individual through the Soul-Star chakra.

Kyanite accepts any light frequencies coming from the Stellar Gateway and the Soul-Star chakras directly. During a Light Body crystal layout, the light coming to Kyanite from the Soul-Star chakra most often passes through Optical Calcite first. Within Calcite, the soul's light and the light of the person's physical-level Oneness are united and then passed on to Kyanite. As Calcite creates a new frequency incorporating both soul and third level light, the new frequency presented to Kyanite is slightly different from the Oneness originating within the individual. As Kyanite accelerates any soul frequency offered to it, these frequencies, as well as, those from the Stellar Gateway, are accelerated by Kyanite to pass through the person's etherics and into the Soul-Star chakra.

The person using the four stones of the Light Body invocation, Selenite, Optical Calcite, Kyanite and Hematite, receives a strong mix of soul-level and physical-level Oneness frequencies, as well as, the divine Godhead light coming through the Stellar Gateway chakra. All three types of frequencies are thoroughly mixed within the Soul-Star chakra, which then circulates this precious most highly charged light, not only into the conscious body, but also throughout the entire chakra distribution system.

While the primary focus of these frequencies involves the consciousness, they also serve the physical body's seven chakras and its general bodily essence. Light frequencies created on the physical plane, such as those created within the individual's own Oneness, resonate fully with the physical body and are easily infused into each of the chakras. When the light of the physical-level Oneness is combined with light from the soul and the Godhead, the mixture is carried into the chakras and bodily essence by the indigenous vibration of the physical Oneness. As a result, the light from the highest sources comes to permeate the essence of a person's physical being.

The primary focus of the combination of soul-light frequencies, physical-level Oneness, and Godhead light frequencies is to enlighten the mind's consciousness. However, each infinitely tiny speck of the person's lighted essence carries the consciousness within. To offer light in such an all pervasive way works to bring the consciousness of the mind, in its entirety, into the higher vibration of the larger universal self. Reference is not to the cranial brain, but to the mind of universal-conscious-being that is omnipresent throughout the universe and endowed within the individual's essence. While enhancement of the mind's consciousness is the outcome, because the consciousness is so totally pervasive throughout the physical body, awareness on the physical plane increases with the influx of every additional light frequency. The increase occurs in an incremental and gentle way, as the person gradually adapts to the new and most divine and high frequencies.

Kyanite serves the process by accelerating the available divine light and aura-level light frequencies, thus removing negativity and overcoming impending blockages from the mind and etheric magnetic field. The light then reaching the mind, chakras, and body is most empowering indeed.

Labradorite

Consciousness Healer and Expander

Scientific Properties:
    Crystallography: Triclinic
    Chemical formula: $(Ca,Na)[Al(Al,Si)Si_2O_8]$
    Mohs hardness: 6-6.5
    Density: 2.74 - 2.76 g/cm^3
    Colour: Sub-Vitreous, green, blue, gold-yellow

Labradorite is among the most precious of the inward looking stones. It resonates with the light frequencies of consciousness and offers a vibration that works with the gentle pulsing rise and fall of the mind. Labradorite is capable of bringing light to the conscious body from outside the aura, thus making frequencies available to the mind, body, and chakras. From this external light, Labradorite draws both green and gold frequencies. The green consciousness light frequencies work to heal the mind's conscious body of the problems created by negativity. The gold consciousness light frequencies work to enhance the creative function, which creates and expands the space within the conscious body to accommodate more and higher light frequencies. Labradorite's other colour is an iridescent blue vibration. The blue frequency range, in this instance, is the blue light of consciousness. While the green and gold frequencies have specific roles, the work of Labradorite hinges upon its blue light.

Labradorite's Iridescent Green

Before endeavouring to explain the mechanics of Labradorite's green healing function, here is a bit of background. Because of the meagre amount of light available to Earth throughout its third dimensional life-span, the best source of light for a person's self-awareness has traditionally been from within. "From within", however, is also from within the myriad of delusional veils[1] that tend to blind the earth-bound human being from the truth about existence. Regardless of the problems, individuals do evolve and grow from within. Unfortunately, veiled consciousness often blocks a person's ability to make the inter-dimensional connection with the enlightened universe beyond the third dimension. When the light of truth is restricted to the light available on Earth, the scope of the conscious mind is also restricted. The mind uses whatever light is available resulting in distorted perceptions of life and truth, with which the individual struggles until liberated by healing or death.

Truths on the physical plane are not excessively flawed, but the purity of the light of truth can easily come into question. The light of Earthly wisdom, as it came down through the ages, did not always have the same distilled cleanliness and purity that is found on the enlightened side of the universe. Light on Earth can be divine, but can also be quite impure, tainted, distorted, and damaged. When polluted light frequencies enter a person's consciousness, they bring their own variety of influence to the mind and conscious body. Polluted light is part truth and part impurity, and gives the mind poor quality light frequencies with which to work.

The conscious body vibrates within a frequency range between heaven and Earth. It bears the connection with the higher realms, as well as, with the Earth. The conscious body brings the light of consciousness from the heavens to Earth and from Earth to the heavens. The light of consciousness is most delicate and subtle and is easily distorted and damaged, especially upon entry into Earth's density on the third dimension. Certain aspects of the in-coming light are affected to a greater or lesser extent than other aspects, thus creating warps in their flow and in the frequencies themselves.

---

1   In Sanskirt, the delusional veils, usually labeled 'illusions', are called 'Maya'.

Because the in-coming light frequencies are often warped and distorted, they are disharmonious and difficult to receive.

Warps, damage, and distortions in the in-coming light also cause distortions in the delicate structures of the conscious body. Thereafter, the conscious body suffers imbalances that produce further distortions in its reception of light. Eventually, the conscious body's structural distortions ossify. The problem that originally began as the uneven densification of light, leading to distorted and damaged light frequencies, expands into the problem of damage to the conscious body, and further subsequent damage to the in-coming light. A damaged conscious body also has difficulty receiving light.

A further problem that arises from the damage done to the conscious body is the poor quality of the light that it attracts and receives. A damaged conscious body carries a much lower vibration and attracts a much lower range of light frequencies. Warps in the light and warps in the conscious body, combined with low vibrations of light, result in ideas, thought-forms, perceptions, and world views that are also of a very low quality. To access undamaged light of a higher vibration, the conscious body needs healing. Healing clears the blockages in the conscious body and reduces the distortions in the light frequencies used to generate the mind's thought-forms.

Labradorite's iridescent green light frequencies are designed to heal the conscious body. They meander through it bringing healing to areas of its vibration that need healing. To help enable entry into the conscious body, Labradorite's green healing light is attached to Labradorite's iridescent blue light frequencies. The green light piggybacks onto the blue light. The iridescent blue light of consciousness is indigenous to the conscious body. It easily enters therein, carrying the iridescent green healing frequencies along with it.

The iridescent quality of Labradorite's light frequencies is indicative of high vibration and is consistent with the consciousness.

This iridescent and high quality allows light to reflect deeply into the substance of the stone and contributes to the mixing of frequencies. The stone's blue and green frequencies unite, then enter the conscious body.

Labradorite's green frequencies work in the same way as the green frequencies of Bloodstone, Serpentine, Peridot, or any other green healing stone. Healing green light accelerates and raises the vibration of lower and denser vibrations of form, thus making the form better able to accommodate more and higher light. Labradorite's green iridescent frequencies conform perfectly to the vibration of the conscious body—better than any other green healing stone. Labradorite's green frequencies accelerate and open the conscious body to higher and subtler light frequencies. Healing follows from the light that enters.

The conscious body contains a matrix of light receptors, which attract and receive light frequencies. The green frequencies heal individual receptors within the matrix at the most basic level, as well as, accelerate and heal the increasingly larger aggregations of receptors at successively higher levels. Healing is a by-product of the flow of light into form, which otherwise blocks light and retains negativity. Wherever the conscious body is warped, damaged, or distorted, Labradorite's healing green vibration re-balances and re-enlightens by accelerating and opening the form of the conscious body, thus allowing light to enter, heal, and cleanse.

Labradorite does not add to, or fill in, the blanks of sketchy thought-forms built with damaged, warped, distorted, and missing light frequencies. Distortions and damages to the structure of the conscious body, which then attracts and receives distorted and damaged light, not only lead to damaged thinking, they also leave gaps in thinking. The damaged conscious body cannot receive and store many of the light frequencies that are needed to create whole and balanced thought-forms. The light goes missing, and so, too, do portions of the mind's concepts, ideas, and thought-forms.

Although Labradorite's healing light removes distortions and negativity present in both the light and the conscious body, human perceptions of truth rely on a full complement of the light frequencies of consciousness. Without all of the necessary light, some of the pieces to the puzzle are simply not available to the mind. Gaps remain in a person's perceptions even after the consciousness has been healed and cleansed. To fill in the blanks, a further infusion of the light of consciousness is needed.

The light available to Labradorite from the consciousness of the universe enters the conscious body, but is unevenly distributed therein. Consequently, the wisdom brought by the light of consciousness is, at first, sketchy to the mind's intellect. Labradorite's iridescent blue substance picks up the available light in the conscious body and mixes it with the green healing vibration. Using the conscious blue vibration to carry the healing green light deep into the conscious body, Labradorite opens the channels for the greater flow of light, and thus creates balance through a more even distribution.

Further, by using the available light of consciousness present in the aura, but not yet within the conscious body, Labradorite brings light into the healed areas of the conscious body where distortions, and the illusions they bring, had formerly occupied space. It fleshes out the balance within the structures of the conscious body with many of the needed light frequencies of consciousness. Still further, once the healing is complete, Labradorite's blue iridescent structures carry the available light of universal consciousness from outside the aura into the conscious body to re-enlighten its essence. With more, balanced, and higher quality light available to supply the mind's contemplations, the quality of thought improves substantially.

Labradorite's Iridescent Gold

Labradorite presents a blue and green iridescent sheen, but has a gold sheen as well. The golden light frequencies of consciousness that flow through the gold aspect of Labradorite's crystalline structure attach to the blue light frequencies in the same way as do the green frequencies. The blue light moves swiftly into the conscious body carrying both the green and gold with it. The golden ranges of the light frequencies of consciousness arrive on Earth from much higher planes. They are not found readily within the aura, but resonate perfectly with the vibration of Labradorite's iridescent golden structure.

The primary task of the gold light of consciousness is to empower Labradorite to bring into the conscious body frequencies that create and re-create themselves. The gold light also works directly with the conscious body itself. The conscious body is imbibed within the physical body and pervasive throughout. Wherever the gold light enters the physical body, it causes the form of the conscious body in that location to grow from within. The conscious body both grows anew and expands.

Similar to the green frequency, Labradorite's gold frequency meanders throughout the physical body to do its magic. It leaves a trail of light vibration behind in its path, the purpose of which is to make the journey easier for more of Labradorite's golden light to follow. The subtle polarized magnetic push and pull within each of these two bodies, conscious and physical, causes the golden ray to migrate. The golden ray then works it way through to all parts of the physical and conscious bodies.

Some parts of the physical body may not have an established conscious body. Wherever the vibration of the physical body has variations in its density, variations also occur in the presence of Labradorite's golden ray. If density is too great, the golden ray is absent. In places of lesser density, where the golden ray concentrates its effect, the conscious body can establish itself. The golden ray also helps the conscious body to grow and expand.

Labradorite's golden light rays work in the same way as the golden frequencies of Citrine. The primary contribution of the golden range of light frequencies is the expansion of form. Consciousness light frequencies are destined to enter the conscious body, but often, they cannot, because the conscious body's vibration is too limited. Labradorite's iridescent gold frequencies empower the Oneness of the conscious body's form to create more of itself. The conscious body's form thus expands. The expansion of form means that there is more room for more light frequencies. As does the navel chakra under the influence of Citrine, the conscious body's vibration opens to more light and rises under the influence of Labradorite. The newly created and expanded form of the conscious body can then accommodate light frequencies for which it previously did not have room, along with frequencies that were previously blocked from entering because their vibrations were too high.

The light, previously prohibited from entering the conscious body, remains at-hand within the etheric magnetic field (aura) that surrounds the physical body. It hovers near that part of the physical body for which it was intended. Although these are consciousness frequencies, they do not come from or through Labradorite. They enter the newly established or newly expanded conscious body through the adjacent physical body. Each frequency carries a polar charge that is opposite to the charge of the intended body part. The newly-arrived frequency's charge sets up an attraction for Labradorite's golden ray. The consciousness frequency does not attach itself to the golden ray. However, upon arrival, the golden ray attaches to the intended conscious or physical body part to do its work. It further helps the conscious body to establish, grow, or expand, as applicable.

The expanded conscious body resonates immediately with the light frequencies of consciousness that initially attracted the golden ray from Labradorite. The light then enters the conscious body to become frequencies of consciousness within its inventory. The frequencies of consciousness are available to the mind's contemplation, whenever it endeavours to create thought-forms or interact with the intellect or intuition. With an expanded space in the conscious body to accommodate more of the higher light frequencies of consciousness, the person's mind has more and higher light with which to construct its world view.

Labradorite's role is to heal and expand the conscious body[2]. The healed conscious body is distortion-free and attracts and accommodates light that is also distortion-free. The expanded conscious body makes a plethora of higher and more diverse light frequencies available. With light frequencies of higher quality, higher vibration, and in greater quantity, the mind can create its thought-forms with much greater scope, balance, and quality. Quality light means quality thinking.

---

2   Because Labradorite is so very intimate with the conscious body, the reader may wish to discover, or review, the discussion about the consciousness, mind, consciousness light frequencies, contemplation, intellect, and intuition in *The Story of Light, Through Heaven's Gate*, Chapter 14, entitled: "Consciousness". A further reading in this same volume involves how the emotional body plays a role in strengthening the attraction for the light of the mind's contemplations. It can be found in the very next chapter (15), entitled: "The Emotional Body".

Lapis Lazuli

Consciousness Expander

Scientific Properties:
> Lapis is a mixture primarily of Calcite, Lazurite, and Pyrite

The loving blue vibration of Lapis offers a most sincere way to penetrate deep into the crevices of the mind. Through its influence, the love and grace of the heavens is brought into an individual's conscious knowing. Lapis is most effective when placed on the third eye chakra.

The mind consciously works within a specific range of light frequencies whenever it focuses its contemplation, or transcends into the spiritual realms. The mind, however, is limited to the range of frequencies that are within the reach of its vibration. Lapis influences the mind to broaden, widen, and heighten this limited frequency range. It moves light frequencies through its crystalline third dimensional matrix, and helps them traverse into the innermost places of conscious endeavour. Wherever the mind entertains contemplative thought or spiritual awareness, Lapis expands the normal range of frequencies available to the consciousness process. It moves the energy of the mind, as a channel medium might, to bring forth light beyond the usual limits available to the mind.

Enhancing Mundane Skills

In situations of mundane activity where a person is performing tasks such as peeling potatoes or driving a car, using Lapis within the aura allows the mind to transcend the normal boundaries of awareness. This leads to a greater intensity of conscious awareness, which is directed ultimately towards the task at hand. Peel more potatoes faster; drive accident-free! Under the influence of Lapis, the mind penetrates its established and limited envelope of conscious activity. It attracts more light frequencies into the conscious body. More light allows the mind to expand its awareness of the environmental context and the more subtle motor skills of the given task. Thus, the hands of the person using Lapis, now controlled by a mind with an enhanced conscious awareness, are capable of moving at a far greater speed. The hands holding the potato peeler fly into the task; and the mind's awareness of the more refined and subtle vibrations of the driving scenario significantly enhance the driver's skills.

Lapis expands the mind beyond its usual limits of conscious awareness by allowing the mind's energies to be channelled through openings it creates at the periphery of the conscious body. To perceive how this is done, envision a sphere full of water with a hole allowing the water to spill out, except that the light spills in. The sphere represents consciousness. Lapis creates this 'leak' by penetrating the veils of denial, illusion, and ignorance that often surround our conscious awareness. It creates an intensity of light at the point of contemplation, wherever that may be on the circumference of the sphere. By concentrating its light frequencies in alignment with the subject of the mind's contemplation, Lapis opens the gateway of the consciousness, through which an expanded range of frequencies can enter. Light leaks into the conscious body.

The mind's contemplation may or may not be directed by conscious mental effort. Rather, whatever the mind is focused upon will determine the place at which the penetration, or concentration, of Lapis' blue light of consciousness will occur. By bringing an excess of blue light to bear upon the consciousness, the limits of consciousness are surpassed. Light penetrates the veils of illusion and ignorance that keep us from greater awareness. The mind can then move its focused energy beyond the usual barriers that restrict a person's knowledge of the subject at hand to enter into an awareness unavailable without Lapis.

As a practical example of how to use Lapis for enhancing daily activities, the prospective employee might wear a Lapis pendant, broach, or ear rings to the employment interview. The effect of the Lapis is to provide an expanded awareness of the immediate subject to which the employer is referring. The interviewee then has an expanded resource of light frequencies with which to formulate answers. Improved answers give the interviewee a greater chance of obtaining the employment being sought.

In a further example, the university student takes Lapis to his examinations. His mind is already focused on the course subject matter because of the time spent studying and cramming for the exam. Lapis, therefore, readily aligns with the strong mental focus. With Lapis, the usual limitations of consciousness are exceeded. The mind opens to the flow of more and higher light frequencies that are directly related to the course material upon which the mind is so focused. With the influx of light, the student better recognizes and formulates the   correct answer. The student's mark is likely to be 5-10% higher than if he had not taken Lapis to the exam.

Expansion in all Directions

The mind might want to focus on a particular finite subject. It can also focus on infinity, which has no specific subject of focus. If a person contemplates in a meditative state, his focus moves beyond the veils of illusion and ignorance in the same way as simply thinking about something. The power of the meditative state is expansive. With the addition of Lapis to bring the blue light to bear, expansion is even further enhanced. This is different from what happens regarding the mundane contemplation related to potato peeling and driving previously mentioned. Rather, the mind holds an infinite and universal focus, instead of a singular and limited focus. In effect, Lapis' blue light is moved to the outer edges of the sphere of the mind's consciousness. It encompasses the entire sphere, without concentrating in one local area. The mind's entire consciousness is moved beyond its previous limits as a result of the expansion caused by Lapis. The greater the expansion, the more in touch the stone's user will be with the vastness of the omnipresent enlightened universe of all.

In truly advanced meditation, Lapis enhances the expansion of the meditation to the very limit of the mind. Lapis was offered with reverence to the initiates and Lamas of Tibet for this expansion enhancing characteristic. However, once the mind goes beyond its outer limit, Lapis has no further influence.

When Lapis' blue light flows into particular aspects of daily activity, the random shifting of the mind's focus slows down. Lapis' frequencies narrow the possible topics available to the mind for contemplation by concentrating and narrowing the range of light that prevails in the consciousness. The mind deals with one topic at a time. Such a concentration of light illuminates the mind's meandering ways, thus taking its focus to the place where the light is greatest. This is comparable to a two-edged sword. Slice one way and the mind moves with the light as the light illuminates the way forward. Slice the other way and the light is brought to bear by the focus of the mind's own will to contemplate a particular subject of thought.

Lapis the 'Protector'

Lapis is sometimes seen as a stone of protection, which could mean many things. What does 'protection' mean using Lapis?

The protection brought about by Lapis is basically a mundane skill, and works similar to any other mundane skill. When the mind is prompted to concentrate its focus of attention out of some sense of danger or some negative energy to which it has been drawn, Lapis' blue light concentrates in alignment with the mind's focus. It adds light to the focus and opens the mind, thus ensuring greater awareness of the subtle nuances that the perceived danger brings.

The danger may result in a significant concentration of the mind's energies. As a consequence, the quantity of Lapis' blue light that comes into the mind's consciousness is also significant. The mind's access to light frequencies from the realms of consciousness, due both to its concentrated focus and to Lapis' blue light, is most penetrating. It works with light in all three dimensions to give the affected individual an understanding of the breadth, depth, and height of the danger.

For example, if an individual is facing the danger of being run over by a bus, Lapis expands the range of light available to the mind to sense the approach of the bus. Lapis does not stop a bus. Rather, alleviating the danger means stepping out of the way. In another example, the lawyer, who is bent on proving the innocence of his client in a civil lawsuit needs to be aware of the many nuances of the case. His mind will concentrate its energies on the subject of the case. If he uses Lapis, the energies of the stone will come into alignment with his concentrated mind and open his consciousness to the flow of related light frequencies. The acquisition of case-oriented frequencies expands the limitations of the light to which his mind is exposed. It expands his awareness of the possibilities and details involved in the litigation. He can better serve, or protect, his client by formulating a more comprehensive legal defence.

Lapis in Combination with other Crystals

Lapis creates an opening into greater consciousness. When a second crystal is used in conjunction with Lapis, the second crystal has greater influence on the mind than when used without Lapis.

Lapis opens the consciousness, which then aligns with the second crystal and acquires the second crystal's light frequencies. The combination of crystals gives the mind access to light that is not normally within its vibrational range, especially with regard to the specific frequencies belonging to the second stone.

For example, when Rose Quartz is placed on the heart chakra with Lapis on the third eye chakra, the mind perceives the loving influence of the Rose Quartz. The combining of the two crystals does not enhance the Rose Quartz influence directly. Rather, the combination enhances the mind's conscious awareness of the influence. Rose Quartz frequencies increase the mind's magnetic attraction for more of the love frequencies of Rose Quartz, and thereby, draw the mind into a contemplation of greater depth in alignment with love. In turn, the mind's deeper contemplation strengthens its attraction and brings more of Lapis' blue light of consciousness to bear. The greater amount of blue light further increases the contemplative focus, which brings even more blue light and love light to bear. Each frequency acts upon the mind to deepen the contemplation, which strengthens the mind's attraction for yet more light. The mind becomes consciously aware of the love at-hand.

As another example, using Malachite in combination with Lapis results in an elevated vibration, as also happens with Rose Quartz. However, the effect of Rose Quartz is specific to love and the heart chakra. The effect of Malachite, on the other hand, is generalized throughout the body. This is because Malachite is basically a light cleanser for light flowing through the stone, wherever it is placed on the body. If Malachite is placed on one or other of the chakras or body parts, the light flowing through the chakra or part is cleansed by Malachite, thus raising the overall vibration. Lapis' contribution is to open the mind's conscious awareness of the particular characteristics of the light frequencies of that chakra or part. Malachite's contribution is its cleansing action, which improves the quality of the light of the chakra or body part and provides a more pristine infusion of light to the mind's contemplation. Malachite is mentioned here to draw attention to the capacity of the stones to bring the light of consciousness, and thereby, to bring the mind's awareness into a chakra center or body part in conjunction with the mind's contemplation.

Wherever the mind is focused is where Lapis is at work to expand the limited reach of conscious awareness.

Larimar

My Spirituality... Past, Present, Future

Scientific Properties: (Variety of Pectolite)
Crystallography: triclinic
Chemical formula: $NaCa_2(HSi_3O_9)$
Mohs hardness: 4.5-5
Density: 2.84 - 2.9 g/cm^3
Colour: transparent, translucent
white, pale blue, greenish

Where *are* you positioned on your spiritual path? Where *were* you positioned on your spiritual path, and where are you *going*? Larimar can help your conscious mind to see the past, present, and future of your spiritual journey.

Larimar is a most divine and precious stone that offers one of the most exquisite vibrations of consciousness available on Earth. Its light is mixed with the frequencies of purity that originate from among the frequencies attracted into the crown chakra. Larimar presents as a pale sky blue, through slightly darker sky blue (Larimar can, at times, be greenish in colour) vibration accompanied by white inclusions. The whitish material is comparable to that found in Howlite. As does Howlite, Larimar's white inclusions empower the crystalline substances, to which they are adjacent, with a feminine vibration that enhances the attraction for light. The feminine influence strengthens the polar charge of the location in which it is placed, and hence, strengthens the attraction for the frequencies brought forward by Larimar's sky blue substance.

Larimar's sky blue vibration brings a range of light frequencies to enhance a person's intuitive awareness. Its frequencies first enter the person's conscious body, where they are stored in anticipation of being used in the third eye chakra. Larimar does not provide consciousness frequencies that offer a new perspective on greater knowledge. Rather, Larimar's light opens the intuition to the higher light vibrations of consciousness related to one's own state of affairs. It empowers the intuitive side of the third eye to perceive one's own true place on the spiritual path.

Awareness of the perspective, relative to one's position on the spiritual path, entails a broader understanding of the directions one's personal truth is taking. The spiritual devotee travels a journey that has a past, present, and future. 'Perspective' implies the illumination of where one has been in the recent past, where one is right now, and where one is going. The means, by which a person can be aware of his journey's perspective, comes from the light frequencies of consciousness of both Larimar's white vibration and its sky blue vibration.

Larimar's blue frequency brings illumination to the person's awareness of the truth of consciousness as it is in the present. It also illuminates the truth of the consciousness as it was recorded in the person's conscious body at the time of its occurrence. The truth of both the present and the past are brought forward from consciousness into awareness. Larimar illuminates the wisdom, lessons, and joys of a person's real truths, past and present.

As mentioned, Larimar's white frequencies introduce a feminine vibrational influence to the stone. The feminine influence polarizes the stone's crystalline matrix. Larimar already has a magnetic attraction for light, but the addition of the feminine aspect sets the stone up to be even more effective. Specifically, it attracts the light vibrations of the past and present. The light of the past and present creates a vibration that, respectively, has either a negative (bad life choices) or a positive (good life choices) polarity. The polarized matrix, firstly, attracts light frequencies with which it resonates. Secondly, and more importantly, the matrix attracts the light frequencies that carry the polarity, which is in opposition to the polarity of the projection of the vibrations of the past and present. The explanation continues.

The light of the past, in one polarity, sets up an opposite polarity as it projects through the present and into the future. The presence of both polarities within the same set of frequencies creates a composite whole frequency. The composite whole gives one's path both the negative and positive aspects of the past and future in unified time. This is almost fourth dimensional because of the unification of time. However, the operative aspect is not the unification of time, but the polarized projection of light frequencies from the past, through the present, to the future. Past polarity plus future polarity result in a completed whole frequency of light.

Conditional to its finding its way into the conscious mind, the unified frequency contains the contributing frequencies that illuminate the past, present, and future, and can then be read by the conscious mind. The frequencies involved are high vibrations, which do not resonate readily with individuals who are in denial about their spirituality. Illumination of where a devotee has been, where he is now, and where he is going in the future is reserved for the individual whose vibration is high enough that his third eye chakra is consciously attuned to the light frequencies of the past, present, and future.

Larimar's whitish crystalline inclusions further add the feminine vibration to the consciousness. It works with the conscious mind to set up a magnetic field within the mind. The magnetic field enhances the mind's attraction for the polarized projection of the light frequencies of future possibilities, which are then deposited into the conscious body. The future is an event that has not yet happened and is, therefore, a projection emanating from what has and is happening. It is the projection of the past and present. Larimar transfers the light frequencies of third dimensional time from within the etheric magnetic field into the conscious body. The conscious body then offers that light to the third eye. The light vibrations of the future—the projection of the past and present— are thereby revealed to the consciousness. Through the third eye, the light frequencies of the future find their way into the person's intuitive awareness. Voila! The user of Larimar comes into an awareness of the future possibilities on his spiritual path through third eye intuition. Larimar shows the user his place in the greater scheme of divine purpose.

Placing Larimar at the third eye, or in near proximity, is optimal, because the frequencies brought forth by Larimar are from the highest levels of vibration in the third eye and crown chakra. Although best suited to understanding a person's place on the spiritual path, Larimar is also useful to an individual's understanding of his place among associates, clients, friends, or any other form of societal relationship. Larimar illuminates the future possibilities based on the vibrations of what was and is now, within whichever venue it is called upon to serve.

Lemurian Seed Crystal

Steps of Consciousness

Scientific Properties: (Variety of Quartz)

Lemurian seed crystals began as ideas within the minds of the ancient inhabitants of Lemuria. The seed crystal is a six-sided clear quartz crystal with a termination, characterized by an opaque exterior and a very clear interior. Another feature usually present is one or more shaft sides having parallel offset steps, which appear to be parallel lines running perpendicular to the length of the crystal.

The Lemurian seed crystal took form as a result of the precipitation of conscious energy. It descended to Earth at the point that the ideas of the ancient Lemurians manifested. The ancients understood the connection to the heavens, but had to contend with the perils of the physical plane. They could not overcome the density and negative vibration that pervaded Earth. They succumbed to the dark energies that led them to a violent destructive end, even though they understood the path to the light and enlightenment very well.

Because the ancient Lemurians were so well connected to the heavens, conscious knowing came easily. When their ideas crystallized into quartz crystals, what they imposed within the crystals were the keys, or steps, to conscious awareness. The keys or steps were a set of directions to help the spiritual devotee in his journey from the darkness all the way to his immediate connection directly with the Godhead. As a result, the user of the Lemurian Seed Crystal is a student of enlightenment. However far the student has travelled, and however evolved he has become on the spiritual path, he will be introduced to the ideas that pervade the stone at the appropriate level of his own vibration. He will receive instructions from his higher-self to move forward on the path from wherever he is currently. Hence, steps of consciousness. The steps of

195

consciousness correspond to the horizontal lines, or parallel offset steps, on the shaft(s) of the stone.

The ancient Lemurians understood the path from the beginning of darkness to the highest level of enlightenment, and this was the core of their intent—to teach the way. Because they laid out the entire spiritual path, the evolutionary development of the person using the stone was not then, nor is it now, a factor in the stone's effectiveness. Any individual using a Lemurian crystal receives exactly the right lessons for his growth, and at the level of enlightened awareness appropriate for his current state of vibration and conscious awareness, whether evolved or unevolved.

Lepidolite

Balancing Stone of the Crystal World

Scientific Properties: (Member of the Mica Group)
Crystallography: Monoclinic
Chemical formula: $KLi_2Al(Al,Si)_3O_{10}(F,OH)_2$
Mohs hardness: 2.5-3.5
Density: 2.8 - 2.9 g/cm^3
Colour: transparent, translucent
pink, light purple, light rose red

The vibration emitted by Lepidolite has its own graceful way of bringing forth pure and loving light frequencies to those who use the stone. Lepidolite gathers the light available from within the aura and gives it to the stone's user. The light involved is mostly the user's own including soul frequencies. Lepidolite's fascinating feature is that, as light frequencies are brought into the stone, they are emitted without delay. The light passes through to the body and chakras almost simultaneous to its collection. The benefit of the rapid flow of the light in and out again is that the turnover of frequencies makes room for more light. As light moves out of Lepidolite, more light moves in to fill the void.

Lepidolite works with light that is immediately available, but also works with the soul frequencies belonging to the person using the stone. It attracts the person's soul frequencies in their polar equivalent. Each light frequency available to Lepidolite has a polar opposite frequency at the vibrational level of the soul. The soul light attracted is not indigenous to the Earth and originates in the polarity opposite to the bodily form upon which Lepidolite is placed.

The soul's light needs protection as it travels to and from Lepidolite on Earth and the soul in the heavens. For protection, it transitions through a spiraling vortex of consciousness energy.

When a light frequency is projected through the spiraling vortex, its polarities reverse. To explain, if Lepidolite attracts positively charged light frequencies from the soul to balance its own negatively charged frequencies, the in-coming soul light changes to a negative charge upon entering the spiral vortex en route to the third dimension. The soul's light arrives on Earth in the same polarity as the light in the stone. However, its polarity is reversed again upon leaving the spiral vortex, as it enters the Lepidolite crystal. Light, coming to Earth, is often damaged upon encountering the extreme density of the third dimension. By changing polarity and by coming to Earth on a spiral vortex, light frequencies are gently ushered onto the physical plane, thus avoiding most of the damaging effects of crossing into the third dimension.

Lepidolite allows and encourages the presence of all light frequencies within the aura—both soul and non-soul. The soul's light frequencies provide an additional benefit for the other light frequencies moving through Lepidolite. As each of the non-soul frequencies are gathered into the stone from the aura, they undergo a cleansing in the presence of the soul's high and subtle frequencies. Soul light energies remove the distortions, damage, and warps present in the non-soul frequencies.

Further, the soul's light frequencies balance the light within the stone's matrix. First, the soul frequency is attracted by the vibration of its identical polar opposite, as projected from the attracting form on the Earth plane. Second, the intensity of the attraction for the soul's light conforms precisely to the strength of the attraction emanating from Lepidolite. Therefore, the light coming to Lepidolite from the soul is perfectly balanced because it is the same frequency and has the same intensity.

The in-coming soul frequencies mirror the light vibrations already present in the stone. The stone's frequencies are in balance, in the opposing polarity, and at the same intensity and strength as the soul's frequencies. The soul's light changes its polarity twice, first as it enters, and second as it leaves, the connecting spiral vortex on the way to the Lepidolite crystal. This ensures that the soul's frequencies are in perfect synchrony with the frequencies of Lepidolite as they enter the stone.

The light frequency that is specific to Lepidolite is purple. As with any purple light frequency, it works directly with the soul inviting the soul into the mind's conscious awareness. Lepidolite's purple frequency resonates specifically within the middle range of frequencies of the third eye chakra, as might be expected from a balancing stone.

Lepidolite's use of the purple ray permits all of the soul's available energies to enter its matrix. Lepidolite then moves its own light, which includes the soul's light, outward and into the chakra distribution system of the person using the stone. With the fast movement of light into and out of Lepidolite, other frequencies from the soul are also attracted to their specific place in the body. Because each in-coming frequency arrives in precise accord with the soul's response to the stone's force of attraction, balance is assured in exact proportions, whenever light moves into the chakras.

Lepidolite's balancing of light is unrelated to the person's etheric magnetic field, which is usually responsible for the attraction and repulsion of light to ensure the physical body's optimal vibration. Rather, balance occurs with the light of the aura in total, as the light runs through the chakras. Each soul frequency is paired with its identical corresponding frequency in the opposite polarity in the chakras. Both soul and chakra frequencies are united within Lepidolite's crystalline structures. With the help of the soul, Lepidolite creates balance within the body in every way—polarity, quality, and quantity. It brings or removes the exact frequencies needed by the body and chakras, and in the exact quantity and quality.

In the practical application of Lepidolite, placement at the crown and third eye chakras is most effective. The crown channels the light into the chakra distribution system, while the third eye best resonates with the stone's purple ray. Greater effect is attained when Lepidolite is placed upon both chakras. Placing the stone in the hand or elsewhere is somewhat less effective, but still works reasonably well. A further suggestion is to use it under the pillow at night.

What benefits accrue from balanced light? Centering is a notable feature, along with the complete reduction of the stresses resulting from excessive or inadequate light. Balancing is offered in accordance with the light of the chakras as it becomes available. Because the human mind is continuously programmed and reprogrammed by the soul, it draws upon the light held within the conscious body. The soul has the responsibility to provide the specific frequencies needed and in the exact measure of intensity. The in-coming light is attracted by the magnetic configurations of the mind and physical body, which communicate to the soul through vibration. The soul then knows exactly which frequencies are plentiful and need removal, which are in short supply and need replenishment, and which are too strong or weak in the yin or yang polarity. Following its assessment, the soul then sends precisely the quality and quantity of light in the exact intensity and strength required to balance the light energies and frequencies of the individual.

The frequencies of the body and chakras are not simply brought into balance, rather, they are also balanced with what the soul perceives is correct.

Malachite

Cleansing Stone of the Crystal World

Scientific Properties:
Crystallography: Monoclinic
Chemical formula: $Cu_2(CO_3)(OH)_2$
Mohs hardness: 3.5-4
Density: 3.6 - 4.05 g/cm^3
Colour: bright green through dark green to black

Malachite moves light like no other crystal. It stands very much alone.

Malachite can be placed anywhere on the physical body. It works best at the solar plexus, where it densifies the light flowing from the upper chakras to the lower chakras. When placed on individual chakras, Malachite causes the higher vibrational light frequencies that are coming into the chakras to transmute into lower vibrational light frequencies. Thereby, it also facilitates the flow of light from the upper chakras to the lower chakras. When placed at the crown chakra, it acts as a filter that allows light of a purer form to enter the entire chakra distribution system.

As light frequencies flow through Malachite, the stone separates them into their negative and positive aspects. Malachite absorbs the negative aspect, but only temporarily. More accurately, it deflects negative energy outside of the aura. Deflecting negativity allows the purer forms of light energy, the positive aspects, to move from higher to lower chakras.

Malachite's patterns of bright green crystal, marbled with darker green and black shades, all contribute to the way light is processed. Its bright Earthy green shades move light from higher to lower vibration in the same way as the Earth moves light from the heavens through its grounding effect. Light moves down in the direction of Earth. Light from the heart moves to the navel chakra;

201

light from the crown moves to the throat chakra, and so on. Light, however, does not move upward as a feature of Malachite. Neither does Malachite provide a grounding effect. It is simply a channel for light causing directional flow in a consistently Earthly direction.

As light is routed through the stone's matrix, it enters the area of the stone's darker green shades, and thereafter, the areas of the black shades. Malachite's black areas temporarily hold the negative aspect of the light, which was separated from its positive aspect within the stone's matrix structure. Once a sufficient quantity of negative energy has accumulated, the black portion of the stone directs or pushes it out past the edges of the user's etheric field. Malachite removes negativity.

The efficiency of the outward flow of light frequencies, in both negative and positive aspects, is dictated by the design patterns within the individual piece of Malachite. If the stone's design has strong, smooth, and even lines that are thick and straight, light moves faster. The filtering capacity of such a stone makes it a strong light purifier. Pieces with random splotchy patterns or inconsistent choppy lines are less efficient in directing the light, thus reducing the value of the piece.

Malachite works with the light frequencies flowing through the space or body part upon which the stone has been placed. It separates the negative aspect and sends it out of the aura and makes the positive aspect available for assimilation into form. Malachite also works with the light found in the immediate area of its placement. If placed on a chakra, the localized light is drawn into the stone where the same process takes place. Malachite removes existing negative light energies, thus cleansing light frequencies wherever it is placed.

Malachite splits light! No other crystal performs the task of splitting a stream of light into negative and positive aspects. The significance of the task is truly something to appreciate. The splitting action places considerable stress upon the essence of the stone at the most refined molecular levels of its structure. Excess stress eventually leads to the breakdown of those molecular structures. Therefore, Malachite, more than any other stone, requires vigilant and careful cleansing using the sun-water method. A few granules of sea salt—never more than ten—added to a crystal stemware glass of clean water provides more than enough polarized ions to facilitate effectively the balancing and removal of negativity from the stone. The need for properly cleansing Malachite's fragile matrix is not prompted by the presence of negativity. Rather, the need arises from the stresses placed upon the stone's molecular essence by the extremely delicate filtering action of splitting individual light frequencies.

The primary role for Malachite is to open those chakras that are plagued by density and blockages. The infusion of pure light, untainted by the presence of negativity, allows 'healing'. Chakras that have blockages are cleansed and bathed in the cleanest light possible. Once the initial cleansing of the chakra's essence with Malachite has taken place, the chakra opens further and easily. The chakra can then acquire and assimilate the light intended for its empowerment. Thereafter, the use of other crystals, which bring the light frequencies needed for the chakra's empowerment, becomes effective.

Marcasite

Age-Old Light Harmonizer

Scientific Properties:
Crystallography: Orthorhombic
Chemical formula: FeS_2
Mohs hardness: 6-6.5
Density: 4.887 g/cm3
Colour: opaque
pale brass-yellow,
tin-white on fresh exposures.

'Marquisite' is the common name used when denoting jewelry for sale. A slightly different spelling is Marcasite, which is the correct modern scientific name for what is sometimes called white iron pyrite. Marcasite is iron sulfide (FeS_2) with an orthorhombic crystal structure. This is distinct from pyrite, which has a cubic crystal structure. Classifications and proper naming aside, Marcasite is basically pyrite and does what pyrite does. Using it in jewelry usually involves placing a stone of some kind within a Marcasite setting. For the purpose of moving light, jewelry consisting of several different gem stones set in Marcasite can have a most beneficial consequence.

The piece that was used to channel the information about Marcasite for this section of the book involved a dark green gem stone within a Marcasite (orthorhombic structured iron sulfide) setting. From the channelled information, the Pyrite inclusions harmonize the user's etheric magnetic field, and the dark green crystal is a healing stone, which prepares the user's form to accept incrementally more light passing into the third dimension.

In the long history of moving light throughout the planetary grid system, there was a need to help light frequencies attune to persons who were willing and able to accept and work with light.

Light flows via the magnetic field patterns of the Earth's etheric body. Reception of the light depended, and still depends, upon the attraction set up within the essence of the individual for whom the light was destined. By using magnetic polarity to attract, and a magnetic field to route the light to its destination, the in-coming light frequencies were conditioned prior to their arrival. That is, upon passing through the etherics, the in-coming frequency was filtered by the etheric magnetic field, and, to some extent, pruned of its less desirable qualities. The part of the frequency that made its way into the third dimension was only a limited portion of the available frequency. As well, the remainder of the higher aspects of the frequency remained in stasis in the immediately higher fourth dimension.

Marcasite facilitates the arrival of an incrementally greater portion of the higher aspects of a light frequency and of higher frequencies that do not otherwise descend onto the physical plane. Its primary, functional, material composition is its pyrite inclusions. The pyrite flecks work to align the etheric magnetic field of the person, who is receiving the light, with the etheric magnetic field patterns of the Earth. The Earth's etherics then route the light to the person's body for which it was intended. By harmonizing the planetary and the personal etheric magnetic fields, there is a reduction in the turbulence experienced as light frequencies enter the third dimension en route to the body. With less resistance, a greater portion of the in-coming frequencies and parts of frequencies move past the third dimensional threshold and into the physical form of the receiving person. Further, the in-coming light experiences less damage and distortion.

By working with the green vibration of the gemstone used for the channelled information, the person's vibration accelerates somewhat. This action is the standard mode of healing for crystals and any other healing modality. Accelerated essence offers an expanded space into which more light can enter. Light then does its healing work. Between, first, the harmonizing and aligning of the etheric magnetic field's access points through Marcasite's influence, and second, the acceleration of form through the green gemstone's influence, significantly more light enters the space of the receiving person.

The gemstone within the Marcasite, used in the channel for this information, is of a darker green variety, and therefore, works with the slower, lower vibrations of a person's body. The frequency ranges that are pertinent to the Marcasite setting reflect its use during a very long period of Earth's history. Similar to the dark green stone, Marcasite's frequency range is also slower and lower. While the higher and subtler, exotic frequencies of the new age are now in fashion, getting to the vibration we experience today took a great deal of work with numerous stones within Marcasite's frequency range.

Is placing gemstones within a Marcasite setting appropriate to help the spiritual devotee find her way to enlightened consciousness? Perhaps gold and silver settings might work better. Gold and silver, however, are energy conductors that do not harmonize the etheric magnetic fields of differing forms. Marcasite reaches out to bring light that otherwise remains aloof from the physical form.

Moldavite

Pulse of the Celestial Heavens

Scientific Properties:
> Officially considered to be a Tektite
> Moldavite is in a class of its own.

The arrival of Moldavite occurred early in the Earth's history, and only in one location. Fragments of Moldavite were scattered in the area of the Moldova River, primarily in the Czech Republic. Only recently, has it spread across the globe.

The crystalline formation of Moldavite is often labelled a "meteor" in the tektite classification. Almost invariably, it has a translucent, bottle green colour, but its shape has no conformity. Moldavite can be oblong, roundish, or misshapen in many ways, and can be sharp, jagged, smooth, or rough in texture. Its hardness and consistency are uniform within its own tolerances over all specimens.

The vibration of Moldavite is quite specific. Its light frequency range is narrow and unavailable from any other source on Earth. Further, Moldavite is not indigenous to Earth, but, at the same time, carries one of the highest vibrations on Earth. Those who possess Moldavite are almost exclusively among the Earth's highly evolved spiritual beings. A person's vibration must be sufficiently high to even come into close proximity. Moldavite has occasionally been referred to as the chalice of the holy grail.

In the crystal world and elsewhere, healing is the acceleration of mass, thus opening mass to accept light into the body. Light then does its healing work. Although Moldavite is a healing stone in the classical sense, as just described, its healing is a secondary function, and more in the way of a 're-ordering' of the vibrational frequency rates of the body's molecular structures than of an acceleration of mass. Moldavite's healing action brings the body's molecular structures into attunement with their own vibrational frequencies, which are again quite specific and within a narrow band.

Prior to being exposed to Moldavite's extremely high vibration, the human body's ability to work with light is limited to specific frequencies consistent with its vibration. Because of Moldavite's re-ordering of the body's molecular structures, the body surpasses its limits, and a new and different set of light frequencies comes within its range of compatibility. The qualities of the new frequencies promote a new level of healing. In effect, Moldavite accelerates the body into higher dimensional formats. It changes the body so that it resonates with, and assimilates, light frequencies from the highest dimensions.

Conceptually, Moldavite is like a skylight in the house of the third dimension. Through the skylight, the viewer looks out into the vastness of the starry universe. What comes into view are the light frequencies from all levels of the person's multi-dimensional higher-self above the third dimension. Although the light from all dimensional levels is intimately involved with Moldavite's vibration, only frequencies from the first few dimensions above the physical plane—fourth through seventh dimensions—are within the third dimensional mind's scope of rational comprehension.

Moldavite appears to be a meteor, but is far from being a mass of physical material that crashed onto the planet. Its vibration originates in the dimensions from well beyond the beyond. It was sent to the Earth by the Angelic Hosts, and works in harmony with them. It transcends any attempt to categorize its energies into limited logical third dimensional frames of reference. Moldavite's vibration is high beyond comprehension.

Bringing such an extremely high vibration as Moldavite onto the Earth comes with challenges. The vast majority of crystalline formations on Earth are transmitted as light vibrations from their sources in the heavens. They journey through the Earth's etheric magnetic field and arrive on the planet's surface. Once on Earth, they precipitate into their various physical forms over a lengthy time period to become crystals. Moldavite is different. Its vibration is simply too high. It cannot adapt into a physical format in a gradual way. Significantly and, more importantly, realistically, physical density prevents any of the desirable aspects of Moldavite's vibration from entering the third dimension. The Angelic Hosts were forced to use a radically different method than crystalline precipitation to bring Moldavite to Earth.

On Earth, the third dimension has both very high and very low levels of physical vibration. Similarly, every other dimension, higher and lower, has an upper and lower limit to its vibrational influence. At the upper limit of any dimension, form vibrates at its fastest and is closest to the next higher dimension. At the lower level, density is greatest. Form vibrates at its slowest and is closest to the next lower dimension. The procedure involved in bringing Moldavite to Earth is to first bring its vibration to the lowest and greatest density in the fourth dimension, then across the threshold to the third dimension, followed by its introduction to the Earth at the highest level of the third dimension. The precise means was implosion and explosion.

To come to Earth, Moldavite descended to a dense state of vibration causing it to implode upon itself. At the lowest point of densification, the implosion brought its vibration to the threshold with the next lower dimension. As the implosion continued, Moldavite reached its critical mass in the higher dimension, at the greatest possible density, after which it crossed into the next lower dimension. The implosion then reversed. The stone imploded until it was released into the lower dimension at which point it exploded. Upon arrival in the lower dimension, its vibration existed at the extreme highest level possible. Because its vibration was actually above the vibration rate of the lower dimension as it entered, it exploded.

The importance of the implosion and explosion was that, upon entry to the lower dimension, Moldavite retained its essence.

Its light frequencies did not fragment into portions of distorted, damaged, and warped individual frequencies or collections of frequencies. Almost the full complement of its light made the crossing, and therefore, the full value of Moldavite became available.

The use of the implosion-explosion method did not occur in one easy stroke. Attempts numbering in the hundreds to implode Moldavite took place. Further, its vibration had to pass through innumerable higher dimensional thresholds, imploding and exploding at each one, before it finally descended enough to enter the Earth's physical plane. In addition, the Earth's cooperation was necessary to successfully host Moldavite's vibration because the protective shield of the Earth's etherics was an inhibiting factor. The etherics had to be modified, at least temporarily, for the process to work. The innovation, orchestrated by the Angelic Hosts, involved creating a warp or hole in the planetary etheric magnetic field. The angels 'parted the Red Sea', so to speak. Creating this anomaly in the etherics was much easier to accomplish during Earth's infancy than it would have been once the etherics had stabilized and strengthened[1].

The angelic overseers of the Moldavite project brought its vibration into position over the hole in the Earth's etherics. This allowed the imploding Moldavite to enter from the fourth dimension into the third dimension at a place about five miles (or 20,000') above the Earth's surface. Here, the etheric field enveloped the incoming Moldavite, at which point it exploded. At the time of

---

1 Stabilization of the Earth's third dimensional vibration, and hence its etheric magnetic field, took place upon the establishment of the energy grid around the planet. The energy grid was imposed upon the Earth in an effort to narrow the extreme ranges of vibration that created instability and wild vacillations of third dimensional vibration. This grid came into place upon completion of the Giza pyramids, which continue to serve as its anchor.

At the time of Moldavite's arrival, the planetary grid was not yet in place. The third dimension's vacillations made the task of opening a hole in the Earth's etheric magnetic field much easier than if the grid was in place.

conversion to physical density, the mass of the Moldavite vibration was moving at extreme speed. Crossing this boundary into matter reversed all aspects of its structural form from a vibration of the upper dimensions into a vibration of the third dimension. The reversal caused some frequencies to be negated, as was expected. Therefore, although the full essence of Moldavite did not arrive on the Earth, the essential essence came as needed. As with all frequencies of higher vibration, the highest aspects were unable to cross the threshold into physical matter.

As one of the highest frequencies on Earth, Moldavite is not available for use except to those who resonate at the highest levels of human existence. As previously mentioned, Moldavite' contribution enhances an individual's vibration by re-ordering the physical body's molecular structure to attune to its own higher frequencies. Attunement also creates the re-ordering needed to resonate with a very specialized, high, and narrow band of light frequencies currently available on the Earth. This specialized band of frequencies moves with the rhythmical flow of the divine light of the celestial heavens. The cyclical patterns of celestial time and space, and their influences, are noticeable to the person using Moldavite. The attuning of the body's vibration also harmonizes the flow of the person's actions with the energy that emerges from the cosmic celestial planes. *The user of Moldavite ebbs and flows with the pulse of the celestial heavens.*

Because the Earth is essentially in harmony with these celestial pulses, an individual's Earthly activities come into significantly greater alignment with the truths that constitute her being. Moldavite, modifies the body to polarize itself in tune with the matching frequencies of the heavens. The conscious body of the mind is then reordered to accept the in-coming cosmic energies, and the individual's daily activities naturally move into a most graced and harmonious flow.

With Moldavite, an individual's experiences may border on the euphoric. The re-ordered consciousness can usually sense the extreme alteration in the flow of light into the conscious body. The effect on those whose third eye was open can be profound. However, persons who use Moldavite need not be afraid of its power. It simply helps the energies of the highest dimensions to become available to the body's reordered essence. The user then immerses in the cosmic energy that is a part of the Earth's greater truth, and does so at the highest levels of her multi-dimensional self. Events in a person's life then reflect much deeper purpose, and flow with significantly more harmony than ever before.

Moonstone

For the heart's deepest Love

Scientific Properties:
(variety of Feldspar, most commonly Anorthoclase)
Crystallography: Triclinic
Chemical formula: $(Na,K)AlSi_3O_8$ (Anorthoclase)
Mohs hardness: 6.0-6.5
Colour: opaque, pale brass-yellow, blue, grey, white, pink, green, brown

Moonstone is an ancient stone of the night. It provides its bearer with the love inherent to the light and joy of the invigorated heart. Loving hearts radiate to the world a sense of joy, peace, and laughter, along with the pleasure of being with others. Although Moonstone is the stone of emotional love, the name Moonstone comes not from any significant connection with the moon or the emotions, but rather from the peace that pervades a clear night when the moon's brilliance casts its light upon the Earth.

The heart that suffers the betrayals of love, so common on the Earth, needs serenity from the turbulence of the physical plane. Moonstone's frequency enters the heart to create peace. It has been on Earth since the earliest of times, and has a long history of providing the calm that peace brings. Moonstone calms the emotions as a consequence of its action. If the emotions involved are strictly within the frequency range of the heart, they also resonate with Moonstone. Using Moonstone to activate the heart chakra's emotions strengthens the energies of the heart chakra.

The frequency emitted by Moonstone resonates in the heart chakra as a means to bring the moonlit reflection of the heart's own peace. The stone casts a filmy vibration of light that surrounds the heart chakra. Its colours of near peach, opaque white, or light brown bring frequencies that resonate with the vibrations

213

at the very periphery of the heart chakra. Moonstone works with light frequencies and not the etheric body as does Pyrite. However, similar to Pyrite, Moonstone creates a calmed ring of vibration to still the turbulence that surrounds the heart.

Moonstone attracts light and holds it within its substance. It acquires light from many Earthly and heavenly sources, and then transfers that light in combination with its own light frequencies. Its own frequencies merge with any light frequencies seeking to enter the heart chakra. As light frequencies coming into the heart cross Moonstone's path, they emit a polar charge that triggers the stone's frequencies to join with them. Each set of frequencies is in polar opposition to the other. By combining the otherwise erratic in-coming light frequencies with Moonstone's frequencies, the result is light that is in polar balance. Moonstone's polarity does not prevent light from entering the heart chakra. Rather, it helps light to enter free of polarity. The newly created, balanced light is a calming, soothing, and peaceful addition to the heart chakra.

The clean, loving, and joyful vibration that lies deep within the heart makes its way outward to the external world, but usually with great difficulty. Light from the deepest crevices of the heart may never find its way out. The difficulty arises because the light frequencies in the deepest parts of the heart are not sufficiently energized. They cannot move of their own accord. They need their empowerment frequencies to become active. Alternatively, they need the extra energy of Moonstone. Moonstone reaches into the heart's deepest caverns to open and activate the heart's many passageways that need to be traversed before the light frequencies of the heart can enter or be liberated. Once opened, the light for empowerment penetrates and energizes the deepest parts of the heart chakra. Once empowered, the light from deep within finds its way to the outer world to express the heart's deepest and purest of love vibrations.

The deepest heart frequencies are loving vibrations that are most finely attuned to the soul. As a person's deepest love finds its way out, she expresses it in the way the soul approves and encourages. To fully appreciate the great gift that these deep frequencies of the heart chakra truly are, envision the heart as the link with love in the heavens. The human heart is the bridge between the love on Earth and the love of the soul. The heart's deepest frequencies have the greatest connection with the soul. They permit a person to offer an expression of love that is literally love from beyond—deep love, soul love.

Moonstone's own light frequency resonates only with the heart chakra frequencies that are most profoundly protected by the heart's etheric magnetic fields. The etheric field at the heart's innermost depths make the penetration of almost any light frequency impossible. Only the purest frequencies of love find their way past to enter the inner heart. When the light that resonates with Moonstone is drawn into the heart, that light is then available to accumulate and radiate. The etherics allow some of this light to pass. The degree to which Moonstone's vibration moves past the etherics and into the depths of the heart depends on the love that empowers the heart. The more that light comes into the heart, the more the heart is empowered.

The heart's empowerment receives further enhancement through the support of the emotional body[1]. The emotional body aligns its energies with both the light coming into the heart and the light of the Moonstone, as well as, their combined frequencies. It contributes to the flow of light through its polar magnetic charge. The emotional body accelerates the flow past any remaining turbulence in the heart's passageways, and through the heart's etheric magnetic field. Light goes to the deepest recesses to empower the heart's love, thus bringing forth the most soul-attuned frequencies within the human heart.

---

1   The emotional body is not the emotions. It has a specific location, organization, and function, all of which are discussed in detail in *The Story of Light, Through Heaven's Gate*, Chapter 15, entitled: "The Emotional Body".

Because Moonstone is a heart chakra stone, it is best placed at the heart in a crystal layout, or worn around the neck as a pendant. Placement within the aura offers reasonable benefit as well.

Morganite

Love, pure Love

Scientific Properties: (variety of Beryl)
Crystallography: Hexagonal
Chemical formula: $Be_3Al_2(Si_6O_{18})$
Mohs hardness: 7.5-8.0
Density: 2.63 - 2.92 g/cm3
Colour: translucent, transparent, pink

How shall my spirit guides describe this most exquisite vibratory frequency of precious uplifting love? Shall they offer that Morganite inspires the heart? Shall they maintain that its pulse throbs with the celestial heartbeat in perfect rhythm? Shall they offer that sharing the loving heart with Morganite leads to a graced and blessed path of love? Indeed, yes, they shall, and much, much more!

While Morganite is not a truly new arrival to Earth, its grace has been savoured for its acclaim during this current period of the new age. Morganite's most gentle crystalline form comes to the Earth, not so much as a new age stone, but as a stone reserved for the new age. Morganite's structure manifests in its crystalline form during a lengthy period of thousands of years on Earth. It has been well hidden, and has simply not exposed itself to the world-at-large until very recently.

The reason for the lengthy period of its crystallization, with only very recent exposure, is the need for the careful accumulation of Morganite's pure energies in an Earthly form. Because of the exceptionally high quality of love coming through Morganite, its vibration needs to be well acquainted with the physical plane. Its structure needs to be perfected to carry its loving light frequencies forward. Purity is its trademark feature. To appreciate the clarity of Morganite's vibration, contemplate the stillness of the high

Tibetan Lama, meditating into the Oneness of all. The Lama becomes stillness—the most serene of vibrations. Morganite, too, sits in absolute stillness and serenity awaiting its moment to emerge as the vibration of divine grace that it is.

As do many other stones, Morganite accumulates many of the light frequencies it attracts. It then makes them available to the heart chakra. Morganite also creates its own light frequencies and crystalline structures from its own Oneness within—more so than almost any other crystal. By creating most of itself from within, Morganite retains a much higher vibration of purity. Its purity permits a much greater expression of love.

The specific frequencies, with which Morganite resonates, are located at the highest levels of the heart chakra. Its light is among the highest of the divine love vibrations available on Earth at this time. Although Morganite's vibration is available and resonates with anyone, only persons with the most loving hearts have the vibration needed to reflect the energies of the stone outward.

A person, whose heart has less than purity at its core, can accept Morganite's vibration, but unlike the high Lama, that person does not possess the serenity that allows the light to work its joy into the fabric of her heart. On one hand, in the underdeveloped heart, the vibration of the stone is lost in the turmoil and turbulence of the heart chakra's swirling energies. On the other hand, in the developed heart, the presence of serenity creates a steadiness with which the stone's frequency connects with ease.

The analogy may be likened to riding a boat on a sea of perfect tranquillity. The boat is moved on the glass-like surface by pure will, with no need for paddles. In another analogy, the stone's vibration is spread thin over the water's surface without a break in continuity, in the same way that oil spreads over water. Similar to the undisturbed mountain lake that exudes serenity, Morganite's vibration spreads and expands in a most thin layer of tranquil love. As its vibration expands, so too does its grace. The subtlety of love could not be more exquisite.

The heart chakra that is empowered by Morganite is given a place side-by-side with the divinity of all. Its vibration sits immediately beside the vast ocean of Oneness. It is not of the Oneness, however, nor is it able to create a pathway therein. From its most Earthly vantage point of love, the heart empowered by Morganite converses with ease with the heart of the creator.

Moss Agate

Throat Healer

Scientific Properties: (Variety of Quartz)

The agate crystal used to channel the information in this section is primarily an Earthy green, blue, grey, and cloudy quartz specimen. The way an individual piece of Agate works with light depends on its colour and pattern. Therefore, while a similarly structured piece will share the same qualities as the piece used herein, each variation of Agate[1] works with light differently.

The "moss" of the Moss Agate refers to the inclusions within the stone's quartz base of red, green, blue, grey, white, and clear quartz crystalline structures. Together the colours give the stone a "mossy" appearance, but each colour variation has its own particular frequency. Soft blue is for the higher frequency ranges of the throat chakra. Earthy green is for healing. Grey is somewhat different because it is essentially a cloudy quartz. Cloudy quartz implies the presence of a strong yin or feminine polarity, which usually offsets the presence of clear quartz, and which is masculine or yang in nature. White is merely a variation of the cloudiness. Other colours may also be present such as different shades of green and red or ochre, which works with the second (pelvic) chakra.

Light frequencies naturally flow into a person's auric field. The frequencies that correspond to Moss Agate's colours are attracted and made available to the chakras and bodily essence. Moss Agate mixes all of the light frequencies present within its crystalline structures. The mixed light forms a unified presence, which moves as one through the body and chakras.

---

1   Agates are a variety of Quartz. Variations in the sub-minerals within agate usually give the individual stone its different colours and patterns of formation. Many types of quartz share the name agate, but work with light in significantly different ways.

In most instances, a crystal will yield its one and only specialized light frequency to the body for assimilation. Thereafter, a specific set of receptors within one or another of the chakras attracts the crystal's light. In contrast, Moss Agate offers an array of different coloured light frequencies. The only frequency that corresponds to a specific set of receptors is the blue vibration, which resonates with the receptors in the throat chakra. The stone's other coloured light frequencies are part of the mix of frequencies that bond with the blue light. Because the blue light resonates closely with the throat chakra, it enters the throat easily. It carries all of Moss Agate's other light frequencies along with it.

While only Moss Agate's blue colour hue is indigenous to the throat chakra, each of the other colours offers a specialized service. The green part of the crystal offers healing. Healing through crystals means that the stone accelerates the vibration, in this instance, of the throat chakra's molecular mass, which then opens to allow light to enter to do the healing. The green vibration piggy-backs onto the blue vibration, which carries both vibrations into the throat chakra. The green frequencies then proceed to accelerate and raise the general vibration within the throat. The chakra opens to more and higher frequencies of light and is healed.

The cloudy (feminine, yin) or clear (masculine, yang) quartz crystal within Moss Agate creates gender polarity by skewing its polar balance to the dominant presence, either yin or yang. A stone that has a greater presence of cloudy quartz is yin or negative, which bears an attracting force. A stone with more clear quartz is yang or masculine, which expresses light outward rather than attracting it. In Moss Agate, the tendency is for a stronger presence of the yin or feminine vibration.

The value of having greater yin energy is that Moss Agate works to attract more light. Because the quartz aspect of the stone also piggy-backs onto the blue vibration, it, too, enters the throat chakra. Its role is to enhance the polar attraction of the throat for light. The arrival of light in response, not only brings light to the throat, it neutralizes the throat's polarity. It therefore brings the throat chakra into balance.

If red or ochre shades are present in Moss Agate, the stone works with the second or pelvic chakra in a way that is identical to the blue hues of the throat chakra. Red light frequencies are indigenous to the second chakra. A reddish Moss Agate's mixture of light, including red, green, and clear or cloudy quartz, penetrates into the pelvic chakra. It brings healing, which is the green vibration, as well as, gender polarization and balancing, which is the clear or cloudy quartz.

Colours, not already mentioned, relate to other chakras or places in the body. In each Moss Agate, the green healing frequencies piggyback the chakra's indigenous colour vibration to enter deep within to heal the body's physical essence, and the clear or cloudy quartz effects balance.

Obsidian

The Living Soul of the Earth

Scientific Properties:
>   Obsidian is naturally formed volcanic glass that cools quickly into an igneous rock.
>   Chemical composition: SiO_2 plus MgO, and Fe_3O_4
>   Mohs hardness: 5-6
>   Colour: translucent, black, brown

In the early moments of Earth's existence, there was very little light. Obsidian was, and still is, the most potent grounding force available. Through Obsidian, Earth acquired the light frequencies needed to establish its Oneness. It initiated Earth's journey to enlightenment. Obsidian was therefore honoured with being the carrier of the living vibration of the Earth's soul. Through Obsidian, the Earth offers its love and light.

Within Obsidian, the light frequencies of the Earth's soul merge with the light frequencies from the consciousness of the person using the stone. Obsidian serves as the bridge between. Earth's inhabitants offer their own light frequencies to the healing and raising of Earth's vibration, and in turn, receive the light of the Earth's soul. Obsidian embodies the seed of the soul of the Earth in the same way that the base chakra embodies the seed of the soul of a person[1]. As the emissary of Earth's spirit, Obsidian offers its owner the blessings of the full radiance of the planet's indigenous light frequencies.

By using Obsidian, a person can better integrate Earthly love. The person possesses her own light of Oneness within her base chakra—that is, the soul-seed. When this sacred kundalini energy

---

1   The discussion about the base chakra and the soul seed within can be found in *The Story of Light, Path to Enlightenment* (volume one), chapter 3, sections 3.4 and 3.5.

mixes with the light held within Obsidian, the result is the love of both heaven (soul frequencies) and Earth (person and planet frequencies). Because the Earth's soul resides within the stone, the individual using Obsidian undergoes a most potent experience of the grounding of Earth energies. The person's vibration attunes with the pulsing flow of the Earth's soul.

The energies of the Earthly soul come into the heart, mind, and body of Obsidian's user. The great presence of the Earth's soul vibration creates the soul-level resonance that invites the person's own soul vibration into the stone. Soul resonates with soul. The full strength, power, love, and vibration of the Earth awakens within the stone's user. The person experiences a new and powerful energy force. She comes into a state of unified Oneness, as a consequence of the love offered by the Earth. She experiences Earthly heaven, as her energies and the Earth's energies merge. The soul light of the individual, coming from the heavens, and the light of Earth combine to create the Oneness of heaven on Earth.

When individuals resonate with the combination of their own soul's energies and Earth's soul energies, they naturally brighten on their path. The strong presence of the two soul energies does not leave much room for the ego. Soul light displaces the ego. The ego recedes into the background and eventually disappears. Disempowerment of the ego may or may not be disruptive. It can cause distortions in the individual's sensory perceptions and in her conscious interpretations of the external world. Because the disempowerment of the ego results from the presence of the two souls within Obsidian, the disruption itself is only temporary. The souls dominate, and the ego yields.

Temporary or not, for a person who has had limited progress in her spiritual development, an experience with Obsidian can be discomforting. This is because the ego suffers the equivalent of an electric shock treatment. The disharmony between the ego and the soul can leave residual effects. Ideally, a person uses Obsidian long enough to completely displace the ego. Once the use of the stone begins, its use must continue until the experience, lesson, or issue, which is at the core of the disruption, comes to its conclusion. If the use of Obsidian is halted prematurely, the experience, lesson, or issue will be left unresolved, with the ego most eager to fight its way back to prominence. If the ego can regain its former place, the person will regress back to her former vibration.

Ego aside, when the person's and the Earth's soul forces combine, life's experiences proceed with gracious and loving harmony. Obsidian's user truly attunes to the love inherent to the Earth. Using Obsidian leads to the cessation of the disharmonious and misaligned way in which individuals stumble through life, continually arriving at points where the will of the Earth and the will of the individual are in conflict. However, finding the alignment and harmony with the Earth does not necessarily mean that a person also achieves alignment and harmony with other persons, especially with persons whose egos are still intact. Further, the life experiences of many individuals renders them out-of-sync, and therefore, incapable of the integration of soul energies.

The great alignment and harmony with the Earth, brought forward by Obsidian, leads to a life, which is full of the abundance offered by the Earth, as well as, the gracious grounding and use of one's own soul energies. Obsidian is the grounding stone of the soul and the ego destroyer.

Okenite

Angelic Starlight

Scientific Properties:
>Crystallography: Triclinic
>Chemical formula: $CaSi_2O_5\text{-}2H_2O$
>Mohs hardness: 4.5-5
>Density: 2.28 - 2.33 g/cm^3
>Colour: transparent, translucent
>>white to slightly yellow, blue

Okenite is a crystalline lattice network of filaments that radiate outward from its centre in a roundish shape.

Okenite is the soft, delicate, whisper of the hair of angels wafting in a gentle summer breeze. Watch for it passing through clouds, for its vibration is the radiant expression of angels. Each tiny projection of its fragile countenance is a crystalline light-bearer that carries love from the angelic realms on-high to persons on Earth who would have it for their own. Okenite crystals are nodules of angel love.

By way of background information, the section in this book entitled, "Quartz", describes some of the influences of the light of the stars in the heavens. Briefly, their influence on clear quartz is to provide each of the crystal's six shaft sides with the connection and characteristics of one star. A six-sided crystal is influenced by six different stars. The star's particular characteristics, which might be warmth, honesty, love, joy, harmony, understanding, or clarity for example, are expressed on the third dimension through its light frequencies. Stars express themselves through a variety of means including clear quartz crystals as mentioned, as well as, crystals such as Okenite. Each Okenite of globe-like filaments, therefore, is the presence of the light of a star in the heavens, and as such, reflects the characteristic nature and influences of that star. The frequency, held in reverence within Okenite's crystalline matrix, is the highest of the star's light frequencies possible on Earth.

Okenite begins as a fragment of starlight vibration that crosses the threshold of the third dimension to enter the physical plane. Its extremely high resonance is not capable of remaining on Earth, with the exception that its presence is retained by the fantasies of human thought-forms. The creative mind's thought-forms anchor Okenite's crystalline physical form onto the Earth. The highest physical vibrations of a star are consistent and compatible only with thought-forms that resonate with the angelic vibration in its softest and gentlest aspects.

The vibration of Okenite is not a star's light frequency, nor is it the vibration of the human thought-form. It is the combination of both. The star fragment of light assimilates into the thought-form created by persons on Earth. Such persons invariably display angelic qualities. Once manifest, the combined frequency is given its Okenite format of crystalline filaments of angels' hair.

The aesthetic pure white ball of filaments is Okenite's greatest asset for transmuting starlight to Earth. For the person to whom it belongs, it holds great reverence. The frequencies of the owner's affectionate thought-forms resonate in harmony with the star frequencies coming to Okenite. The person, who owns Okenite, has a special affinity for it. However, the human thought-form, with which the star frequencies originally assimilated, may or may not belong to Okenite's owner. If not, the owner's thought-forms only need to be reasonably close in harmony for her to work with the crystal. With harmony, Okenite's combined vibration of starlight and human thought-form can be offered to the owner as it passes into the third dimension.

Okenite reflects the characteristics of the starlight, which, as mentioned previously, can include warmth, honesty, love, joy, harmony, understanding, clarity, and more. These characteristic qualities become available to the crystal's owner through the light present in Okenite's crystalline lattice of filaments. The owner's harmonious thought-forms provide the vibratory resonance that allows the crystal's heavenly angelic light to transfer into the owner's physical presence. Thereafter, the owner takes on the qualities of the angels as offered through Okenite.

Opal

Emotional Emphasis

Scientific Properties:
Crystallography: amorphous
Chemical formula: $SiO_2 - nH_2O$
Mohs hardness: 5.5-6.5
Density: 1.9 - 2.3 g/cm^3
Colour: colorless, white, yellow, red, orange,
green, brown, black, blue

Who needs an Opal? Opal boosts the emotions. Persons with a tendency to erratic, unstable, and manic expressions of the emotions, or who are highly charged emotionally, do not need further emotional charge. They need to be cautious when using Opal. For the person living a sedate, calm, tension-free existence with little outside stimuli, the get-up-and-go emotional lift coming from Opal may be quite desirable and beneficial[1].

The Opal family offers the vibratory pulsing throb of emotional energy! Opal's vibration possesses the same fluidity of motion as the e-motions themselves. Opal's flowing light creates pulses that move through the aura in the way that waves on water rise and fall. Opal does not emit a steady flow. Consequently, a constant adjustment to the rise and fall of emotional energies needs to take place within the physical and subtle bodies of the person wearing the stone.

The tides of emotional energy wash in and out upon the substance of a person's being, just as the tides of the oceans rise and

---

1   The emotions and the emotional body are not the same. For the comprehensive discussion about how the emotions and emotional body work with the physical body to generate energy-in-motion, e-motions, please see *The Story of Light, Through Heaven's Gate*, Chapter 15, entitled: "The Emotional Body".

fall. At times, the emotions are high and, at times, low. The energy flow is constant, even though it ebbs and flows, rises and falls. The emotions bring more or less energy to the process of gathering light frequencies. The light is then presented to the mind. The focus of the mind's contemplation is energized in proportion to the light brought forth by the emotions.

Emotional energies empower a person's magnetic attraction for light exponentially. They push the person's own energy flow to the furthest reaches of its limits. For example, the threat, created by the red light of anger, is empowered many times by the addition of emotional energy. The emotions turn a mild threat into something to be reckoned with. Similarly, when accompanied by the presence of emotional energies, the passions that energize each of the chakras have a much greater effect. When the tide is in, per se, the passions surge forth. When the tide is out, the passions subside. The writer, for example, writes from dawn to dusk for a week straight without eating. She is running on the emotional energy of passion. Then, for the next week, she experiences writers' block. Emotional energy flows as an ocean wave with distinct highs and lows.

Opal affects the rise and fall of the energy driving the emotions. It enhances the flow of light frequencies that empower the chakras, and with ever greater effect. Opal, together with emotional energy, brings a much greater quantity of empowering light to the body. Opal and the emotions, however, do not affect balance. A person's vibration remains constant and in balance, even through erratic emotional mood swings. To illustrate, the waves of the ocean are continually rising and falling, but sea level is constant and in balance. The key to wearing an Opal, then, is personal balance.

The will works through the mind and its contemplative focus. When the mind is focused upon enhancing the flow of light to a particular chakra, the emotions join in. They make the light that empowers the chakra truly effective. For example, the pink hues of the light of love in the heart are impassioned by the addition of charged emotional energies. The passion drives the love vibration into its full radiance. Each of the other chakras is also effectively empowered by the addition of emotional energy. The lower chakras are affected most. As another example, the anger of the second chakra can be quite devastating when charged by the emotions. An angry person, who is emotionally driven, is not someone to whom reason will make any difference. Emotionally charged anger may lead to destructive or violent behaviour.

The mechanical means by which Opal contributes to the emotional empowerment of the chakras is through filtration and the refraction of light. Because the emotions are of the water element, Opal's crystalline structure contains a watery substance within. The water in Opal filters the light as it passes through the crystal. The frequency range not governed by the emotions is allowed to pass out, while frequencies of the emotions undergo further processing. The filtering action brings forth a purer form of the light frequencies of the emotions. With no frequencies outside the emotions to generate an influence, Opal's watery substance works to concentrate the emotional vibrations present.

In addition to filtering and concentrating emotional energies, Opal's watery substance refracts the light into an array of frequencies. The refracted emotional frequencies[2] move out of the stone and start moving through the chakra distribution system's passageways (ida, pingala, sushumna). They become available to which-

2   The benefit of making refracted light available is the energy saved by breaking up the aggregate of frequencies into free-floating individual frequencies. The body assimilates individual frequencies, not aggregates or groupings of frequencies. By refracting the flow of light, the body receives the individual frequency without having to draw upon its own energies to split the frequency away from the light flowing by. The discussion on how refraction plays a part in energizing and empowering the body involves the inter-dimensional three-sided pyramidal vehicle of light, and is truly fascinating. Please see *The Story of Light, Through Heaven's Gate*, section 8.9, entitled: "Refracted Light, Light Energy, and the Aura".

ever chakras are open to receive them. The frequencies of the emotions are then drawn into a particular chakra, as the will exerts its intention through the focus of the mind's contemplations. Emotional energy, directed by the will, produces an enhanced effect upon the target chakra's expression of its purpose. The outcome is the impassioned speech of zealots (throat chakra). It is the genius of the creative expression of the artist (navel chakra). It is the threat turned into effective anger (second chakra). It is the will to survive extremely undesirable living conditions, or to go through the most harrowing of traumatic experiences (base chakra). The contribution of Opal is the concentration and amplification of emotional energies to enhance the effectiveness of the work of the opened and empowered chakra. 'Emotional emphasis' are the keywords in understanding Opal.

The blue, rainbow, and iridescent variety of Opal, known as the 'common' Opal, has the ability to mix the light frequencies of the emotions together with specific chakra frequencies. Opal carries both emotional light energy, plus a given chakra's indigenous frequencies. The light that then passes through the chakra resonates readily with the most subtle parts of the chakra. It enters the chakra easily, and is assimilated without delay.

The 'common' Opal's individual features (the blue, rainbow, and iridescent aspects) each has its own specialized role. The blue vibration resonates naturally with the consciousness. When the blue vibration is pervasive in the stone, the light frequencies of the consciousness are added to the mix. The person using Opal receives the grace of an enhanced consciousness. Opal's iridescent aspect, similar to Tiger's Eye and Hawk's Eye, moves light from receptor to receptor within the structure of the Opal, thus giving the flow of light momentum. Iridescence hastens the flow. In contrast, the rainbow appearance of Opal is not structural. Rather, it is the result of light refracting through water. By filtering out the non-emotional frequencies and splitting the emotional light into the colour bands of the rainbow, Opal processes the light of the emotions. Opal does the work of separating individual frequencies from the flow. Processing within the crystal, as opposed to processing within the physical body or chakras, requires less energy and makes the light easier to assimilate within the physical body.

Opal greatly empowers the chakras by the addition of emotional energies. Not all uses of the stone, however, result in empowerment. Emotional energies ebb and flow. Therefore, when the energies are ebbing, the chakras may experience disempowerment as energies withdraw. When the emotions are flowing, the chakras are empowered as energies accumulate.

If a chakra is empowered, the potential to work with emotional energies increases. By enlightening and empowering a particular chakra with its own frequencies, usually done through exposure to an additional crystal, the potency of the emotional energies increases significantly. As an example, Rose Quartz can be used in conjunction with Opal. The Rose Quartz brings a vibration of self-love, and the Opal brings an emotional charge to empower the love. As the refracted light of the emotions from Opal integrates with the love of the heart chakra empowered by Rose Quartz, the outcome is that the great passions of self-love arise within.

The rise and fall of emotional energies, is determined by the many factors affecting the movement of light into a chakra. The use of Opal and other crystals each contribute to the total amount of light.

Peridot

Prestigious Traditional Earth Healer

Scientific Properties: (a variety of Olivine)

Crystallography: Orthorhombic
Chemical formula: $(Mg, Fe)_2SiO_4$
Mohs hardness: 6.5-7
Colour: translucent, green

The translucent green to dark green vibration of Peridot has a long history on Earth. It uses light from the aura to heal the physical body through the classical method of crystal healing. It accelerates the body's molecular structures, which then open to receive light more readily. Healing follows the flow of light. Peridot works best when placed on the immediate location where density is severe and the body is in need of healing.

There is a difference between Peridot's vibration and other Earthly green healing stones. Peridot is translucent, while other stones are not. Therefore, its crystal structure allows a greater amount of light to pass through. Consequently, once the body's molecules accelerate and open, its healing is also greater. Because Peridot permits light to flow through its crystalline matrix, it shares a place of prestige among the advanced of Earth's traditional healing crystals. It cannot, however, compare to the recently arrived ascension-era stones such as Green Tourmaline. Nonetheless, Peridot is a most valuable vibration of grace that has made light available to the physical body throughout its long tenure on Earth. Peridot has earned its reputation as a respected and honoured healer.

As a third dimensional stone, in the same way as Green Adventurine, Peridot is about to depart the Earth for the regeneration and re-creation of its vibratory powers. It will then be redeployed to some other third dimensional planet.

Pink Halite

The Love Vortex

Scientific Properties:
>   Crystallography: Isometric
>   Chemical formula: NaCl
>   Mohs hardness: 2.5
>   Density: 2.168 g/cm³
>   Colour (all Halites): transparent, translucent
>   colourless, whitish, yellow, red, purple or blue

Pink Halite brings a glorious vibration of love in the shade of the pink ray. This is the light of loving hearts. Any, who are able to share their light freely and wondrously, offer a vibration of love that corresponds to Halite's pink ray.

Halite shares the same loving pink heart chakra vibration as that of Rose Quartz. The difference in the hue and core vibration between Pink Halite and Rose Quartz is almost negligible. The difference, then, is not found in the quality of the pink ray, and hence not in their vibrations. Rather, the difference is found in their presentations. The light coming from the Rose Quartz passively radiates outward in all directions. In contrast, Pink Halite's light follows its shape. Halite has a basically square shape that is created by the layering of its pink substance on the outside and perpendicular to each of the previous layers. The stone is structured with successive layers in a progressively spiralling stepped staircase that begins at the center and moves upward and outward. Each layer is superimposed upon the one before in a balanced and orderly manner. The result is a growing but ever balanced form.

Pink Halite's energies expand from the center outward following the pattern of its shape. The pink light vibration first enters the crystal at its core—the heart of the stone. Entering the heart is the way of love. Only the most minutely formed core substance of the stone is empowered to accept the light frequencies of love. At the first step of the spiral staircase, the energy is slight and hardly able to reach out beyond its own physical space. The energies of the first step are drawn upward by the second step. The first step is thereby emptied of its light energies, but by doing so, space is opened up for more of Pink Halite's vibration to come from the core. At the second step, the energies are strengthened and take an abrupt 90° turn. This is the first of many right angle shifts in energy flow as the light follows the steps of the spiralling staircase.

Once the pink light of love enters the staircase, it flows from step-to-step in an ever expanding spiral. The momentum of its movement increases with each step as light moves upward and outward, faster and faster. The directional flow of the light is not easily contained by the stone's right-angle patterns. It moves ever faster and with less conformity to the square shapes that define each successive step. In a well developed Pink Halite crystal, light is whipped around the stone in a clockwise manner creating a spiral vortex of the pink frequencies of love.

Pink Halite's beauty is its attraction. Its vortex sends light outward in an ever expanding spiral. When the pink love vibration leaves the stone, it makes itself available to the external world and to the environment in which it is placed. As a crystal for invoking the pink ray in a layout of crystals on a person's body, there is no appreciable difference in its effect compared to Rose Quartz. In a room, however, it brings its light into gracious harmony wherever it is placed. Pink Halite serves love well on the living room coffee table. It offers the love vibration with abundance to any who choose to occupy the room. Place Pink Halite in all the rooms of a house, and love, spiralling forth to its occupants, will indeed transform the hearts of those therein.

Pink Halite needs no prompting to send its love from the space in which it dwells outward to the world. Once placed, watch it offer its loving charm.

Prehnite

Healer for the Heart's Emotional Body

Scientific Properties:
> Crystallography: Orthorhombic
> Chemical formula: $Ca_2Al_2Si_3O_{12}(OH)$
> Mohs hardness: 6-6.5
> Density: 2.8 - 2.95 g/cm^3
> Colour: translucent, light green to yellow, but also colorless, blue or white

Prehnite is a vibration of the heart and brings a joyous, happy, and satisfying vibration of love. It provides a healing glow of warmth and accelerates vibration, as do most other green healing crystals.

Prehnite originates in a hydrothermal environment. When the Sun shines upon shallow waters, there is significant amplification of the Sun's light through the water element. Water acts as a filter. It allows a select band of light frequencies to pass, while excluding most other frequency bands. The deeper the water, the greater the filtering effect. Prehnite comes from great depths within the Earth, where the water involved in its formation carries only the very core band of light. It, therefore, manifests into form following a highly effective water filtering process. Because only highly filtered light frequencies reach into the Earth's and the oceans' greatest depths, Prehnite's frequency is quite pure.

The link between water and the emotions has long been established. Because the light frequencies that eventually precipitate into Prehnite first journey through water, Prehnite aligns with the emotional body. In particular, the stone's lighter shades of green resonate with the emotional body of the heart. Prehnite's vibration has the same modus operandi as other green healing stones. It accelerates the infinitely minute essence of third dimensional form, thus permitting greater amounts of light to enter. However, there is a difference in the structures involved. Acceleration occurs, not in the heart's actual physical form, but in the essence of the emotional body[1] of the heart.

Rather than facilitating alignment and balance, Prehnite opens the heart to receive more and higher light frequencies. If the heart of the individual is already aligned with the heart of the soul, additional healing occurs through cleansing. Alignment allows even more higher dimensional light to enter the heart. The frequencies attracted by Prehnite are specifically from the emotional energies of the heart of the soul. They act upon the emotional body of the heart of the individual. The incoming light cleanses the emotional body by displacing the lower and slower frequencies of light that might be causing problems. The cleansing action forces problem frequencies to leave.

Light made acceptable to the person on Earth is filtered by his physical body's etheric magnetic field. However, the body's etherics are not the only filter involved. For example, Apophylite works with the elemental frequencies of the Earth—wind, Earth, fire, and water. The frequencies of the elemental energies are filtered by the etheric magnetic field of our local solar system as they enter the physical plane. They are influenced by several planetary etheric magnetic fields, and filtered again by the Earth's own etheric magnetic field. Similar to Apophylite, the divine light frequencies that work with Prehnite are filtered and influenced by the etheric magnetic fields of the person, the Earth, the planets, and the solar system. What is not similar stems from Prehnite's role. Prehnite makes room in the person's heart for the infusion of

---

1   The emotions and the emotional body are not the same. The emotions originate as thought-form energy, while the emotional body is one of the many subtle bodies. It has specific design characteristics that affect its contribution to the flow of light. The structure, design, and operation of the emotional body are discussed at length in ***The Story of Light, Through Heaven's Gate***, Chapter 15 entitled, "The Emotional Body".

greater amounts of the light and love from the Godhead. As light frequencies journey from the Godhead, they are filtered in addition by the etheric magnetic field of the emotional aspect of the soul. Prehnite brings a very high vibration of the Godhead made pure by the filtering action of the soul.

In conclusion, Prehnite's complexity is minimal, because it works in the same way as any other classical healing crystal. Prehnite works its healing miracle by accelerating the emotional body of the user's heart chakra. The light that it brings to do its healing includes the highest frequencies of the soul and Godhead. As the light rushes in, the emotional body heals and emotional pains subside.

Pyrite

Etheric Field Manipulator

Scientific Properties:
Crystallography: Isometric
Chemical formula: FeS_2
Mohs hardness: 6-6.5
Density: 4.8 - 5 g/cm^3
Colour: metallic, pale brass-yellow

Pyrite is of Earthly origin. It first offered its grace during the great upheavals of the planet's surface. Since those earliest of times, Pyrite's vibration has evolved significantly. It has emerged to work with its human companions. Pyrite, however, does not serve the movement of divine light frequencies in the same way as a crystal. Pyrite does not work with light frequencies.

Pyrite's initial form primarily took the shape of a sun-dollar. Since that time, the cuboidal shape has emerged. The cube brings a few variations to the stone's original purpose. As most of the literature indicates, Pyrite is a stone that offers protection from the environment. In Earth's earliest days, protection was of greater concern than it is now. Currently, Pyrite has more to offer than simply protection.

Pyrite and Protection

Protection in the Beginning

Prior to the stabilization of the Earth by the planetary grid centered at the Great Pyramid, the light frequencies on Earth fluctuated within a wide range of high and low third dimensional vibrations. The highest of the high frequencies were quite disharmonious with the lowest of the low frequencies. The difference was extreme. Incarnating beings entered the density of the physical plane at significantly different levels of vibration within the third dimension than might be imagined in today's world.

The differences in density created the need to ensure that the friction between Earth's varied creatures was kept at a distance. Each living being required space to live out their own experiences. To help maintain the distance between these early beasts, Pyrite created a cosmic wall, so to speak. It created an 'armour plate' at the edge of an entity's etheric magnetic field. The armour plate was the equivalent of a force field that did not allow entities, who were of radically different vibrational density to come into each other's physical space. This was a very early use for Pyrite indeed![1]

Protection as it is Now

In today's world, there is no further need for this 'armour plate' type of protection. Protection is much more refined and reflects the state of the Earth's evolutionary progress. Pyrite's protective capacity still creates an armoured layer at the periphery of the etherics. However, the need to register the differences in density and deal with them is not as relevant (with some exceptions) as it was long ago. Instead, Pyrite's protective function is similar to osmosis. The stone imposes an etheric screening process that registers the vibration level of a potentially invasive being. If the being's

---

1   During the earliest of times on Earth, the high and low vacillations of the Earth's vibration necessitated some means to stabilize the third dimension. The highest third dimensional vibrations had difficulty remaining on the physical plane without slipping back into the fourth dimension, while the lowest third dimensional vibrations made little evolutionary progress and subjected other vibrations to chaotic negativity. Neither high, nor low vibrations shared harmony. The building of the pyramids at Giza in Egypt anchored a planetary energy grid, which served to narrow and stabilize the third dimensional vibration of the physical plane as a whole. Thereafter, individual vibrations could evolve without the overwhelming disruptions experienced when the vibration of Earth was less stable.

vibration is within a reasonably acceptable range, the etheric magnetic field configuration allows the user of the Pyrite and the being to share harmony.

Entities, whose vibratory frequency is not acceptable to the etherics, experience vibrational disharmonies with the user of the Pyrite. Pyrite deflects, reflects, absorbs, and otherwise manipulates the etheric magnetic field of unacceptable entities. The etheric field then creates disharmony by not allowing them a stable focus or steadiness of faculties, primarily of the mind, but also of the electric impulse energies controlling their motor functions. The Pyrite-empowered etheric field creates disjointed etheric balance, causing the invader to be rendered vulnerable to the will of the user of Pyrite.

Protection using the Sun Dollar Pyrite

In the case of the sun dollar Pyrite, the stone empowers the etheric field of the stone's user in the layer in which it is placed. The layer fully surrounds the user's body in a spherical radiating fashion, and potentially surrounds his environment as well. This is the same type of protection that comes from the armour-plated, force field of the past. There is no need to dwell on this model of protection because the density of mass is now relatively stable. The gap between highest and lowest vibrations has narrowed considerably since those ancient times when the protective function was needed to ensure that living beings had the space to live and thrive on Earth. The sun dollar Pyrite strengthens the outer layers of the etheric magnetic field to do their job of attracting and repelling energies, but falls well short of creating an armour-plated force field.

Protection using the Striated Cuboidal Pyrite

The striated variety of cuboidal Pyrite is firstly shaped into a square cube. Each of its six sides has a number of raised lines that are perfectly parallel to each other. The lines on each side run perpendicular to the lines of the sides at each end.

Striated cuboidal Pyrite works to cause a person's etheric energies to flow along the lines of its parallel striations, generally in a straight line. It does not cause the etherics to create the same disharmonious imbalances that arise from the protective effect of the sun dollar Pyrite. Rather, the cube, having numerous parallel striations on each of its sides, causes the invader's etheric field to be rendered at an angle perpendicular—broadside—to that of the user. Protection comes as a factor of the angle at which energies flow. The Pyrite user's energies flow in straight lines directly at the exposed breadth of the invader and, therefore, have full effect. The invader, on the other hand, does not have a comparable ability to channel its energies in a focused linear pattern and, therefore, cannot directly oppose the Pyrite user's etheric field.

Pyrite's striations help the user's etherics to come into concentrated focus at any line upon the breadth of the invader's etheric field. In the battles of conflicting energy forces, the user's ability to focus his own resources increases due to the enhanced etheric field configuration as a result of using the striated Pyrite cube. As such, the marshalling of more energy and the direct focus upon the invader's opposing energies allow the user a distinct advantage. To understand this advantage, one might draw a line into a second line and consider the concentration of energies that can occur at the intersecting point.

Protection using the Smooth Pyrite Cube

When the Pyrite cube is smooth instead of striated, the protective function occurs as a result of a reflection upon the invader's place in the scheme of vibration. The use of the smooth-cube Pyrite indicates that the beings involved are mature, and well past the evolutionary state involving simple manipulations of energy flows.

Pyrite, at this stage of vibrational maturity, causes the invading vibration to enter into reflection, both from the inner world of the mind, and from the external world of action and form.

Under the influence of Pyrite, the etheric field of the invader is limited to reflections upon his own actions. The etheric field configuration prevents the invader from seeing past this reflection, and thereby prevents him from assessing the actions of the Pyrite's user. Further, Pyrite helps the user to acquire the ability to read the reflection of the invader's actions. The reference at the end of the previous paragraph to the inner world means that the invader can only see self. The reference to the external world of action and form means the user can sense the invader's developing intentions and actions. The mechanism at work causes the Pyrite's user to intuitively feel vibrational shifts within the etheric energy fields of both the invader and himself. A quick assessment of the situation follows and allows strategies for preserving well-being to develop accordingly.

To adequately use the protective potential of Pyrite, a person needs to rely upon the intuitive feeling that arises from reading the etheric energies of the another person or entity. When the reading indicates that the other person or entity is at 'odds', Pyrite is working. It causes the invading person's etheric body to be manipulated into a state of detectable disharmony, thus alerting the stone's user to the radical difference in the other person's vibration from his own. A person's intuitive sense of this disharmony is the warning bell for some inequity. Pyrite has a vibratory frequency range that tolerates similar vibrations, but obviates dissimilar vibrations. It then manipulates the etherics causing them to be out-of-sync with undesirable vibrations. It prompts the user to the need for active, conscious, scrutiny.

As an example of the protective potential of Pyrite, a crystal store owner might place the stone at various locations throughout the store. He can then listen more confidently to the disharmonies that arise when customers with ill intentions enter. If the store owner heeds his intuitions and takes strategic actions, the Pyrite will have served its protective function by the prevention of inventory losses. Under the influence of the Pyrite cube, the imbalance that results in a thief's etheric magnetic field is to his disadvantage. In some ways, a thief's intuitive senses, which are usually highly attuned in order to mask his misdeeds, are distorted by the Pyrite. The store owner can take a more aggressive approach in dealing with undesirable persons as the apparent etheric imbalances offer their warnings.

In contrast, the well intended person vibrates within the harmonious range of the smooth-cube Pyrite's etheric scrutiny. In the same crystal store, Pyrite works to facilitate the exchange of energies. The Pyrite-enhanced harmony can be expected to help a person to attune better to the light of particular crystals, which serve that person.

Pyrite and the Mind

In addition to protection, Pyrite focuses the mind. Pyrite has the ability to create the environment necessary for accelerated and elevated focus through the smoothing and caressing of the mind's etheric magnetic field. The vibrational configuration and polar charge in the etherics, as set up by Pyrite, attracts the light frequencies that feed our thought impulses. The in-coming frequencies arrive in the opposing polarity, thus establishing etheric balance.

A person may choose to balance his etheric magnetic field using a biocircuit or copper energy bed[2]. If Pyrite is used in conjunction, its manipulation of light contributes to greater harmony between the polar tensions, which exist in the etherics of

2   The discussion about biocircuits and the copper energy bed can be found in *The Story of Light, Path to Enlightenment*, Chapter 2, section 2.3.3, entitled: "Energy Conductors". The description of a crystal healing, balancing, and empowering layout, using a copper energy bed, can be found at www.angelsandancestors.com/crystal.php.

the physical body. With the resulting increased flow of light, love comes naturally as part of the enhanced harmony and higher vibration. The mind, which needs light frequencies to create thought, can also play a role. It shifts its focus to attract light frequencies to the place in the etherics where harmony and higher vibration, and resulting love, is strongest. At that place, the mind has greater focus and less flightiness, as well as, greater continuity, strength, and depth of contemplation. Pyrite creates an etheric balance that then allows steadiness of thought and the focusing of the mind where love is prominent.

The Mind and the Sun Dollar Pyrite

The layers of the etheric body look somewhat like the rings of an onion. The sun dollar shaped Pyrite works with the ring upon which it is placed. For example, in a typical crystal layout, placing the sun dollar Pyrite 12" from the body, while the person is lying down, concentrates the effect of the Pyrite at the ring layer of the etheric field, which is 12" out from the body. Pyrite balances the entire layer at the 12" mark. In a most uncomplicated way, Pyrite attunes the etheric magnetic field to a specific range of light frequencies throughout its circumference. Consequently, the enhanced etheric field more effectively attracts and repels light, acting as the filter it was designed to be.

Light frequencies, which contribute to the creation of thoughts, filter in past the etherics. At the 12" mark, they encounter a uniformly radiating cocoon-type magnetic field surrounding the physical body. All frequencies passing through this layer are treated in an equivalent manner no matter how diverse the light frequencies might be, or at what angle they might be arriving from. The Pyrite-empowered etheric field, then, better attracts and repels a set range of light frequencies according to the person's vibration rate.

The effects of the etheric body can be viewed from the perspective of the conscious body. The mind concentrates and directs its focus on a given subject at a specific angle outward. The sun dollar Pyrite alters the etherics to concentrate its magnetic energy, for any particular thought pattern, to a few degrees or so within the 360° circumference at the place on the etheric body to which the mind is directing its focus. As the mind concentrates its energies in the narrowed pattern of its focus, light frequencies for the synthesis of thoughts are attracted in greater quantity by the increased strength of polarity in the etherics. Thereafter, the light moves quickly into the conscious body[3] and is available to the mind's contemplative focus.

Some of the mind's created thought-forms find their way into the awareness, but not all. To enter the awareness, a thought must be strong enough to do so, and is, therefore, higher in quality, with depth and strength of vibration. The depth of the subject matter results from the greater penetration of the light drawn into the consciousness in alignment with the particular angle of the mind's focus. When the mind concentrates its energies on a particular subject or interest, it narrows its focus to a single set of thoughts in greater depth, and thereby, receives much greater clarity on the topic in question. The sun-dollar Pyrite's role is to enhance the flow of desirable frequencies that feed the mind's interest.

The Mind and the Striated Cuboidal Pyrite

When the striated, cube-shaped Pyrite is used, the mind gains easy access to light frequencies to explore the tangents that are relevant to a given topic. The cube's parallel striations manipulate the etherics, as well as, the etherics of the mind. Pyrite creates linear etheric magnetic field patterns that develop along each striation.

---

3   The conscious body is the construct from which the mind draws light frequencies to create thought-forms. It is a storehouse for light. The background discussion on the conscious body and how the consciousness works can be found in ***The Story of Light, Through Heaven's Gate***, Chapter 14, entitled: "Consciousness".

By following the etheric patterns, the mind's focus is drawn into a linear perspective. In-coming light frequencies, needed to create thought-forms, penetrate the etheric body filter along the lines set up by the striations. The mind's focus aligns with the topic of interest to acquire depth, breadth, and height—the three dimensions of the cube—in linear fashion. Each topic is revealed to the mind in keeping with the etheric field configuration. Focus follows the lines of depth, breadth, and height. Along any one striated line, each idea leads to another idea, then to another, and so on, until that line of thought ends.

Each line of thought corresponds to one or another of the Pyrite cube's many parallel striations. However, the etheric magnetic field is configured to help the mind jump to another adjacent parallel striation on the same cube face, and at will. On the new striation or line of thinking, the mind explores the stream of linear thought impulses that run within the same general subject matter, but parallel to it. Each of the six cube faces correspond to a general subject, while each striation is a line of thought within the subject.

For example, the business accountant uses the striated cuboidal Pyrite to process his client's annual tax return. On one side of the cube, his mind works in the breadth dimension, as he builds his understanding of the scope of the return. Breadth involves income, expenses, and deductions. Once he has determined the breadth of areas to be processed, he shifts his focus to one of the areas in depth. The influence of the Pyrite then comes from a different cube face. Expenses, in depth, include car mileage, meals, and office equipment purchased. Height, which involves a third side to the cube, might follow the line of the cost of the office equipment. Purchasing a dozen computers takes higher priority over purchasing staples, as it is a capital expense as opposed to an operating expense.

The striated cuboidal Pyrite helps the accountant stay focused on each subject without straying from that specific line of thought. It contributes to disciplined thinking processes. At the moment, the mind wishes to contemplate a different line of thought, the Pyrite enhanced etheric field quickly shifts the mind out of the first line of thought and into the second. His mind moves from the influence of one striation to the influence of the adjacent parallel striation. The new focus becomes central to the mind, and the accountant experiences little distraction, as he reviews his client's capital expenses.

Breadth, height, and depth involve three different sides of the cuboidal Pyrite, but there are six sides. Breadth, height, and depth also involve the other three sides, but differently. Each line of thought has two sides to it. On any given subject, there are pros and cons, or negatives and positives. The cube side that works in the dimension of depth can be either the positive or negative perspective of the subject-in-mind, while the opposite cube side will be the opposing polarity. If one side is positive, the other is negative. To continue the example of the tax return, on the positive side, the accountant decides that the receipt for lunch at the cafe across the street from the business location can be claimed as an expense. On the negative side, he decides that the lunch at the ski chalet on a weekend, and 100 miles from the business, is not a claimable expense. The accountant is influenced by one side of the cube in his decision to add a claim for one expense, and by the other side in determining not to include a claim for a different expense.

Continuing with the discussion of the striated cuboidal Pyrite, when the mind's focus comes to the end of a line, thought patterns can shift onto the cube's adjacent face. The mind might then explore the lines of thought that follow the new face's complement of striations. The logical shift from one face to another means that the new line of thinking takes a new tack. According to its free will, by following a different face on the cube, the mind might shift its focus from contemplating the depth of a line of thought to contemplating the breadth of the same subject. For example, when the reader of this volume delves into the characteristics of Labradorite, he is working with a line of thought, or subject, in depth. If the reader then focuses on a number of crystals, he is following the line of thought, or subject, in breadth.

The mind's focus follows its alignment with the linear and perpendicular patterns of the etheric magnetic field as set up by the striated Pyrite cube. As the striations on the cube are parallel and at right angles, the patterns of incoming thought on any topic follow similar linear patterns. Further, the journey of the mind's focus travels along several lines of thinking, and can then shift quickly into different dimensions of the same subject.

The Mind and the Smooth Cuboidal Pyrite

The refined, smooth-sided, cuboidal Pyrite is six-sided in the same way as the striated cube. When a person uses the smooth cuboidal Pyrite, the etheric pattern that arises in the mind is also smooth and undirected. The individual surfaces of the smooth cube do not follow clear lines of thought, as does the striated variety. Rather, the smooth cube promotes unity of thought and unity in a person's understanding. The etheric pattern does not limit the flow of light to narrowed and linear thinking.

The light frequencies, which contribute to understanding a particular subject or to synthesizing a set of thought-forms, can coalesce and merge with each other on any of the cube's smooth surfaces. The outcome is that the light synthesizes into a unified and larger thought-form. The smooth surface offers no impediment to the union of a topic's subject matter as a whole. The individual, whole, units of subject matter, contingent with an individual cube side, can be juxtaposed with other whole units of subject matter on another side. For example, academic research, using a refined smooth Pyrite cube, enhances a person's awareness of the unity of the whole of a subject, and provides perspectives from several sides. Topics, having significant complexities, come clear to the conscious mind. Clarity of a subject of interest in the three dimensions of width, height, and depth is the gift of grace of the refined, smooth, cuboidal Pyrite.

Both the striated and smooth variations of cuboidal Pyrite work with the mind and consciousness through their influences on the etheric field. Both work best when placed on the third eye chakra at the forehead.

In summary, Pyrite influences the balance within the etheric magnetic field, which in turn influences the filtering of particular ranges of light frequencies. The sun dollar Pyrite enhances the body's etherics to more effectively attract and repel light frequencies for the physical body in general. The cuboidal varieties strengthen the focus of the mind, and bring awareness to the depth, height, and breadth of the subjects upon which the mind is contemplating. If the cube is striated, the mind can follow the linear patterns of logic within the subject, and tends to disciplined thinking. If it is smooth, the mind can work with the complexities of thought as a unified whole.

Quartz

Purveyor of All Light Frequencies

Scientific Properties:

Crystallography: Trigonal

Chemical formula: SiO_2

Mohs hardness: 7

Density: 2.65 - 2.66 g/cm3

Colour: transparent, translucent, colorless, blue, black, brown, green, orange, purple, red, rose, yellow

Clear Quartz Terminated Crystals

Directed Enlightenment

Godhead's eternal purpose has always been the bringing of light into darkness. It required and still requires the presence of the divine will. Through the divine will, the Godhead bestowed the clear quartz terminated crystal upon the Earth. Quartz crystals fulfill the eternal purpose. They bring light into dark places. Quartz crystals descended onto the physical plane already programmed with the Godhead's divine plan. Consciously aware individuals can also impart their own programming into quartz crystals, if they willingly offer themselves in service to the co-creation of the universe and the Earth. Quartz crystals can be programmed.

Crystalline minerals are the original means by which light frequencies descended onto the Earth. Their structures are firmly anchored in the physical plane, but span the upper dimensions, creating natural pathways between heaven and Earth. Foremost among the contributors from the crystal mineral world, is the clear quartz terminated crystal.

Each quartz crystal functions like the Sun and stars. Each is a portal between dimensions. Each holds open a space through which light traverses onto the Earth[1]. Further, the crystal's primary source of energy in the heavens delivers a basic energy pattern that arrives encoded with the design configurations of the divine plan. The encoding is the passkey or road map for the crystal's light-conducting pathways. A crystal's source frequencies find their way into the vicinity of the crystal's physical structure by following the pathways extending from their original source in the heavens. Crystalline structures on Earth reach beyond their physical forms to interact with higher dimensions.

The light, which surrounds any form, including the human body, is the total of all the light available to that form. On Earth and in the heavens, light is available from every angle of a form's circumference. Is a particular form capable of working with all of the light available to it? When available, all forms work with frequencies that are within the specific range of frequencies consistent with the form's vibration. Extremely few forms work with all of the light that is available. The round quartz crystal ball is an exception.

The round quartz crystal ball coalesces with light at every angle of its circumference without the limitations of flattened sides, which are characteristic to clear quartz terminated crystals. The quartz crystal ball accepts all light into its form. But, unlike the clear quartz terminated crystal, it does not create intensity or directional flow. It accepts all light, from every direction, with an equal attraction for each frequency throughout its sphere.

In contrast, the six-sided clear quartz terminated crystal draws light from all around, but the strength of its attraction vests in its six shaft sides. The strongest pull upon the surrounding frequencies occurs at precisely 90°, or perpendicular to each side. There

---

1   The Sun and Stars are portals between dimensions, or 'holes' in our night sky. For the discussion on the nature of the Sun and Stars, please see *The Story of Light, Through Heaven's Gate*, Chapter 9, sections 9.1, entitled: "Portals of Light: The Stars", and 9.2, entitled: "Portals of Light: The Sun".

are only six frequencies or ranges of frequencies, which occur at 90° to each side. All other frequencies experience attraction, but with decreasing strength the farther they occur from perpendicular.

The size and relative angle of each of the six opposing sides places the incoming light into a specific configuration within the stone. If the physical size of each shaft side is roughly the same as each other shaft side, the configuration of the light attracted will be in balance. However, if the size of one (or two) of the shaft sides is disproportionately larger, it will attract more light, and thereby dominate the equilibrium of the crystal. The imbalanced crystal offers the dominant light frequencies to the external world, along with offerings of proportionately less of the crystal's other light frequencies.

In conjunction with the shaft sides, the termination of the crystal plays an important role in the configuration of light moving through the stone. The termination concentrates the light and directs it out to the physical world through its point. If the facets of the termination are proportional to each other, light will concentrate in the most efficient manner and exit the stone with the greatest strength. The light is in balance. Facets of differing sizes, however, move the light at differing speeds and angles. A dominant facet can skew the flow of light, thus favouring a particular range of frequencies as easily as a dominant shaft side. The larger the size of an individual facet in the termination, the greater will be the flow of light coming from the shaft side to which it is connected. Smaller facets contribute proportionately less to the flow.

Each clear quartz terminated crystal possesses a configuration of shaft sides, which creates its own unique signature from the light frequencies present. The frequencies passing through the crystal do not create an aggregate of separate frequencies. Rather, they merge. The many frequencies, passing through the crystal, rally around the crystal's primary core frequency to become a single frequency. The single frequency given off by a natural clear quartz terminated crystal is unique to that particular stone.

All light descends onto the Earth at a precise angle. It originates from a specific source in the Earth's third dimensional heavens. These are the stars. Stars are inter-dimensional portals through which light descends from higher dimensions. The source of this light is beyond the conceptual ability of the incarnate mind. At source in the higher dimensions, linear concepts do not apply, nor do third dimensional frames of reference, upon which the mind relies. However, once light passes through the star's inter-dimensional portal, it enters the physical plane and assumes physical characteristics. 'Starlight' moves according to third dimensional time and space constraints, and most often, moves in linear progression.

The angles by which light aligns with a particular clear quartz crystal reflect the precise alignment of each of its sides to a specific source of light in the heavens. Each of a crystal's six shaft sides aligns precisely with its own star in the heavens. Each of the six stars sends its own unique primary frequency or range of frequencies. The crystal assimilates this starlight into a temporary manifestation of Oneness within itself. The term temporary applies because the crystal does not retain light. Light transits through the stone and only briefly assimilates into its form. Therefore, the crystal's Oneness continuously manifests and dissipates, in keeping with the arrival and departure of light frequencies passing through.

The characteristic signature of a clear quartz terminated crystal arises from the precise angle of alignment of each of the crystal's six shaft sides to each connected heavenly star. Only six stars in all of the heavens could possibly align precisely with each shaft side. Therefore, only six possible light frequencies or ranges of light frequencies become available. Each of the six stars contributes its characteristic light. Love, hope, peace, joy, awareness, and truth, for example, are a few of the possible characteristics. In turn, after passing through the crystal's shaft and exiting its termination, the combined characteristics of the light from each of the six stars beam out from the crystal.

Crystal Ball

Radiating Light from Everywhere to Everywhere

Because a crystal ball is spherical, it draws and emanates light in all directions. It imparts the wisdom of divine grace in the direction that its user chooses. The light available through the crystal ball comes from 'all'. It comes from all directions, all times, all places, and is at the centre of manifest existence. It brings forth the light of the divine Godhead and, thereby, parades before the attuned user the divinity of knowingness for all queries.

The light involved with a crystal ball is of great significance. When the crystal ball's user is attuned, it helps the user to draw all of the light available for the object of the mind's contemplation. The user, through her contemplation, automatically creates an etheric magnetic field in her mind by which she attracts the light frequencies relevant to the contemplation. When this light enters the aura, it becomes available largely through the third eye.

Gazing into a crystal ball helps the third eye by revealing the nature of the object at the centre of the mind's contemplation. The object may be an idea, concept, or potential physical mass. It displays a unique etheric blueprint, which is apparent to the third eye. The object's light frequencies are its life-force essence, but not its physical form. The contemplation's etheric magnetic field blueprint allows an exact quality and quantity of light frequencies to pass into the aura. As the frequencies circulate within the etherics, they make an impression on the crystal ball. The impression is apparent to the attuned mind. The crystal ball focuses the light received by the mind, thus revealing the object at the centre of the contemplation.

When the ball's user contemplates a particular manifest object, the light or life-force of that object also illuminates the physical aspect of the object. The third eye interprets the light frequencies it receives through symbols and references that it understands. The third eye's acceptance of the illumination presented and the limits, inherent to the light available, are dependant upon the openness and expansion of the vibration of the mind. The crystal ball's user needs to be most clearly aware that the mind must be opened up quite significantly to be capable of receiving the extremely subtle light coming through the ball. When the mind meanders through the various areas of its contemplation, the light that inhabits those areas becomes clear to the user's conscious perception.

The intensity of the light frequencies of a crystal ball will supersede almost any other light source, as it draws light to itself and dispenses light from itself. It will dominate the space wherever it is placed, and undoubtedly will be the dominant force within the user's aura.

In a nutshell, that is how a crystal ball works.

At this point in my introduction to the crystal ball, my spirit guides, the Councilate of the Ascended Light, went on to enlighten me as to the nature and history of my own crystal ball.

Councilate of the Ascended Light: *"Yes, Roger, this is indeed Autig as you, to provide tonight's channel along with MPZATQGSK (Myzat, for ease of use)*[2]*, who has most joyously consented to inform you as to the nature of your particular crystal ball. Would you please welcome our most obliging light brother?*

Myzat offers you his gracious loving greeting and wishes to begin."

Mzyat: *"Indeed, this crystal ball is among the rarest of crystal balls for indeed its near perfect quality is not often found in the size offered. You will undoubtedly see equivalent balls, but with adequate perusal in various shops you will come to appreciate the exquisiteness of your own. Roger, this crystal, Eparastika by name, is most clearly*

2   The entity, MPZATQGSK, Myzat for short, originates somewhere in the dimensions of the beyond. The phonetics of the name are also of the dimensions of the beyond and too difficult to pronounce. The name is a resonance rather than a sound. It denotes a vibration, therefore pronunciation of a 'word' is almost inappropriate.

yours as you incorporate its vibration with your own from the times that gave Atlantis its origins. I, Myzat, offer that it (my crystal ball) emerged from its watery protective sanctuary to be placed in an appropriate location, from which it began its journey through the appropriate distribution system en route to you. The molecular essence of the stone materialized and dematerialized about four times. It needed to be relocated to preserve its place on Earth in light of changes that took place on the planet."

"*The crystal originated with you in Atlantis. Your use of it at that time gave you enhanced powers of will to proceed with the work of drawing light essence into yourself during your descent into the third dimension. Your spirit's body was gradually brought down to its current state of density, which is the vibratory frequency rate you now possess. During this gradual densification, while in Atlantis, you used your crystal ball to draw upon divine source essence light to maintain the wisdom that was known beyond the third dimension. This was its primary use.*"

"*Your full descent into third dimensional vibration occurred during the time span of Atlantis' existence. Upon completion of the descent, the crystal ball was given sanctuary in the depths of the ocean. It needed to rest in this place because the changes to the world necessitated its storage for future use, which is now. The most significant worldly change was the absolute removal of the super-consciousness, which originates with the higher-self. This higher enlightened, super consciousness was most available at the start of the spirit body's densification into the physical plane, and was maintained with increasing use of the powers of the crystal ball. At the appointed time, the ball was stored. The body could no longer tolerate the intensity of light offered from on high. The body descended into density beyond its ability to accept light from the great divine source of light.*"

"*Storage of the crystal and the descent into physical density were required to adequately submerge onto the third dimension. Your service to the mission to bring light to Earth needed to acquire the desired frequency and the experiences that thereby became available. The crys-*

tal is now available to you for the purpose of drawing divine source essence light, which your body is most capable of accepting, without fear of harm and in accordance with the way that your aura and etherics cause that light to be filtered."

"Thank you for your loving invitation to accept our message on this most splendid of crystals the sphere, Eparastika."

Dearest most humble Myzat signing off.

Using the Crystal Ball

Because a crystal ball radiates in all directions and with all light possible, it enlightens the entire area in which it dwells. As a ball sits in its humble place, on a coffee table perhaps, the room is filled with light.

The light flowing outward from the crystal ball projects through every angle possible and in any direction. The user can work with the ball when contemplating some idea or subject. The contemplation aligns the mind with a single subject, which naturally involves a single projection of light to or from the ball. The direction of the light within the crystal ball depends on whether the contemplation is focused on a query, meaning that light is inbound, or on a circumstance that does not need a solution, meaning that light is projected outward.

Once the projection to or from the crystal ball has been established, the user of the ball will experience an enlightening of the contemplation. The light frequencies involved follow the alignment created by the mind's contemplation with the help of the ball. The state of vibration of the user's conscious *body* determines the quantity and quality of the light attracted and accepted therein. The conscious *awareness* is enhanced according to the quantity and quality—the limitations—of the additional light available to the contemplation, coming through the crystal ball[3].

---

3   The comprehensive discussion on the workings of the consciousness, including the conscious body, the mind, the intuition, the in-

Enhanced conscious awareness comes from the third eye. Intuition is the means. The crystal ball lights up the conscious body, making the intuitive visions of the mind much stronger and clearer. The mind is then significantly more capable of accessing the recorded events that have shaped the evolutionary journey upon which the crystal's user is contemplating than without the crystal ball. During this journey the experiences of all that happens are written upon the Akashic records of the soul and may be accessed through the light that is focused within the conscious body. The consciousness is capable of moving into itself to illuminate the records that it contains. The conscious body holds all of the records of all of the events that the individual's soul has experienced in the incarnate form throughout the period of that soul's existence on Earth. The complete Akashic record is available at the level of the soul.

At the level of the conscious body on Earth, the crystal ball is capable of offering all light frequencies that are acceptable to the conscious body. As such, the mind can focus on a particular idea or subject with significant clarity, often receiving a definitive vision. When a person contemplates the past, she receives the visions and impressions of that time period to illuminate her conscious awareness. If a person simply focused on her chosen contemplation, light frequencies come into the conscious body. The crystal ball sends the light. The conscious body then opens to it and draws it in. Because the ball cannot offer light beyond that which the conscious body is capable of accepting, its user is wise to open the conscious body up significantly before bringing light in through the crystal ball.

The user may begin her session with the crystal ball through meditation, which creates the stillness that leads to serenity. She can then move the stillness into her contemplative focus. If she

tellect, and the contemplation can be found in *The Story of Light, Through Heaven's Gate* (volume two), Chapter 14, entitled: "Consciousness".

260

wants to bring light to any of the charkas, the heart chakra for example, she can do so through simple mental focus on the heart chakra and through her expression of the will to draw light to that chakra.

Further to the example of bringing light to the heart chakra, the user of the crystal ball might be aware of the changes that are occurring within the chakra and how the chakra is affected. Awareness comes with the will to bring the subtle vibrations of the heart chakra into the third eye, simultaneous to the changes of light occurring within the heart. The third eye reads the vibrational differentials and acquires awareness of the change. The crystal ball operates to bring light to the heart for its empowerment, but also to the third eye for its empowerment. The empowered third eye senses the shift in light and energy as a result of the contemplative focus, and thereby acquires awareness.

The fact that the crystal ball is spherical in shape means that the light available to the third eye, the heart chakra, the mind's contemplation, and more can come from any direction. The light coming into the conscious body can enter through any angle of the full radiating sphere of the contemplative focus. As the focus consciously follows the light, the light can be moved to the appropriate angle to illuminate any particular aspect of the focus, thus giving the awareness access to the totality of the focus as it exists in the conscious body.

The primary outcome of the use of a crystal ball is the complete illumination of the contemplative focus. The will sets up the contemplation to focus on specific queries, ideas, visions, and more. The focus then draws the specific light frequencies from the conscious body to shape the mind's awareness. The crystal ball makes its light available from every direction of its sphere to empower the conscious body. The light actually received is in compliance with the light frequencies needed by the contemplation. The crystal ball helps to empower the mind with awareness.

Generator Crystal

The Floodgate for Light

Light coming to Earth must pass through the etheric magnetic fields of each physical form that it encounters. The planet, local geography, and human body each have an etheric magnetic field, which filters and at times blocks some of the light attempting to pass. The problem of etheric blockage is somewhat alleviated by the bridging function of crystalline structures, but much more light bypasses the etherics when generator crystals are involved.

Generator crystals have the same structural configuration as the six-sided clear quartz terminated crystal. Generators are clear quartz terminated crystals, but they intensify the flow of light. They push pure white light, which carries the full range of all frequencies, onto the physical plane and into the aura. The level of their intensity is high enough and strong enough to overcome many of the problems of etheric filtering. The ability of the generator crystal to intensify the light that it receives is its trademark feature. All clear quartz terminated crystals process and intensify light to some degree, and are, therefore, generators in their own right.

The intensification of the light comes primarily through the generator crystal's ability to balance the incoming light frequencies. Imperative, therefore, true generators must have equally proportioned shaft and facet configurations. The stone's physical appearance needs to look balanced in order to project light in a balanced way. The balance, in turn, intensifies the flow of energies. As light moves towards the generator, the six roughly equivalent shaft and facet sides accumulate light. Each side, in relation to the other sides, has a specific angle from which it draws light. When the physical sides have balance, the angles at which light enters the stone will also have balance. The six different sets of light frequencies refract through a generator crystal in equal quantities and in balance with each other, and therefore, move in the most efficient manner. With balance, light moves through and exits the generator crystal with strength.

The generator crystal works to intensify the light moving through it. Light moves through the crystal's structure entering at the base end and leaving at the terminus end. As the beam of light exiting the terminus moves outward from the stone, it assumes the angle that reflects the balance inherent to the shape of the facets on the terminus. In a perfectly balanced crystal with facets of identical design, the beam emitted incorporates each of the six frequencies equally, and light leaves straight from the point. The light, then, becomes so intense that it penetrates the etheric field at whichever place it is pointed. The significant intensity of the combined beam is more than the etherics are capable of blocking, and so, the light passes through.

All crystals are in essence generators of light. Along with their ability to channel light, crystals may also create their own light from the form and light—Oneness[4]—within. The creation of light is a manifestation in the image of God. Because all lighted beings create their own light from the God-self within, each being, including the generator crystal, manifests creation in its own image.

The generation or creation of light by the generator crystal is no different than any other six-sided clear quartz terminated crystal. The label, 'generator', is a loosely applied term usually given to those stones that are large enough to dominant among other crystals because of the significant amount of light that they offer. While clear quartz crystals produce light, the generator crystal's light is available in sufficient quantities to supply both its own needs and the needs of other crystals. Some crystals, including Malachite, Lepidolite, and Lapis for example, emit extremely little light. Without the generator crystal to empower them with addi-

---

4   Form + Light = Oneness. For the discussion of this principle see *The Story of Light, Path to Enlightenment*, Chapter 1.2, entitled: "Form + Light = Oneness". For the qualities of Oneness see *The Story of Light, Through Heaven's Gate*, Chapter 7, entitled: "Oneness Light".

tional light, fulfilling their specialized purpose may be quite difficult or impossible. Quartz of whatever variety generates light. Crystals outside of the quartz variety, however, do not generate sufficient amounts of light to be effective as generators.

Features to look for that make up a good quality quartz generator crystal include size, balance, and clarity. First, the larger the quartz crystal, the more light it generates. Bigger is always better. Second, the primary determinant in the generation of crystalline light is the quality of the termination. Balance, as previously mentioned, is key. If the shaft sides and termination facets are equal in size, light flows through the crystal evenly and efficiently. The beam of light given off is strongest. The third important feature is the clarity of the quartz within the shaft. Cloudy quartz indicates a crystal that is still in the developmental stage. Much of its energy is focused on attracting light for it maturation. It does not give off light in the quantities, or qualities, given off by the crystal that has clarity. The best generator crystal is large, to ensure a significant quantity of light flow, balanced, to ensure efficiency and strength of flow, and clear, to ensure the quality of the frequencies involved.

All light created is divine-source light[5]. Further, light generated from within the aura is among the cleanest light possible on the physical plane. The quantity of light needed to radically change the body, however, is quite significant. Consequently, the use of crystal generators does not usually result in an amount of light that overwhelms the body. With the exception of the largest and most powerful generators, the light beam from a crystal is not harmful to the person using it. If, however, the generator crystal's light beam is excessively strong, it may create transient distortions in the user's normal auric patterns.

---

5   Light frequencies can be created anywhere within creation and still be divine-source frequencies. The design of a light frequency includes the core frequency, which is always an extension of the energies of the Godhead. The core frequency makes light divine. For the full discussion of core frequencies, please see *The Story of Light, Through Heaven's Gate*, Chapter 4: Godhead Light", sections 4.1 through 4.3.

A crystal can be too strong for the body, but the body can also be too weak for the crystal. If a person's body is not attuned to the high and subtle vibrations of the in-coming light, it cannot tolerate light because its own vibrations are low and dense and open only to low, dense, and slow light frequencies. The body that is not attuned is easily overwhelmed with light, even small amounts. While the transient distortions experienced in the aura or the etheric magnetic field are likely to be more pronounced, given either a strong crystal or a weak body, ultimately, they are not harmful or permanent. With strong generator crystals the cautionary note is to not push their use beyond the innate instructions of the intuition.

The Laser Crystal

Surgical Cutting Crystal

The clear quartz laser crystal has a very distinctive shape. It has six shaft sides and six facets on its termination, as does any other clear quartz terminated crystal. However, its shaft sides are tapered from the base, and quite long and narrow. Further, its facets and termination are always very small. A small laser crystal might be 3-4 centimeters in length, and a master laser is usually more than 10 centimeters. Intuitively, it has the look of a crystal that can move light frequencies very fast—and it does.

In my own collection of crystals are two master lasers. I use them on occasion during crystal layouts. Their job, in this context, is to cut the etheric magnetic field of the person receiving the layout. This cutting action slices through dense vibration and makes way for the light of empowerment. As well, laser crystals bring their own version of divine heavenly light. Such light is securely within the realms of Oneness with little or no taint or negative vibration. Light moves very quickly through a laser, thus preventing any lower or negative vibrations from being part of the flow. Light from a laser crystal acts similar to kyanite because of the speed by which it moves light, and because it leaves negativity behind. Hence, a clear quartz laser crystal brings exceptionally clean light frequencies.

The clear quartz laser crystal performs three main functions:

1. It can cut through the etherics to create an opening that allows light in the near vicinity to pass through the etherics[6].

2. It moves light exceptionally fast, thus removing negativity.

3. It penetrates deeply into physical form. Penetration ensures that the laser crystal's own light frequencies, along with a few 'choice' frequencies having a high and subtle vibration, can move into the form.

The additional 'choice' frequencies (#3 above) must have a sufficiently high vibration to keep up with the laser's own vibration. Therefore, additional frequencies that piggyback onto the laser's own frequencies are always high and subtle and generally free of negativity.

The laser has an additional function which is available, but rarely used by humankind. It can pierce the dimensional barriers outward from the physical plane and into the heavens. As a person holds a laser, the light it gives off travels high into the heavens. Its

---

6   Using a laser crystal to cut or open a person's etheric magnetic field needs to be done with caution and integrity. The etherics serve as a filter, which repels unwanted light frequencies and attracts frequencies that contribute to spiritual enlightenment and growth. When the etheric field is cut, light from the immediate area can slip in—desirable or not. The salient need is to not allow negative light a chance to enter. To ensure that only desirable frequencies find their way within, the room or space, in which the layout is conducted, needs to be cleared and protected. Smudging is sufficient to do the clearing. Invoking the presence of Archangel Michael is sufficient to effect protection.

reach goes well beyond the highest dimensions to which the consciousness of the mind can ascend. The value of this feature is that it can be used consciously.

When a person's will sets an intention, the clear quartz laser crystal can be programmed with that intention. The laser crystal then sends the programmed intention high into the dimensions beyond consciousness. Whereas, the intention is recognized and respected within the dimensions that are within reach of consciousness, sending the intention beyond consciousness by using the laser crystal gives it even greater attention. Not only do the dimensions within the reach of consciousness come into alignment to muster their energies to contribute to the fulfillment of the wilful intent, the dimensions beyond consciousness also come into alignment and contribute their light energy. The net result is a significantly greater participation of a greater portion of the lighted universe in the fulfillment of the intention.

Time-Link Crystal

Parallel Experience Through Time

The Time-Link Crystal is a clear quartz terminated crystal with a diamond-shaped window located at the base of one of its facets. The window allows the user to look into the stone.

Meditating with the Time-Link crystal makes the past available, along with access to much wisdom. A person's awareness of his past-lives gives perspective to the experiences of his soul—experiences that constitute the totality of all of the soul's learning to date. Access to such experience is a treasure, for the insight that is placed before the awareness offers all there is to know.

The method, by which to access the divine wisdom brought forward by the Time-Link crystal, comes through the requests of the stone's user, as conveyed by pondering a problem or curiosity. As the problem becomes apparent within the contemplative awareness, there will be a related past-life experience, which offers a life-lesson contingent to the current experience. To add perspective, consider that all experience occurs simultaneously in the same instance of time. When a person transcends the third dimension, where time is limited to only the now-moment, the great knowledge of timelessness unfolds.

How does a person use a Time-Link crystal? Begin with a contemplation of the current experience-at-hand in the physical plane's time-space continuum. Next, using the crystal, focus on the diamond-shaped time-link window. Consciously project the experience-at-hand into the crystal's window. The potentials of the experience, as it occurred at a time in the Earth's past, then become apparent within the third eye's vision. The events of the current experience are substituted with the events of the past experience. The equivalent or parallel experience, which pertains to the identical lesson, takes place through the perceptions brought forward by the crystal. For example, today's lesson in honesty is experienced through re-experiencing a similar lesson in honesty that took place several life-times ago. By projecting the current contemplation upon the screen of timeless experience, the lesson becomes available in the fullness of its depth and meaning.

To be more specific about using the Time-Link crystal, first bring the mind into a state of peace and calm, then focus upon the lesson of interest. As the contemplation brings light to illuminate the current experience, the consciousness is drawn to the light of the past experience that occurred during some past-life situation. The crystal brings into the contemplative focus a parallel experience, which is connected by the will and spirit of one's eternal being. Whereas the top edge of the window facet's parallelogram reflects the current focus, the bottom parallel line is the past focus offered through the crystal, to the lesson at hand.

By seeing the lesson through the experience of the past situation, the beginning, middle, and end of that experience enter the awareness. The lesson's outcome, and what needs to be learned, become clear. Awareness of the previously unknown or hidden parts of the lesson may then be applied to the current life experience. The person using the Time-Link crystal can heed the wisdom inherent to the past lesson to arrive at an enlightened conclusion.

Again, focus on the situation of interest with intensity while wearing the crystal. Then allow the light of the crystal to move the focus past the time-link barriers to review the fullness of a past situation with the same lesson as the object of contemplation. This does not imply that the practitioner attempts to project conscious intent into some other zone of time and space. Rather, the crystal will cause the contemplative focus to shift from the current experience to the past experience. The practitioner only needs to be calm, to contemplate, and to witness the shift in focus. At times, the person may hesitate to accept the past situation. To overcome such doubts and blockages, openness and acceptance are all that is needed.

Specialized Quartz Crystals

The specialized quartz crystal is a caldron for light. When light passes through a specialized quartz crystal, such as Amethyst[7] for example, the crystal's specialized frequencies merge into the mix of all other light passing through. The frequencies of Amethyst combine with the full spectrum of the great white light provided by the crystal's clear quartz aspect. The person using the stone receives the specialized frequencies, along with all the light needed for growth on her evolving spiritual path.

Terminated quartz crystals merge the vibrations of all light frequencies moving through its structures into a single umbrella frequency. By definition, the umbrella frequency carries all of the other frequencies within. A particular (primary) light frequency

---

7   Other examples of specialized quartz crystals include Citrine, Rose Quartz, Smoky Quartz, Green Adventurine, Chrysocolla Quartz, and Spirit Quartz. This list is not exhaustive.

within the umbrella frequency enters the body part for which it was intended carrying with it all of the umbrella frequency's other (secondary) frequencies. The secondary frequencies, which include the full spectrum of white light from the clear quartz aspect of the Amethyst, are not in conflict with the body part. However, they do not resonate well enough to enter past the body part's etheric shield without help. For example, the specialized primary light frequencies of Amethyst, which are purple, are indigenous to the third eye chakra and resonate with it naturally. Therefore, Amethyst's light enters the third eye easily. The secondary frequencies of the quartz aspect of the Amethyst crystal, the white light frequencies, piggyback onto the specialized Amethyst frequency. Consequently, Amethyst brings the full range of white light frequencies into the third eye chakra. Secondary frequencies then become available for empowerment and assimilation. The third eye assimilates some frequencies. However, most remain unused and eventually leach out.

The additional secondary frequencies that piggyback onto Amethyst's purple light frequencies do not always resonate intimately with the intended body part, but they do contribute to the body's Oneness. According to the nature of Oneness, the light of any frequency is welcome to enter Oneness. Hence, the light is welcome to enter the Oneness that exists within the body part. When the Oneness is at the beginning of its evolution, its form aspect limits the range of additional frequencies that can assimilate therein. If, however, assimilation involves high and subtle frequencies, such as the purple light of the Amethyst crystal, one can safely assume that the third-eye chakra is already open and that the Oneness therein is reasonably well developed. The presence of all light frequencies, as the white light of Amethyst's clear quartz aspect implies, allows assimilation of significantly more light. Not only are there a greater number of frequencies immediately available, they immediately begin entering the body's form in sequence according to their vibration.

The empowerment of Oneness follows the assimilation of acceptable frequencies in the appropriate sequence, frequency after frequency, according to what the vibration of the body needs and can accept. Because the clear quartz aspect of the specialized quartz crystal provides a full range of frequencies flowing into the body's form, albeit in small quantities, assimilation takes place in an orderly fashion. There is no gap in the process. Each frequency needed by the body is available for assimilation, and exactly when the body needs it. In rapid succession, the required light enters the body's various parts as each part becomes ready to receive it. The body's form soon evolves into higher vibrations of Oneness, and its capacity to accept light increases. Eventually, the Oneness of the form merges into universal Oneness. Thereafter, the blockages to the free-flow of light caused by its etheric magnetic field diminish.

Quartz possesses the grace to carry all light frequencies, and combine with them. When a quartz crystal is close to a person's physical body, each of the chakras attracts its own frequencies from the stream of light that flows from the crystal into the body, and then into the chakra distribution system. There is no need to work explicitly with a specialized range of frequencies to empower a chakra. The white light of clear quartz includes all frequencies, and therefore, includes the specific frequencies needed by that chakra. Having the next required frequency for assimilation readily available has profound implications for the spiritual growth of the user of quartz crystals.

Rhodochrosite

Soul Love for the Chakras

Scientific Properties:
> Crystallography: Trigonal
> Chemical formula: $MnCO_3$
> Mohs hardness: 3.5-4
> Density: 3.7 g/cm^3
> Colour: transparent, translucent
> pink, rose, red, yellowish-grey, orange, brown, white, gray;

Rhodochrosite is a treasure in any light worker's crystal collection. It brings love.

Rhodochrosite provides the bridge between the emotional bodies of the third dimension and the emotional energies originating with the creative source, usually the soul, in the higher dimensions. It is a bridge in the sense that the light of the soul crosses through to the Earth plane through its vibration. More important than the bridging function is the relevant range of frequencies. Rhodochrosite resonates only with the heart chakra, and at the upper ends of the heart's vibration.

The pure Rhodochrosite light frequencies come in exquisite pink. Orange (and peach) coloured hues may also be present in some specimens. The orange hues are vibrations of creativity. They are needed to facilitate the descent of the exquisite, high, and subtle pink light frequencies into the third dimension, and are separate from the pure Rhodochrosite vibration. The descent from the heavens into the third dimension is a most traumatic affair for those living light frequencies that bring exquisite vibrations to Earth. Such frequencies are simply too high to enter the physical plane on their own. They often need help to make it across the dimensional threshold, and to adjust to physical vibration. The creative energies inherent to the orange-brown-peach coloured specimens serve to allow the high, subtle, and delicate pink Rhodochrosite vibration to descend to Earth more easily. The orangy inclusions open and create the loving space needed for Rhodochrosite's high and divine pink frequencies to enter into the physical plane. They form the base upon which the pink frequencies crystallize. Their presence indicates the need for the stone's further development before it can function as a properly matured Rhodochrosite stone.

As Rhodochrosite accumulates on Earth, its vibration matures and adapts. Presently, the orange inclusions are no longer needed to open and create space for the pure pink Rhodochrosite vibration. Because these inclusions are exclusive to the creative function, the darker shades of orange and peach do not detract from the quality of pure pink Rhodochrosite. A Rhodochrosite stone, with or without the creative vibration, offers the same effect. When selecting Rhodochrosite for a crystal collection, however, do purchase stones without the orange and peach inclusions. The absence of the inclusions gives the stone a higher vibration.

Rhodochrosite manifests in the depths of the Earth's oceans and deeper freshwater lakes as a hydrothermal vein mineral, therefore emotional energy is present. The watery filter, through which its light passes, accepts the emotional vibrations of love. Rhodochrosite resonates strictly with the heart chakra in the upper frequency ranges and brings an expression of love's purest light. It moves the love vibration of the heart into position in the heart chakra, and then moves it into the chakra distribution system (ida, pingala, sushumna). Thereafter, Rhodochrosite's love vibration is transported to the chakras themselves.

The frequencies attracted to Rhodochrosite are available from the light passing through the human aura. Rhodochrosite resonates at a most exquisitely high level of love. Its love vibration brings the heart chakra into alignment with its light. The light of the loving heart and the light of divine love merge in the same mutual loving way as they do in Rose Quartz. Rhodochrosite's frequencies, however, are not released to the external world or to other persons. They go exclusively to the bodily essence of the person using the stone. Rhodochrosite's love frequencies descend from the soul, not for the purposes of outward expression, but for distribution to the body's chakra centres. The love vibration present in the heart chakra enters each of the other empowered chakra centres, thus ensuring that love is the guiding light within.

Rhodochrosite imbibes love into the process by which each chakra works with its light frequencies. Love opens and accelerates the chakra's essence, thus making room for the light frequencies of the chakra's empowerment. The throat chakra, for example, is enhanced by Rhodochrosite to offer the loving expression of truth. At the crown chakra, where a person's light frequencies first enter the body, the presence of Rhodochrosite's love vibration allows much more light to come through. At the third eye chakra, the enhanced vision of wisdom is the result. At the pelvic chakra, the impulses of sexuality are not inhibited by the need to gain or create an outcome. Rather, the love imbibed into a person's sexuality is given expression through that sexuality. Sexual union is much enhanced by the love that permeates the second chakra by adding Rhodochrosite's contribution from the heart. In the base chakra, the love that enters helps to release the soul from its love cocoon, thus stimulating the kundalini. The love brought into each of the chakra centres by Rhodochrosite offers an exquisite level of enhancement by opening the chakra's essence to receive light.

Because Rhodochrosite's vibration is at the higher end of the heart's frequency range, each of the other chakras experiences empowerment at the higher levels of its vibration. The enhancement offers a love in parallel with the love of the heart chakra. When the light received arises from the love of the person's own heart, it easily passes into his Oneness and chakras.

In a crystal layout, Rhodochrosite is best placed at the heart.

The light, available to the stone from within the aura, is then brought into the heart. Its vibration aligns the heart with divine light frequencies, takes the resulting frequencies of love into the chakra passageways, and empowers each of the chakras to open and assimilate its own empowerment frequencies. Rhodochrosite's love pervades all of the bodily essence with which it comes in contact. Because of its place among the higher frequency ranges, it does not tread upon low vibration where it is unwelcome. It is prevented from entering slower vibrational space. Among those higher vibration ranges with which the stone resonates, its love is welcome whether it arrives invited or impromptu.

Rhodonite

Compassionate Harmony

Scientific Properties:
Crystallography: Triclinic
Chemical formula: $MnSiO_3$
Mohs hardness: 5.5-6.5
Density: 3.57 - 3.76 g/cm^3
Colour: transparent, translucent
red, pink, brownish-red, gray

Rhodonite is the softened way to love.

Rhodonite, stone of the loving and compassionate heart, offers to the world the mellowness of the summer's breeze and the gentleness of the cotton tuft. When Rhodonite is used to bring love, the result is a soft swaying lyrical vibration that lulls its user into the lap of heart's sweet song.

The purpose of Rhodonite is to soften the love vibration and to give love flexibility in the way it is offered to persons receiving it. Rhodonite is love in a hundred different ways and brings the vibration that the joining of two truths can enjoy. As love is truly the middle way, love is what comes between two lovers. The vibrations through which love brings persons of differing truths together is not limited in any way. The only qualifier is that their truths converge and meet with mutual acceptance. As a seemingly implausible example, enemies of war experience love at the peace table. Even with bombs continuing to fall, the experience of the convergence of their truths, for the purpose of making peace, is most difficult, harsh, cold, calculated, and yet love in action.

There are many paths leading to love. To come to love and to know love is best accomplished when love is felt with a sense of harmony and flow, pleasantness and respect, along with numerous other qualities that offer acceptance and encouragement. However, love may also have a presence during moments when facing the jaws of terror. Peace talks with cannon sounds in the distance are one example. Love is not often trusted in circumstances crowded with adversity and mistrust. The presence of mutually inflicted pain, as is war, does not create the environment for love's greatest moments, but love is not denied by such circumstances.

From a different perspective, when the doorway to love suddenly swings open, it can be a blinding flash. Few people can accept love when it presents itself so abruptly. The naked truth of love is easily rejected. Love offered with harmony easily contrasts against love offered with disharmony. While love is present in both instances, the frailty of human understanding and the immense problem of delusions that pervade the human mind often block the potential for love whenever the presence of harmony is weak. Therefore, within the human realm, love needs to be dressed in the illusions of, for example, kindness and warmth. The fine and desirable qualities of kindness and warmth are not herein degraded by the reference to illusion. Rather, a clear distinction exists between the trappings of love and the truth of love. Trappings can be quite positive and desirable, or not. In either case, they are still trappings. They do not influence love in any way.

The will to share the truth of others permits entry into the realms of love. However, the will to love is not always forthcoming. In the absence of the will, the doors to love most assuredly remain closed. By reviewing the sharing of truth, clarity descends upon the most basic and sacred wisdom that dwells within. All truths simply are—are truth. Being-ness is, truth is. The defining point of truth, as it emerges from the original source essence or the Godhead, is the manifestation of divinity. Manifest divinity reaches into all beings and material objects. Manifest divinity is truth. Therefore, whether manifest divinity possesses light or not, it possesses truth. However, when a person denies the truth of the divine manifestation, he is unable to accept truth beyond the scope of his own narrow and limited delusions. In the presence of denial, love is impossible.

In its infinite wisdom and all knowing ways, Godhead has sought to offer a pathway to the truth to those whose limited understanding of truth creates denial. What is offered is that the pathway of convergence with the truth of one person and another has been sugar-coated. The sugar-coating is the trapping of 'compassion'[1]. By extending the trappings of compassion outward from one's own special truth, the limited mind of another person is eased into an harmonious environment within which truth is more readily accepted. Warmth, respect, harmony, acceptance, joy, and peace are some of the steps on the stairway of compassion leading to the temple of love. Through God's gift of the stairway (or vortex) of compassion, the less than self-realized person is given the helping hand by which to come forward into the place of love. Regardless, there is a distinction between the stairway that encourages love, and the love itself.

Rhodonite vibrates within the heart's midrange frequencies in the very first concentric ring outward from the core. While the vibration of Rose Quartz is central to the heart chakra's love, Rhodonite is central to the ways of love. Again, emphasis is given to the ways of love, which are, in essence, vibrations of compassion, as distinguished from the love itself.

While Rhodonite is not truly indigenous to Earth, it has served here during many millennia. Rhodonite works in the same way as numerous other ancient indigenous stones. First, it acquires light that has found its way into the etheric magnetic field of the person using it. Next, from the light flowing in the etheric field, it accumulates its own frequency of harmonious compassion, which it then discharges into the heart chakra. Eventually, Rhodonite's

---

1   Compassion is the vortex that surrounds love and makes stepping through the doorway into love easy. For the discussion about compassion, please see *The Story of Light, Path to Enlightenment*, section 4.5, entitled: "Heart Chakra: Love and Compassion".

vibration of compassion is offered by the heart outward. Compassion then enters the chakra distribution system for expression to the external world in accordance with the user's vibration.

The keywords to describe Rhodonite's vibration are compassion and harmony, or compassionate harmony. For the hesitant person, who would otherwise be willing to share his truth and love with another person, compassionate harmony draws upon vibrations that penetrate his veils of illusion. On the one hand, Rhodonite works with the warmth, kindness, and acceptance—compassionate harmony—to generate a willingness to share truth with another person. On the other hand, its vibration pierces through a person's illusions to join his truth with the truth of another person. Rhodonite makes use of both attracting and penetrating energies to overcome the separation of converging truths. On the feminine side (attracting), the stone polarizes the user to set up warmth, kindness, acceptance, peace, respect, honesty, and more, thus setting up an inviting place of peace. On the masculine side (penetrating), the stone radiates outwardly through hope, and enters through joy. Therefore, Rhodonite's vibration both attracts the hesitant person to itself, and extends out to him as well. Compassionate harmony both ebbs and flows between the stone's user and any person affected by the stone.

As before, Rhodonite is the gentle summer breeze and the soft cotton tuft offering the compassionate and harmonious pathway to love through its warmth and flexibility.

Rose Quartz

Empowering Love

Scientific Properties: (Variety of Quartz)

Rose Quartz is the crystalline channel for divine love. Its soft pink ray invites universal divine light frequencies of love to come quietly into its matrix. Rose Quartz also invites the frequencies of love from the heart chakra of the person using it. Both the vibration of divine love from the heavens and Earthly love from the heart chakra come together in union within the Rose Quartz. Rose Quartz serves the light through its attraction and union of the love vibration.

The vibration of mixed love that collects within Rose Quartz vibrates at a frequency rate below the vibration of heavenly love, but above the vibration of Earthly love. The person using the stone, then, receives love that is higher than the vibration of his own love. The vibration of love within his heart chakra is raised by exposure to the combined love vibration. It not only empowers the heart chakra, it dilutes and displaces with divine love those dark and negative vibrations that hold dense vibration within the heart. With each further use of Rose Quartz, the love in the user's heart chakra continues to rise. The more a person is exposed to Rose Quartz, the more that negative energy is expelled from the heart, and the more that divine love finds a home. As love is truly the middle way, the mixed love vibration of half divine and half heart chakra love has the potential to make a 50% improvement in the heart chakra's vibration each time Rose Quartz is used.

As with any stone, there is a need to clear and recharge Rose Quartz after each use (e.g., the sun-water method). Once cleared and powered up, pure divine love again comes to empower the stone with its pink ray. However, if the stone is subjected to continuous use without clearing and recharging, its matrix weakens and so does the strength of its love vibration. It simply cannot hold the same quantity of love. In wearing it without clearing, the benefits from the mixed vibration of love continues uninterrupted, but at an increasingly slower pace. Ideally, after wearing Rose Quartz for a half-day, place it in the sun for an hour or so. Ask the stone if it needs more or less clearing and recharging.

When the heart is subjected to the difficulties of third dimensional density, negativity has an opportunity to pervade. The dynamic of the stone's action, however, does not change. Rose Quartz continues to mix divine love with heart chakra love. Unfortunately, the heart's vibration may be dominated initially by negativity and thus very dense. If so, it holds a vibration that has very little love. The joy that comes with using Rose Quartz again and again is that it relentlessly moves the heart chakra's vibration ever upward. However, in the presence of significant negative energy, the rate of upward movement may seem slow indeed.

Regarding quality, any variation between pieces of Rose Quartz is insignificant. There is very little difference in the way energies are exchanged or in the strength of those energies from Rose Quartz of one shade to Rose Quartz of another shade. The shape of the stone has a greater effect than any other characteristic. Shape will give direction to the flow of light. While the heart-shape may be very popular, the pyramid is a much more effective configuration in the quest to ground love into the body. The shape, which can attract light from all angles and then concentrate its flow into a narrower band, has the greatest influence. On the one hand, the multisided pyramid has more directional grounding force than a four-sided pyramid. On the other hand, a cone-shaped pyramid has more grounding force than either the four or multisided pyramids. Greater force intensifies the quantity of the divine and heart chakra love vibrations that are available for mixing.

Structural anomalies, within individual pieces of Rose Quartz, may result in distortions of the flow of light into less-than-straight patterns. Also, the heart chakra can be envisioned as having a maze of caverns, some of which carry negativity and dense vibration, and some of which carry loving light. Because there is no way to understand how light might be directed by the stone to specific areas of the heart chakra, or where darkness lurks therein, there is no need to be concerned about the precision of a stone's flow patterns. Particular distortions in flow due to internal structural anomalies are unavoidable. The blueprint of flow patterns and the map of the heart's caverns cannot be matched. The general direction created by the stone's shape is adequate to bring the light frequencies of love to empower the heart chakra.

Shape is an important feature, and so too is size. Quite simply, the larger the piece of Rose Quartz, the greater will be the quantity of the love vibration that can be brought forth.

Within the Rose Quartz crystal, the vibrations of love from the heart chakra and from the heavens mix into a vibration of love that becomes available to raise the love vibrations of the heart chakra. Further, the stone's mixed love vibration dilutes and displaces the heart's dense and negative vibrations. Over a period of continuous use or use at regular intervals, the individual experiences an incremental and continuous elevation of his love vibration.

Ruby

Piercing Red Light

Scientific Properties: (Variety of Corundum)
Member of the Hematite Group
Crystallography: Trigonal
Chemical formula: Al_2O_3
Mohs hardness: 9
Density: 3.98 - 4.1 g/cm^3
Colour: Red

The ancient and prized Ruby crystal has dazzled the eyes of its beholders for the full term of the Earth's physical existence[1]. Prior to the creation of the seven chakra system, Ruby worked with the

---

1   In the original channel given by my guides, the Councilate of the Ascended-Light, my own involvement with the crystal, Ruby, was brought to light. I feel compelled to share this perspective.

Because I am the incarnation of a very old soul that has been on the Earth since the beginning of Earth's sojourn, my soul has participated in several of the major epochs that serve the mission to bring light to Earth. Here is what the Councilate said about my affiliation with Ruby: "Indeed, Roger, your own place in the bringing of the gift of Ruby was significant during these ancient times in early Egypt and the Persian coast. So important was this connection that we offer that a number of your lifetimes were partially involved with the spreading of the light of this most precious of Earth's indigenous vibrations." The time line is roughly 5,000 years before Christ, in the days of the Pharaohs.

The human body was impervious to most of the available light on Earth. Through its capacity to penetrate past the resistance of the body's form, Ruby provided the means to bring light into the body. In those early times, the body's density was great and few frequencies were able to enter. Ruby's red light could penetrate the physical body's form with sufficiently processed light to permit assimilation. Ruby did not begin the enlightenment process, but nursed it through the dark early moments when light was exceptionally scarce.

light frequencies of the primitive three chakra system[2], where only the base, heart, and crown charkas were present. In today's world, Ruby carries the vibrations of the second or pelvic chakra.

Because Ruby is red in colour, it resonates with the higher frequencies of the base chakra, as well as, the full range of frequencies of the pelvic chakra. In the ancient three chakra system, Ruby regulated the light coming into the base chakra. What is meant by 'regulated' is that the in-coming light was distributed by passing through the stone and out into a radiating flow, which then moved to the circumference of the base chakra. Whereas, light normally entered the chakra from a single direction and passed through without being absorbed, the addition of Ruby caused the flow of the in-coming light to break up. The frequencies of lower vibration could then be absorbed by the body's primitive chakras. Thereafter, the light that was acceptable to the body's chakras radiated outward from the stone's crystalline structure. If not radiated, the beam of light entered the chakra as a single stream. The primitive chakra could not anchor and hold any significant amount of this light because the stream was too concentrated. Ruby refracted light frequencies and radiated them outward thus allowing the physical form of the primitive chakra to assimilate the light it needed more readily.

During Earth's infancy, the bulk of Ruby's light involved the highest ranges of the Earth's light frequencies, which were still within the black light frequency ranges. The frequencies that resonated at the lower ends of the second chakra, however, were, and continue to be, primarily within the range of red light frequencies. The light frequencies, which Ruby originally allowed to pass through its crystalline structures, were consistent with the vibra-

---

2   The human body did not have chakras when it first arrived in its primitive forms so long ago. The creation of chakras only happened following a chance discovery of the body's light carrying potential. The discussion on the initiation, creation, and evolution of the first and subsequent chakras can be found in *The Story of Light, Path to Enlightenment*, Chapter 3, section 3.3, "Inventing the First Chakra".

tion of the then new, but still primitive, second chakra. At that time, these were the only light frequencies available with which the second chakra could resonate. This was the earliest of times on Earth—when light of any kind was most limited. Ruby brought with it the first few light frequencies that vibrated above the Earth's indigenous black light ranges of frequencies.

The light within the red range of frequencies is a compelling energy. While black light is simply the lowest form of light capable of reaching into the lowest depths of the physical third dimension, the red frequencies bring fiery energies. These are not the soft blues or purples, or the healing greens, or even the creative yellows. Red works to stir the pot.

Red light creates movement by the irritation of its hue. Physical forms that can accept red frequencies become saturated with the presence of imbalanced light. The imbalance is not because of polarity, however. Rather, the imbalance is caused by the way the light is distributed. Light normally flows toward a point of attraction generated by similar or opposing polarity. In stark contrast, red light flows according to its own impetus, without heed for either polar influence.

Red light acts on physical forms differently than other ranges of light. Once a physical form's vibration evolves sufficiently, it can absorb light. In the case of black light, frequencies move between physical forms. If a molecular structure does not absorb the black frequencies passing by, the frequencies simply bounce off and go to the next structure. In contrast, Ruby's light directs its own flow. It does not softly bounce off physical form. Rather, the flow of Ruby's red light frequencies makes its way by generating intensity that challenges the physical form to either absorb the red frequencies, or reorder its essence. As mentioned, Ruby controls the intensity of light flow through refraction and radiation within its natural crystalline structure. However, if Ruby's light-beams concentrate their strength, they burn through physical form. Both Ruby and the clear quartz laser crystal can burn through form, but

Ruby regulates the intensity and the laser does not.

Ruby's regulated light flow challenges the physical form without causing it to be burnt or destroyed, or even overly burdened. The reduced, or more accurately, the regulated intensity of its flow matches the strength of the vibration of the physical form to a similar degree. The challenged form is bombarded by red light, which moves much faster than black light. The form then either accepts the light by absorption, reflects the light, or undergoes the reordering of its molecular structures. Form is reordered when the in-coming red light refracts again as it moves into the resistant areas of the physical form. Refraction at the micro-molecular level further permits Ruby's light to penetrate even deeper into the form's essence.

While eventually, some light frequencies are lost, the greater part of the light moves into the form, or causes it to be reordered. Reordering refers to the way the polarities of the micro units of the form's essence shift in response to the bombardment by the intense, but regulated, flow. These frequencies do not empower the second chakra. One might envision that the reordering action is that of the splitting of atoms. More accurately, reordering causes the individual internal parts of the body to line up differently. Their polar configuration shifts directions, and therefore, also shifts from one magnetic influence to the other.

The new polarity causes significant enhancement of the attraction and repulsion of whatever light frequencies are available. For example, the red light of anger carries the polarity of repulsion. It reorders the second chakra essence to reject the light frequencies related to the focus of the anger—another person perhaps. Similarly, the red light associated with sexuality carries the polarity of attraction. It reorders the second chakra to attract frequencies related to sexuality, as carried by the person, who is the object of the attraction.

Ruby operates in this current millennium much the same as it did in bygone eras. It brings light frequencies of a lower vibration that resonate with the second chakra. Its reordering action works to enhance both attraction and repulsion, which also corresponds to the way the second chakra manipulates light[3]. Using Ruby in a crystal layout enhances the polarity of the human body by reordering its essence to attract or repel frequencies in near proximity. Ruby does not alter or set up actual light frequencies for attraction or repulsion. Rather, Ruby reorders the physical forms of the body's seven main chakras to enhance their polarity for the light frequencies they need.

Ruby indirectly empowers the second chakra by reordering its molecular structures. As a result, the second chakra sets up a polarity field that causes the person to have an affinity for beneficial light frequencies. Rather than empowering the second chakra, these frequencies cause the person's vibration and energy to move towards a state of balance. For example, enhanced sexual energies, which are consistent with the second chakra, move the person towards experiences that will balance his increased libido. The energy to satisfy the libido is attracted, as opposed to denying and perpetuating the imbalance. Empowerment is the result of the attraction of light for balance by the reordered second chakra essence.

---

3   The way that the second chakra works with light is discussed in *The Story of Light, Path to Enlightenment*, Chapter 4, section 4.3, entitled: "Pelvic Chakra: Attraction/Repulsion".

Selenite

Gateway to the Highest Self

Scientific Properties: (Variety of Gypsum)

Crystallography: Monoclinic
Chemical formula: $CaSO_4\text{-}2H_2O$
Mohs hardness: 2
Density: 2.31 - 2.32 g/cm^3
Colour: transparent, translucent, opaque, colourless to white

Selenite is among the most precious of all crystalline formations, and indeed offers great joy through the refined and delicate frequencies it brings.

Selenite is a bridging stone between the most distant planes of the beyond-the-beyond and the third dimension. It holds third dimensional vibration within its essence, and at the same time, offers access to the light of the soul and the universe to any person with whom it resonates. The light frequencies of the person using Selenite and her soul merge within Selenite's Oneness. Although a similar connection is possible within many other stones, Selenite works with the Oneness of the soul in the way that the master calls the servant. The master on Earth, who is at One with Selenite, has at her disposal a clear channel to the soul, and to the highest levels of self.

Selenite draws Oneness together. The Oneness of the All of the beyond, the Oneness from the soul, and the Oneness from the person using it on the third dimension, merge together within Selenite. All of the universe can have a home within its essence. Consequently, Selenite is similar to Fluorite. Both Selenite and Fluorite present a physical form that is truly enlightened substance, and yet, not simply enlightened substance. Both accommodate the presence of angelic beings. However, unlike Fluorite, Selenite's task does not include accommodating a diversity of higher dimensional discarnate light-workers and spirit guides. As well, Selenite does not need to be fully functioning enlightened substance at all times. Rather, Selenite ushers the movement of Oneness through its physical form, but only when called to do so. When the Oneness of a person merges with the Oneness of her angelic higher-self, Selenite makes the merged Oneness available on the third dimension. Oneness is brought together from separate sources within Selenite, as it is within Fluorite, but, in Selenite, the unified Oneness is also moved onto the physical plane. Fluorite accommodates higher dimensional Oneness and spirit guides, but their vibrations remain within the stone without actually exiting into physical vibration.

Selenite resonates intimately with the physical plane. Understanding how it manipulates third dimensional energies is key to how it works. Over a period of several millennia, the human physical body gradually acquires the capacity to anchor and accommodate light. The capacity to anchor light is primarily accomplished through the expansion of a person's Oneness as the light created from within assimilates into the physical body. The person's Oneness also expands through the light received from the higher planes and the higher-self, whenever that light is available.

Using Selenite allows a person to focus her Oneness into the stone simply by its placement nearby, preferably at the head about 12" above the crown. Giving one's vibration over to the stone, by wilfully using it, joins a person's third dimensional Oneness with the substance of the stone. At this initial point of union, the stone assumes the precise vibrational frequency rate of the user. The vibrations of the stone and the user merge into one, thus becoming the same.

In the resting state, Selenite is dormant. However, upon holding Selenite or having it in near proximity, the user's unique frequency rate is programmed into Selenite after only a very few seconds. With the newly acquired frequency rate, Selenite projects its vibration of unified Oneness (the user's Oneness and the Oneness of the stone) into the lighted universe. Because the stone has assumed the exact frequency of its user and no other, the pathway into the heavens strictly follows only the alignment with the specific soul energies of the user's higher-self. No other soul or higher dimensional entity could possibly attune to Selenite's frequency rate, as based exclusively on the user's frequency.

Accessing the vibrational frequency rate of the user's soul is the primary task assigned to Selenite. Selenite also facilitates the soul's union with its incarnation's Oneness on Earth, and helps anchor the Light Body. In the current new age, the Light Body does not need to be beckoned. The Angelic Ones, the souls of Earth's evolved beings, await the union of higher and Earthly selves from places that are close at hand.

In bye-gone ages, when very few souls were evolved and the light was scarce, Selenite was used in the same way to draw the Light Body from the beyond-the-beyond into the physical body. The results, however, were rarely satisfactory. The connection with the higher-self requires that the vibrational quality of a person's Oneness be adequately high. In the past (as now), if the soul's angelic light was present, and if the enlightened Earthly will to call forth the higher-self was true, the Light Body[1] was anchored. These simple conditions were not easy to fulfill, however. The way was most difficult because light was available to only a very few of the most adept individuals on Earth.

In this most precious moment of the new age, Selenite is emerging to take its rightful place. It builds the bridge between Earth and heaven, and increases the potential to join the Oneness of the person on Earth with her soul, but not just her soul. Selenite

---

1   Light Body includes the soul, which is part of the higher-self. It also includes the physical body once invoked. This is the essence of enlightenment. For the comprehensive discussion of the soul, higher-self, and the process of enlightenment, please see *The Story of Light, Path to Enlightenment*, Chapter 5, entitled: "Enlightenment".

reaches up to the highest levels of a person's angelic self to the very highest place of separate and identifiable being, immediately outside of the Godhead. Selenite works with every level of the Light Body.

To prepare the physical body to resonate at a frequency high enough to accommodate the Light Body, a person's etheric body must be in balance. Balance comes either through the disciplined practice of meditation, or by the use of other enlightened technologies such as the copper energy bed[2] and crystals. The state of a person's karmic lessons must also be acceptable. The lessons of karma are written as a vibrational blueprint upon a person's etheric magnetic field. In response to karmic imbalances, the etheric field sets up blockages to light frequencies that may be needed for spiritual growth. Excessive blockages, caused by unresolved karma, indicate an unacceptable level of a person's evolutionary progress and vibration for the purposes of anchoring the Light Body.

The Angelic Hosts are now swarming upon the Earth ready to be invoked into their respective physical bodies. In this new age, with easy access to the awaiting angelic light, Selenite works with the soul's energies surpassing the limits of age-old density to bring about the union of the physical body with the Light Body.

Although Selenite brings together the Oneness of the individual and her higher-self, its loving purpose is not exclusively for the benefit of the individual. The individual's responsibility within the divine plan is to bring light onto the physical plane. Light, however, can also flow in the other direction. Once Earthly Oneness has been adequately lighted, its connection with the heavens allows light from Earth to transcend to the heavens. The Heavenly Hosts then experience the joyous flow of loving light coming from the

2   The copper energy bed works directly with a person's etheric magnetic field to accelerate it and bring the person's vibration into balance. For the background discussion, see *The Story of Light, Path to Enlightenment*, Chapter 2, entitled: "The Etheric Body". The way that the copper energy bed works with the etheric field is specifically discussed in section 2.3.3 entitled: "Energy Conductors.

third dimension³. The new age is indeed also a celebration for the enlightened ones in the heavens.

Selenite's contribution to the service of the light goes beyond accommodating the presence of Oneness. Its vibration allows the Oneness of the person using it to connect with the highest levels of her higher-self. Selenite opens the door to the person's soul in the heavenly planes. Within the structures of Selenite's substance, higher dimensional light frequencies create pathways to the beyond. The pathways are simply the manifest forms of higher dimensional substance. The forms of the pathways are present within the stone, but are not lighted nor active when Selenite is not is use. The physical form within Selenite is void of light, and therefore, lies dormant when not in use. Without an empowering source of light, Selenite cannot offer any connection to any other source of light. Once the light frequencies of the user enter Selenite, for the mere act of picking it up, the pathways also light up to become Oneness. However, the pathways become Oneness only in the exact frequency of the user. It is as if a switch is turned on, and the stone lights up like a light bulb.

Upon activation with the user's light frequencies, Selenite's pathways open to the celestial origins of soul-level Oneness. The user's own unique frequency determines which pathway is used. Quite quickly, within seconds at the absolute most, the Oneness is linked between the user and her higher-self. The pathway is cleared and ready, and awaits the coming of the Light Body.

Selenite permits the Light Body to enter its substance, but does not serve as a holding station. Rather, the Oneness is so thoroughly connected between the person, the stone, and the angelic presence of the person's soul and higher-self that the Light

---

3   Sending light into the heavens is paramount to the acceleration of Earth's enlightenment. For the discussion that will help connect the dots to explain the elation of the Angelic Ones, who are receiving light from the Earth, see *The Story of Light, Through Heaven's Gate*, Chapter 6, Section 6.4, entitled: "The Value of Duplicating Earth Light".

Body simply transits through the stone into the lighted essence of the person's physical body. There is no real time delay. The pathway opens and the Light Body moves at the speed of its own light frequencies to assume a place within the user's third dimensional body.

Enlightenment! The Angels sing with Joy! Enlightenment!

The invocation of the Light Body is the pinnacle of the person's third dimensional mission accomplished. It is the ticket home to the ascension in this most graced new age.

Selenite's initial dormancy and its exclusive attunement to the user's vibrational frequency rate are an important feature that is essential to safe invocation of the Light Body. Light Body invocation is the physical body's accommodation of the presence of the soul and higher-self. The objective is to ensure that the soul and higher-self belong to the person that is undergoing invocation. The potential exists for a mischievous lower fourth dimensional entity to slip into the physical body and take over. Such malignant beings are the cause of delusions of grandeur seen in persons suffering from schizophrenia. Having two higher dimensional beings vying for the same physical body is chaotic and contrary to the will of divinity. Selenite effectively eliminates the possibility that any vibration, except the user's vibration, plays a part in the Light Body invocation process.

As to Selenite's many other talents, Selenite has access to the full vibration of a person's third dimensional body. Selenite's vibration, specifically Selenite's Oneness connection, has the capacity to move into the deepest parts of the physical body, as well as, move on its pathways to the farthest reaches of the user's highest origins. Selenite coalesces with self from top to bottom. With such a broad range of possibilities, only the will constrains the work of Selenite. The person's will is the means by which the knowledge within the stone is acquired. Selenite offers the knowledge of the light of universal Oneness and eternal wisdom.

The light of eternal wisdom enters the consciousness of the

stone's user. The presence of Oneness, enhanced by the stone, implies an intimacy with universal knowledge. To activate this knowledge, a person need only contemplate the self, wisdom, and love. Thereafter, the light of consciousness is given. Responsibility for initiating the contemplative will rests with the individual. By contemplating any chosen topic, the light attracted becomes available, through the Oneness of the user and Selenite, to enlighten third dimensional awareness in the ways of the heavens. The choice of topics is only limited by the scope of the mind, but limited nonetheless.

Selenite is intimate with the Earthly emotions through its connection with the water element. Water is, at times, trapped within the stone's substance, and its crystalline development takes place in watery environments. The emotional vibration taken into the stone is Oneness complete—from the fullest extent of Earthly expression to the highest resonance in the heavenly beyond. Because the Oneness within Selenite carries emotional vibrations, the emotions are intimately connected with the divine light brought forth from the higher planes. When an evolved person uses Selenite, the intent of the universe is placed clearly before her consciousness. The less realized person is only capable of partial awareness of the divine intent and is likely to suffer emotional pain. That is, the use of Selenite gives a person the will, but not the knowingness or the balance, to align with the emotional light of the soul. An imbalance in the emotions foretells significant pain for its incarnate victims.

Selenite offers the chakras the full range of light frequencies from the soul's Oneness. Each chakra acquires the frequencies it needs for empowerment. The quantity of light involved is not so overwhelming that the stone's user experiences kriyas[4] or other such

---

4   One meaning of Kriya is the outward physical manifestation of the awakened kundalini. Kriyas can also be spontaneous movements resulting from the awakening of Kundalini energy. When I attended the Siddha Yoga ashram in Ganespuri, India several years ago, kriyas were easily observed among many of the ashram's devotees, who were

problems. Rather, the energies involved are those, which constitute the union of the higher-self with the physical self. Harmony, therefore, reigns. The guidance of the soul is omnipresent, and so, the measure of light entering the physical body is precisely correct. The person's own soul ensures that the exact amount of light needed is sent to empower the bodily essence and chakras. When the light of a chakra either lags in growth or is exceptionally ahead of the person's spiritual evolution, the soul automatically sends the correct measure of light to create the balance required.

In summary, Selenite is capable of preparing the pathway for the entry of the Light Body through its ability to resonate with the full range of Earthly and soul level frequencies. It attunes to the user's unique vibrational frequency rate, following which, it actually vibrates at the very same frequency. Because Selenite's reach into the heavens is comprehensive, it brings together all of the evolved Oneness of the person's physical body with the Oneness of the highest levels of self and all parts of self between. Using both the very highest and the very lowest frequencies of the user's vibration, the stone draws Oneness from the infinitely tiniest conceivable essence deep within the body's third dimensional molecular structures.

By comparison, whereas Fluorite is enlightened substance, so too is the Selenite. However, Selenite becomes enlightened substance only when used. A very rapid transformation takes place within Selenite, as soon as the light of the person using the stone merges with it. Selenite, therefore, is not a pillar of light and does not accommodate a host of light beings, as does Fluorite. Instead, Selenite draws the Oneness vibration of the user into itself. When held in the hand, or when in near proximity, Selenite attunes strictly to the very unique frequency of the user. It magnetizes the person's Oneness thereby attracting it into its own substance. There

---

seen shaking, rocking, or bouncing to some degree. While kriyas may be mistaken for epilepsy or Parkinson-like symptoms, they are not harmful, especially under the Guru's roof.

is no change in the frequency of the Oneness. Once imbibed with a person's light, Selenite's vibrational frequency rate is the same as the person. Immediately thereafter, Selenite connects to the universal source of Oneness. Through the universal Oneness comes the wisdom of the dimensions of the beyond. Additionally, if the physical body is adequately prepared, the person's physical body anchors its Light Body.

Selenite, Diamond-shaped and Radiated

Light Body Layouts on the Fly

Diamond Selenite comes during this moment of the New Age bringing the blessed offerings of Selenite. Diamond Selenite has been radiated, and therefore, also carries the divine frequencies directly from their original source the Godhead.

As a form of Selenite, Diamond Selenite facilitates the union of the incarnate person with his higher-self. Because Diamond Selenite is also radiated, it takes the user's essence further into the dimensions of the beyond. It brings about the union of the person and his Light Body, as does Selenite, but also establishes the union of the self, including the self in every dimension, with the Godhead. As laid out in the divine plan, radiated Diamond Selenite also grounds the energies of absolute divinity into the frequencies intended for Earth.

The in-coming light from the Godhead includes the Earth's black band of light frequencies, as well as, frequencies reflecting the higher states of Earth's planetary evolution. By using Diamond Selenite, the Oneness of the Godhead and the black light frequencies of the Earth mix together. Earth's black light is indigenous to the base chakra. It can easily penetrate taking the divine light of the Godhead with it. As Selenite works to unite a person with his multi-dimensional self—the soul and Light Body, Diamond Selenite goes one step further by uniting the person with the light of the Godhead. The additional Godhead frequencies greatly enhance the person's Oneness throughout his multi-dimensional being.

To use the Diamond Selenite, place one piece about eight inches above the head, and a second piece about five inches below the feet. Using two pieces ensures that the person both attracts the divine light, as well as, grounds it. Diamond Selenite is constructed with a slightly indented rough groove, which runs from point to point along its length. This grooved line is the route by

297

which light moves through the stone to the chakras. Ideally, when used in a crystal layout, the groove running the length of the stone and the center line of the body need to be aligned.

If a person leaves home, travelling to far away destinations, and cannot access the stones of the Light Body layout (Selenite, Kyanite, Calcite, Hematite), Diamond Selenite can stand in as a substitute. It can provide a mini-layout that ensures the invocation of the Light Body. However, in the full power layout involving all of the crystals that are normally used for invocation, as named above, place one piece of Diamond Selenite on top of (or near to) the primary Selenite piece being used to invoke the Light Body. Place another piece between Hematite and the feet. Using this configuration allows the Diamond Selenite's Oneness to carry and ground divine Godhead light directly into the human body.

Selenite that is not radiated uses the unique frequency rate of an individual's Oneness to encode its substance for the purpose of connecting with the Light Body. In contrast, Diamond Selenite encodes its substance in an identical manner, but the light attracted by the Diamond Selenite is from the Godhead. Using the radiated Diamond Selenite ensures the connection to the Light Body, but also achieves a much stronger connection to the divine original source of light—the Godhead.

A crystal layout using Diamond Selenite brings grace to a person's vibration. Once the initial crystal layout to invoke the Light Body has been completed, incorporating Diamond Selenite into future Light Body layouts ensures the presence of the Godhead vibration.

Seraphinite

Medium to the Angelic Universe

Scientific Properties: (Trade Name for Clinochlore)
Crystallography: Monoclinic
Chemical formula: $(Mg,Fe^{2+})_5Al(AlSi_3O_{10})(OH)_8$
Mohs hardness: 2-2.5
Density: 2.6 - 3.02 g/cm^3
Colour: Green, blackish-green

Seraphinite's iridescent dark green hues open physical form for light to come in. Light moving through Seraphinite begins its flow from its source at the centre of the stone's structure, then follows the stone's semi-radiating patterns along roughly straight lines. Once the light passes out from the stone, it radiates in all directions.

As do classic green healing stones, Seraphinite opens the essence of form on the physical plane. However, healing is not Seraphinite's primary purpose. Rather, Seraphinite carries its own very distinct vibration, which offers the light of the Seraphim Angelic Kingdom. Seraphinite does not bring the light of any one spirit guide or angel, but rather the light of the entire realm of Seraphim angels. Seraphinite's vibration is a very high and specific range of angelic vibration, which resonates on the Earth plane with whoever has the openness to receive it.

The Seraphim angels offer their angelic light to serve the awakening of humanity. However, the benefit of receiving Seraphim angelic light is not limited to what it will do for the awakening. The entire spectrum of Seraphim light is very helpful with the every day needs of individuals, who are attempting to harmonize with each other and to progress in their spiritual evolution on Earth.

Awakening begins with the opening of the dormant light of

the soul, as it rises from within the love cocoon of the base chakra to open the upper chakras. This is the uncoiling of the serpent of the kundalini. Awakening allows the base chakra to create the shift in personal energies to place the individual into the flow of light needed to initiate her ascension process.

The Seraphinite crystal itself opens the physical body of an individual to light frequencies, which facilitate her spiritual awakening. In particular, the opened and empowered base chakra causes the relocation of the individual to places on Earth having the needed light frequencies for further empowerment. This implies that locations and individuals that have the ability to facilitate spiritual growth become centres of attraction for the growing spiritual devotee. The user of Seraphinite follows the lead of the empowered base chakra[1] by gravitating to places where light is available for spiritual growth. The user is thereby positioned in alignment with the light frequencies she needs. The empowered base chakra enhances the will and propensity of the user to seek out environments that contribute to growth.

The Seraphinite crystal functions as a bridge between centres of light and the individual. First, it opens the individual to receive light. Then, it creates the flow of light from the light centre to the person using the stone. The light centre can be, for example, a vortex of light frequencies or a master light-worker. It serves as a platform or medium through which the Seraphim Angelic Kingdom transfers light frequencies from its realms and other realms in

---

1 The base chakra plays a significant role in a person's spiritual growth by creating vibrational tensions that cause relocation to venues having light frequencies for growth. For the foundation discussion on the role and function of the base chakra regarding its relocation feature, see *The Story of Light, Path to Enlightenment*, Chapter 4, section 4.2, entitled: "Base Chakra: Environmental Compatibility".

The opening of the love cocoon mentioned a few paragraphs before may also be of interest. The explanation of the base chakra's mode of operation at the time of opening is discussed in the same volume, sections 3.4, "The Seed Light", and 3.5, "Awakening the Seed Light".

the heavens into the physical body of the person using Seraphinite.

Seraphinite establishes its primary vibration, which is the light of the Seraphim Angelic Kingdom, within both the medium of the light centre (vortex or master light-worker) and the person using the stone. As the Seraphim angelic vibration is a continuous vibration that extends from the heavens, through the medium, and into the user's essence, all of the Seraphim Angelic Kingdom's light frequencies become available. Light can come from any part of the universe. Whenever an individual emits an attraction for specific light frequencies, the Seraphim angels direct the needed frequencies into the user's space with the help of its ally, Seraphinite.

The exchange is not a drain of light from Seraphinite caused by the acquisition of the personal store of light of an unwitting individual. In the flow of light from the medium to the user of Seraphinite, that is, from the vortex of light or master light-worker to the user, there is no drain of energy, because the only light frequencies available, or even possible, are Seraphinite's own frequencies. Seraphinite sets up the opening and the energy shifts within the person's physical body, and then generates the flow of light to the body. The flow generated by Seraphinite is exclusive of the medium's own light sources because it comes from the heavens, as directed by the Seraphim angels. There is no dependency on the mediums' light reserves, therefore the potential quantity and quality of light is infinite. Further, the medium benefits because it acquires some of the light that flows through the Seraphinite crystal to the individual.

The master light-worker or light vortex, which serve as mediums for the light moving into the Seraphinite user's space, are willing participants, as determined in the heavens by the soul. If the soul's incarnation is also a conscious participant, the process is readily expedited. If she is not consciously aware, her soul takes over to facilitate the outcome. Because the mediums in-question are, of necessity, willing light-workers, the soul has the freedom and permission to direct the process, whenever the conscious awareness of the person on Earth falls short.

Light flows from the high heavens, as directed by the Seraphim angels, through the medium of the light-worker or light vortex, into the Seraphinite crystal, and is received by the user's physical body. To the willing user of the Seraphinite crystal—to someone who honours the Seraphim Angelic Kingdom—the light available is virtually limitless. Indeed, the grace possible is the full potential of the physical consciousness.

Serpentine

Meandering Healer

Scientific Properties[1]: (for group name Lizardite)
Crystallography: Monoclinic
Chemical formula: $(Mg,Fe)_3(Si_2O_5)(OH)_4$
Mohs hardness: 2.5-4
Colour: light green, green, blackish-green

Serpentine is a healing crystal. The healing from its particular shade of green has specific characteristics. The frequencies of Peridot or Adventurine, for example, bring healing without complexity, and in the classical way. They accelerate physical form, into which light enters more easily to perform the healing. In comparison, Serpentine is also a healer in the classical sense of accelerating and opening form to light, but it begins its healing by winding its way through the physical body until it encounters vibrations with greater density—blockages.

Serpentine's work proceeds without a uniform sense of purpose. It meanders through all parts of the body. When it runs up against blocked physical form in need of healing, it goes to work on the periphery of the blockage. Serpentine's own frequencies initiate the healing. Serpentine causes the edges of the dense form to vibrate ever faster, as its healing light gradually works its way towards the core. The form's density dissipates and eventually opens, allowing light to enter.

Serpentine continues its healing contribution in another way. Its crystalline matrix acquires the light frequencies originally intended for assimilation into the blocked mass upon which it is

---

1 Serpentine is the name of a group of some 20+ crystals. The group may be referred to as the Kaolinite-Serpentine Group. The stone used for this channel is best understood as a Lizardite, although stones in this group are not clearly delineated within the group.

performing its healing. Frequencies for assimilation that normally enter the body directly cannot overcome the blockage. They enter Serpentine first, before they enter the person's body. From Serpentine's matrix, the newly acquired light frequencies are passed into the newly opened vibration of the physical body, where they act to do further healing. The restoration of light within the dense and blocked masses of the physical body creates balance and returns the body to its healed state, in harmony with the overall state of the afflicted person's vibration.

The physical form's blockage generates polarity that is negatively charged. Polarity is what attracts the light frequencies of Serpentine into position to do its healing at the periphery of the dense mass. After a gradual acceleration and loosening of the dense form on its periphery, some light from Serpentine finds its way past the blockage, thus initiating the healing process. During the next step, the more highly charged positive light frequencies within Serpentine's crystalline matrix enter the blockage to balance the negativity. The light frequencies of the stone and the light intended for assimilation into the physical body eventually neutralize the negative polar state within the blockage. The strength of the negative charge dissipates in proportion to the density remaining within the blocked form.

Serpentine accumulates a positive charge until the blockage is cleared. Actually, the negative polarity of the dense mass is forced to balance the vibration of Serpentine, which increasingly accumulates its positive charge until the blockage is cleared. Serpentine discharges its positive energies into the blockage. Following the discharge, higher light frequencies, available from within the person's etheric magnetic field, provide the recharge. The discharge and recharge of the stone occurs simultaneously. The negative charge of the blockage yields to the relentless pulse of positive Serpentine frequencies. The speed of the healing depends upon the capacity of the stone to transfer light. As the balancing takes place, the blockage is removed by the acceleration of the physical form.

Serpentine's major distinction from other healing stones is that the healing vibration moves at a leisurely pace throughout the physical body. It moves from one polarized charge to another, thereby flowing by attraction. Because only the negativity of a blockage creates an attraction of any significance, the speed of moving through a healthy body is relatively slow. In a physical body that has no blockages, there is no negative charge to set up an attraction, and Serpentine does not move anywhere. In contrast, a body with significant blockages is highly charged and brings Serpentine to its task without delay.

Upon encountering a blockage, the stone's vibration becomes absorbed by the dense, unhealed mass. It stays fixed, unable to move away from the blockage. Healing then proceeds. The speed of healing is faster in the early stages of the encounter than it is when the healing is near completion. Negative and positive charges cancel each other out, as the blocked mass comes into balance. As the strength of the negative charge decreases, the attraction of Serpentine's positively charged light frequencies also decreases. Nonetheless, the two polar charges eventually come into complete balance, density dissipates, the body's vibration rises, light enters, assimilates, and empowers, and the healing resolves the original density.

Smithsonite

Wilful Heart Chakra Healing

Scientific Properties:
>Crystallography: Trigonal
>Chemical formula: $ZnCO_3$
>Mohs hardness: 4-4.5
>Density: 4.42 - 4.44 g/cm^3
>Colour: translucent, white, grey, yellow, green to apple-green, blue, pink, purple, and brown

Smithsonite comes from deep within the loving heart of One. It brings love into bloom. It offers soothing and healing light frequencies to the intrinsic will to change the course of one's life path. Smithsonite works to alter the ravages of Earthly life that reek havoc with love.

Individuals are often exposed to impure negative energies that corrupt their vibrations. In the normal course of living on Earth, a myriad of traumas suppress peoples' vibrations and subject them to low, dense, and negative light frequencies, and the horrors of darkness. Wars, famine, injustice, and being abused in adolescence, for example, are a few such traumas[1]. Because the will to survive these ravages is empowered with the quality of great determination, the affected person coils tightly into a defensive posture. The will plays a part in the person's defense.

The patterns of the body's etheric magnetic field concentrate to act as a protective shield. For as long as the individual must en-

---

1   Smithsonite was offered to me to channel by a friend, who, in adolescence, had been berated, beaten, and emotionally abused by an alcoholic parent. My friend's prominent memory was that his parent continually referred to him as the "thing". After obtaining the channel, it was not difficult to understand why this individual had acquired a piece of Smithsonite.

dure offensive vibrations, the concentrated etherics serve well the need for protection. Tightly bound etheric patterns generate a significant barrier to the unwanted light frequencies. Unfortunately, while harmful frequencies are repelled, so too, are beneficial frequencies. Without light of any kind bypassing the etheric shield, the spiritual progress of the person slows down or stops.

All things on Earth begin and end. So too, do the effects of traumas. When the individual emerges from the darkness of her ordeal, she needs to resume her place in the light of her spiritual path. The protected heart blocks light, both desirable and undesirable. In order to permit the entry of desirable light frequencies for spiritual growth, the etheric body must be reconfigured and reopened. The etheric patterns begin to change when the will of the mind applies its influence. Smithsonite's frequencies resonate with the consciousness within the heart. They draw the will that is resident within the mind's consciousness into the consciousness of the heart chakra. The subsequent involvement of the will works to create polar balance within the heart's molecular essence. The will, thereby, initiates the opening of the concentrated etherics to greater light.

Smithsonite vibrates with the heart chakra in much the same way as Aquamarine does with the throat chakra. It allows the subtle and exquisitely higher light frequencies of the heart chakra to pass through the etherics. The presence of light in the heart chakra triggers the subtle mind consciousness to create space for more light. The involvement of the mind consciousness is usually above the level of the person's awareness. The mind consciousness initiates a change in the heart's etheric magnetic field patterns, thereby reducing its concentration and eventually dissipating its protective posture. By dropping the defensive shield, the etherics open to the range of frequencies that are consistent with the person's current vibration, and intended for assimilation. With the availability of light for spiritual growth, the heart chakra resumes its progress on the evolutionary path.

Smoky Quartz

Environmental Compatibility
Kundalini Opening

Scientific Properties: (Variety of Quartz)

What charm and grace is Smoky Quartz?

Smoky Quartz' dark shades bring to the mind's eye visions of the darker planes. It intrudes upon the shadows of the darkness by casting the grace of its light into the lower heavens. There is no other stone quite like it. It may be the most complex crystal in the crystal world, even though it works with the simplest, slowest, and lowest light frequency—black light. It also works with extremely complex light—soul light. From the simplest light to the most complex light, Smoky Quartz works directly with the heavens and Earth. It is the initiates' stone. It opens the base chakra to begin the spiritual path.

The Love Cocoon of the Base Chakra

Understanding the role Smoky Quartz plays in the spiritual awakening begins with problems encountered when the angelic light workers discovered that their Light Bodies could not descend into Earthly bodies. The human physical body was just too dense to receive the Light Body. Numerous attempts to bring the Light Body into the human body met with failure. With each attempt, the insertion of the Light Body into the physical body caused the vibration of the physical body to shift upward radically, even if only temporarily. Because the shift in vibration upward was well above Earth's vibration, either the Light Body bounced out of the physical body and back into the higher dimensions, or the merged

Light Body and physical body took on higher vibrations and then, together, shifted back into the higher dimensions. The thought of bringing the soul or Light Body into the physical body in one grand infusion was quickly abandoned.

The angelic caretakers of the Earth tried several different experiments[1] in an attempt to bring the Light Body into the physical body. Nothing worked until they turned to the soul, which is a smaller part of the Light Body. Even then, the soul energies used were scaled back drastically. A small, but manageable, amount of the soul's light was seeded into the base chakra. When all was ready, the soul's 'seed-light' was deposited into the base chakra and surrounded by a 'love cocoon'. The love cocoon's role was to protect the seed-light from premature release, and to ensure that the seed-light's release followed a sufficient application of love. Love was the key to opening the base chakra (kundalini opening) and releasing the seed-light, and thereby initiating the devotee's spiritual awakening.

The angelic caretakers of the Earth pondered the problem of initiating the spiritual awakening as soon as the light of the soul was encapsulated in the love cocoon in the base chakra. The seed-light was firmly established in the base chakra, but how was it going to get out? What would bring enough love to get through the protective layers of the love cocoon?

Several means are available to bring love to bear to release the seed-light from the base chakra. Smoky Quartz is confirmed as one

---

1 The discussion of the experiments to bring the Light Body and soul into the physical body, the decision to use the base chakra, the characteristics of the love cocoon, and the spiritual awakening, are rather large and complicated topics, which have been presented herein with extreme brevity. These topics are discussed at length in *The Story of Light, Path to Enlightenment*, Chapter 3, entitled: "Starting from Scratch". The discussion is sprinkled in several other places in other chapters of this same book. Of particular interest are the definitions advanced as to what exactly is the soul, Light Body, and higher-self. See Chapter 5, entitled: "Enlightenment".

of the means. It is the crystal of initiation, and the only crystal of initiation.

Creating Smoky Quartz

By now the role of Smoky Quartz suggests a strong involvement with the base chakra, the Light Body and soul, the Earth, the divine light of the Godhead, and love. Smoky Quartz is involved in spiritual awakening. The question arises as to how it can be intimate with so many varied vibrations. How is Smoky Quartz created so that it can work with the extremely high vibrations of the Godhead at the same time as it works with the slowest and lowest light on Earth—black light?

Smoky Quartz begins as a deposit of clear quartz. Clear quartz is not Smoky Quartz, of course, but gives the stone all of the properties and characteristics that go with clear quartz. Of particular note, the stone can make available the white light of clear quartz, implying that all light frequencies are available. Smoky Quartz always has a 'smoky' appearance, which can range anywhere from extremely black to slightly darkened. Its smokiness is the result of divine radiation. At times, the Godhead emits black light frequencies intended specifically for Earth. These black frequencies carry the vibrations of divinity, and, at the same instance, are the indigenous frequencies of Earth. Smoky Quartz' divine radiation with Earth's light brings it into direct resonance with both the heavens and Earth.

The very black specimens of genuine Smoky Quartz and the slightly dark specimens of genuine Smoky Quartz are both radiated by divinity, but at significantly different times in the Earth's history. The slightly dark specimens are indicative of the effect of radiation applied in recent times. In the recent past, the highly stable vibration of the Earth's third dimension, along with a much more sophisticated etheric magnetic field, do not allow powerful bursts of divine cosmic energy to bombard the Earth. During our current millennium, divine radiation comes in a gentle, non-disruptive flow. The result is mild, hence the slightly darkened appearance of the more recently radiated clear quartz deposits.

In contrast, the near-black specimens of genuine Smoky Quartz were radiated at the very beginning of Earth's existence as a planet. In the earliest times, the Earth's vibration was quite unstable and its etheric magnetic field vacillated wildly. With only a minimal effort, the discarnate angelic caretakers of the Earth could wilfully time the opening of the planet's etheric magnetic field to coincide with the pulses of the divine black light frequencies sent to Earth from the Godhead. At these times, the Earth itself consciously and cooperatively manifested etheric field patterns that created a funneling of light directly onto a particular deposit of clear quartz. In this way, both the Godhead and the Earth played a responsible part. Further, some deposits of clear quartz were radiated multiple times. These strong rushes of black light produced some very dark specimens.

Protection by Light Resonance

A feature of the radiation of Smoky Quartz is that it draws the black light frequencies out of the light flow to which it is exposed. The Godhead's divine core light is also collected by this same darkened crystalline formation. Smoky Quartz carries the white light of all frequencies, together with the black light, which is indigenous to the Earth and is sent from the Godhead. Within the stone, the Earth's light unites with the Godhead's divine light. Divine light frequencies piggyback onto the black light, which resonates in harmony with the lowest vibrations of the base chakra. The merging of the light of heaven and Earth provides the opportunity for the slow and low black light frequencies to carry the high and subtle frequencies of divinity into the base chakra.

Because Smoky Quartz is radiated with Godhead frequencies, it attracts light within a range of frequencies not normally available.

It anchors the Earth's black light, which resonates strictly with the Earth itself, and with the base chakra. No other light frequencies harmonize with both the Earth and the base chakra directly, and at the same time. Therefore, no other frequencies have access to the base chakra's love cocoon, or the soul's seed-light. The design of the base chakra uses the resonance of its light frequencies to protect the soul's seed-light. The only vibrations that can penetrate the love cocoon are love and the light of Smoky Quartz.

Base Chakra/ Kundalini Opening

When light enters the base chakra, the opening and release of the soul's seed-light initiates the spiritual awakening.

Smoky Quartz carries both the white and black light frequencies, and so does the base chakra. In the base chakra, white light is the essence of the seed-light of the soul, and black light is the grounding frequency of the Earth imbibed within the chakra's physical form. Because they have the same frequencies in common, Smoky Quartz and the base chakra share a profound harmony.

Love is the key to the opening of the base chakra. In every other instance, the opening comes through love, not through frequencies of light. Except for the light frequencies of Smoky Quartz, light that is readily available on the Earth vibrates at its own frequency rate, which is much different from the frequency rate of the base chakra. Smoky Quartz is the exception because it alone carries the exact frequencies needed to work with the base chakra to initiate a person's spiritual awakening. As the base chakra and Smoky Quartz share identical frequencies, there is no resistance to their exchange of light. Smoky Quartz is the crystal of spiritual initiation.

Smoky Quartz requires more time to open the base chakra than does the grace of the true Guru, who can open the base chakra in an instant. Further, Smoky Quartz does not break through the layers of the protective love cocoon in the same single burst of energy, as does the love from the Guru. Rather, light frequencies from Smoky Quartz merge with the base chakra and its protective love cocoon. The crystal creates an osmotic flow of light to and from the seed-light therein. There is no dramatic penetration of the chakra, and therefore, no definitive opening. Upon using Smoky Quartz, light seeps gently into the base chakra. The result is an interface between the base chakra and its external environment. Light moves through the interface into the chakra causing it to open.

In each lifetime given to the pursuit of the spiritual path, opening the base chakra (awakening the kundalini) from its dormant state is required before the arrival of the light frequencies for the chakra's empowerment. Once opened, the soul's seed-light begins its journey along the chakra distribution pathways en route to opening each of the other chakras. Smoky Quartz is the crystal that opens the base chakra, but it does not open the other chakras. Smoky Quartz' affect on the other chakras is incidental and dependant upon the white light it carries. Some of the frequencies inherent to Smoky Quartz resonate with various body or chakra parts and bring empowerment. However, other crystals are more likely to have greater effect, as their specializations focus on the empowerment of particular body parts.

As each of the seven chakras reaches full empowerment, the physical body's vibration rises to the level needed to attract the Light Body.

The Problem of Artificial Radiation

Even though Smoky Quartz is the only stone of initiation, it can be copied artificially by radiating clear quartz. The artificially radiated stone may have noticeable dark bands or veins, but can also be very difficult to distinguish from natural Smoky Quartz. A Smoky Quartz that is very dark and comes from the commercial marketplace is likely to be an artificial specimen.

Unfortunately, the artificially radiated stone inflicts damage rather than gracing the start of the spiritual path. This is because the frequencies of the fake Smoky Quartz are not from the Godhead, but they do resonate with the base chakra. The artificial Smoky Quartz has no love. The base chakra opens and the seed-light disembarks, but with no love, the awakening takes place long before the person's vibration is ready. When the very high and subtle vibrations of the seed-light infiltrate the dense and slow vibrations of the unprepared person's physical form, disaster follows. The fake piece causes etheric distortions and chakra damage that may take multiple lifetimes to correct.

Upon discovering an artificially radiated Smoky Quartz, the only option is to place it in the trash. To give it away to someone is to create unwanted karma.

Human Racial Groupings and Smoky Quartz

Smoky Quartz generates an interest beyond its service as the initiate's stone. The crystal's primary purpose continues to be that of mixing the light of heaven and Earth, which then penetrates the barrier of the love cocoon that surrounds the base chakra. The following twist to its service comes from the story told by a most exquisite piece of Smoky Quartz from the author's own collection.

First, during the development of this particular piece of Smoky Quartz, a number of akashic records were set within its crystalline matrix, even before being radiated by the divine light. Once the stone had been radiated, its records came into alignment with the divine plan. Consequently, each of its records unfolds in accordance with the schedule set down in the divine plan by the Godhead. While the effect of radiation is offered in reference to the author's crystal, the alignment to the divine plan is characteristic of all Smoky Quartz. Being on a schedule gives greater perspective to the order in which knowledge arrives on Earth.

In a further twist, from the previous discussion on Smoky Quartz, its formation results from the radiation of a deposit of clear quartz, and at such times as the Earth's etheric magnetic field opens to allow divine light to enter. The specimen from the author's collection follows the normal procedure, but was not radiated in only a single burst. Rather, this piece received the light of divinity not once, but in four separate waves. During four different moments in Earth's history, the divine projection of the Godhead's black light frequencies penetrated or bypassed the Earth's etherics to enter the deposit of clear quartz to which this crystal was attached. Each time, the specific range of in-coming black light frequencies carried a different set of energies from the Godhead.

The four variations in the energies of each of the waves of radiation correspond to the four primary human races—red, white, yellow, and black. During one opening in the etherics, the Godhead's black light frequencies intended for the red race of humanity (the native American Indian) descended upon the author's Smoky Quartz. During another opening, the frequencies for the yellow race (oriental peoples) came. All four races were implanted in their turn. The infusion of light that resonates with the base chakra of one race is at variance with each of the other races. Having a Smoky Quartz that can resonate with the vibration of each of the four human races is a divine blessing that ensures that the crystal will work effectively for anyone who comes for base chakra opening and empowerment.

The radiation of the author's Smoky Quartz at four different times gives it the capacity to mix the light of the four different vibrations of humanity. The frequency range of such a piece is extraordinary. It is capable of bringing light to persons of each of the four major racial groups on the planet, as well as, persons of any combination of the four races. What follows is that the creation of each of the Earth's four racial groupings occurred at different times. The same arrival of divine light that defined each race also radiated Smoky Quartz. Therefore, there are four sets of frequencies that each resonate with the base chakras of one of the races and with Smoky Quartz.

While the stone in the author's crystal collection resonates with all races and racial mixes, other pieces of Smoky Quartz may only resonate with a single race, due to the slight discrepancy in the frequencies with which it is radiated. For example, the piece that was only radiated by the divine light intended for the white race will still open the base chakra of persons in each of the other races. However, the strength of the opening will be greater for the white race than for any other. The spiritual awakening of a person of a different race, then, needs greater exposure to the 'white-race' Smoky Quartz than she would if the stone carried the specific frequencies of her own race.

With the help of Smoky Quartz, when light enters the base chakra, the opening and release of the soul's seed-light and the spiritual awakening begin.

Sodalite

The More Light Stone

Scientific Properties: (Member of the Sodalite Group)
Crystallography: Isometric
Chemical formula: $Na_8(Al_6Si_6O_{24})Cl_2$
Mohs hardness: 5.5-6
Density: 2.73 g/cm^3
Colour: transparent, translucent, colourless, white, light yellow, green, light to very dark blue, gray, pink to violet

Sodalite's dark blue hues[1] illuminate the ebb and flow of life. Vibrational energy surges into the aura. A person moves into the light and evolves.

The planetary timekeeper heralds change with each new age. The moment of divine grace, which is currently enveloping the Earth, comes with significant changes in the historical patterns of light. At this time, the predominant change is the availability of significantly more and higher light frequencies. The new light frequencies mean that the recipient's bodily vibration must make an adjustment before assimilation is possible. During the close of this millennium, the inhabitants of Earth will go through numerous major changes. Earth's beings are being exposed to light vibrations, which are characteristically foreign to the flow of Earthly light. The enhanced vibratory pulse of the Earth has brought forth a great deal of higher dimensional light. The new light necessitates adjustment. To help with the adjustment, the evolving person is given the vibration of Sodalite.

The frequencies within the chakras of the seven chakra system play a significant role. Each chakra has a number of frequencies

---

1   The channelled information about Sodalite for this section refers to the dark blue variety.

that are relevant to how the chakra functions on the third dimension. Light both empowers the chakra's activation and its ability to function. Once there is an adequate amount of the empowering light frequencies available within the aura, each of the body's chakras becomes fully functional. When the chakras and body are empowered sufficiently and have the high vibration necessary, the person can invoke her Light Body.

In the past, the empowerment of each chakra usually occurred over a significant number of lifetimes. The light frequencies necessary for Light Body invocation were assimilated, but only in minute quantities. The invocation of the Light Body, therefore, was a lengthy process, and success was cause for joyous celebration. There was no need for help in making an adjustment to a sudden influx of light frequencies. The physical essence of each chakra was more than capable of dealing with the trickle of empowering light. In the new age, however, the light available to Earth's inhabitants is far greater in quantity and of much higher quality than ever before. There is now a need for a major adjustment in the ability of the body's essence to accept and assimilate the newly available light frequencies.

How does Sodalite facilitate the adjustment of a spiritual person to the rapid influx of the new and different light frequencies?

Light that enters the aura is always filtered by the body's etheric magnetic field, including light of an exquisite nature that is high enough not to be inhibited by the etheric field. The etherics are a checkpoint or guard station for the passage of light. Whenever significant quantities of light enter into the Earth's physical dimension, the evolving spiritual person needs to take advantage of the extra light available. Sodalite works to step-down the vibration of the new in-coming light frequencies to bring them into harmony and alignment with the recipient's etheric field. Once aligned, a much greater quantity of higher divine light becomes eligible for assimilation into the body and chakras.

The range of frequencies available on Earth is determined by the blueprint of the planet's etheric magnetic field patterns. In the current age, the filtering action of the etherics has shifted to work with higher ranges of light than ever before. A much cleaner and purer form of the divine original source light is now available on Earth. Its arrival heralds the coming changes and the ascension. In contrast, the new light vibrates at a faster rate than is acceptable within the person's physical body. The body's etheric magnetic field is programmed to work with the traditional ranges of light frequencies and blocks the entry of the newly available higher light frequencies. It filters the new light out. However, the range of light frequencies, which is currently acceptable to the human body and chakras, does not always lead to significant evolutionary spiritual progress or the ascension. The change in light quality brings the need to change the vibration of the physical body. The body needs to work with the new light.

Sodalite offers the subtle energies of consciousness that alter a person's will to accept the higher, divine frequencies now available. The alteration of the will is not necessarily directed to the person's conscious mind on the third dimension. Awareness is not a prerequisite. Rather, the individual chakras and the bodily essence are imbibed with the will of higher dimensional consciousness. They are programmed to accept the higher light frequencies, independent of the mind.

Sodalite brings frequencies of consciousness to the body. These same frequencies of consciousness also resonate with the soul. They create a connecting pathway between the soul and the body. Through the pathway, the soul is aware of the physical body's vibration. The soul is attuned at all times to the light available to its incarnate extension (person). It is quite aware of the presence of the higher frequencies surrounding the physical body, and in what quantity they are present. When the soul senses the presence of a significant amount of higher dimensional light, it is most willing to accept the light when it knows that the body is willing and able to receive it.

Because the soul is willing to place its incarnate extension onto the accelerated spiritual path, as promised by the arrival of the new and greater light, the need arises to communicate the soul's will to the physical body. Through the consciousness, the will is expressed from the soul to the body. The role of Sodalite, then, is to usher in a vibration of consciousness to the molecular essence of the physical body. This vibration of consciousness carries the alignment with the will of the soul. The result is that the will of the physical essence is aligned with the will of the soul for the purpose of accepting the available higher light frequencies[2]. Once the body has been exposed to Sodalite, the consciousness at the soul-level aligns with the consciousness within the body's molecular essence. In this unique alignment, the body surrenders its will to accept light, and thereby, bypasses the inhibiting filters present in the etherics.

There is no danger with accepting the light frequencies that surround the aura. Any light that can bypass the etherics and is accepted into the physical body has already been scrutinized by the soul. The soul wills the acceptance of only those frequencies of light, which it deems to be desirable. Because the will of the soul is in alignment with the will of the bodily essence, only frequencies that are appropriate are assimilated. Any other vibration, not graced by the will of the soul, is not part of the soul-body-conscious-will alignment and is, therefore, unacceptable.

Once aligned, the body takes on the available higher light frequencies in accordance with the will of the soul. The extra light then goes to work to accelerate the person's spiritual path. Each chakra undergoes exposure to the new range of acceptable frequencies. As the new age offers a most exquisite array of high and divine light, the salient result is the acceleration of the spiritual growth of the person using Sodalite.

---

2   The act of using Sodalite gives the soul tacit permission to reset the will of the person on Earth within the planet's free-will zone. The integrity of choice is maintained.

The use of Sodalite is best when placed on the chakra of consciousness, which is the third eye. The distribution throughout the physical body of the frequencies, acquired through the alignment of the will of the body and the will of the soul, is the work of the third eye.

Other crystals also have beneficial effects when used in combination with Sodalite. For example, the light of a clear quartz crystal enhances Sodalite's effects. Clear quartz makes greater amounts of the divine light available. As another example, Selenite enhances the soul-body-conscious-will alignment. Selenite strengthens the connection of the soul's will to the third eye, thereby strengthening the alignment of consciousness.

The spiritual adherent need not work with Sodalite on a daily basis. The optimum frequency of its use is the same as the need to balance the etheric body—roughly 2-3 weeks. What is important is that Sodalite establishes the alignment of the will of the soul and will of the physical body to the extent that the body's etherics adjust to accommodate the light flowing between the two. The etherics tend to slip from their desired balanced posture because of normal exposure to life's third dimensional activities. The need to use Sodalite arises as the soul-body alignment weakens due to the stressors placed on the mind. If a person were to meditate on the higher self every day, the need to refresh the use of Sodalite might arise after 5-6 weeks instead. If a person is subjected to socializing with persons of lower vibration, alcoholics for example, a weekly, or even daily, exposure to Sodalite becomes necessary. While these are arbitrary guidelines, a person's vibration is affected up or down by the directions of the mind.

When the will of the incarnate self is fully aligned with the will of the soul and higher-self, more light flows. The soul always wants to send more light. Sodalite sets the alignment. It is 'the more light stone'.

Spirit Quartz

Language of Light Translator

Scientific Properties: (variety of Quartz)

Spirit Quartz is one of the most profound meditation crystals available. It outperforms Amethyst and Fluorite because it works with the mind directly. Both intuition and intellect are bridged within the stone.

Spirit Quartz is constructed with three primary and important physical features. First, its core is a six-sided clear quartz terminated crystal. Second, its shaft sides, but not usually its termination, are encrusted with a matrix of tiny quartz points. Third, it carries a soft purple colour, which is apparent throughout the crystal's surface.

Spirit Quartz offers its soft purple hue as a means to connect with the soul. The softness of its purple colour is intended to create a softness in the connection. Rather than automatically making a strong connection to the soul, the soft purple hue ensures a connection, which does not apply to everyone. Those who are on the spiritual path, but only dabbling in spirituality, will not have a vibration high enough to align with the soul. The soft purple hues on Spirit Quartz' surface helps a little with the alignment to the soul, but not a lot. The soul will not, and cannot, connect unless the person using the Spirit Quartz has achieved sufficient progress on her spiritual path.

Having the soul involved emphatically ensures that the stone only works with loving individuals, who not only have the required high vibration, but are also committed to their spiritual paths. Kundalini open, heart open—this is mandatory. Further, the throat and third eye chakras must be open and functioning. Other chakras merely require their vibrations to be consistent with the body as a whole. The mind, not the body, is the focus for Spirit Quartz. Spirit Quartz, when hand-held, works to make its alignment with the soul. Once the soul connection is established, light from the enlightened universe transits through Spirit Quartz to enter into the conscious body[1]. There is no need to use this light immediately, but it is available immediately. Spirit Quartz is of greatest value when used during meditation. When the mind enters the serenity of meditation and creates a contemplation, it calls upon the conscious body for light. The soul responds to the directives of the mind by sending the light needed to illuminate the mind's focus. The soul's light is specific to the focus and comes from anywhere in the far reaches of the enlightened universe. The flow of light from the soul, to Spirit Quartz, and then to the conscious body, indirectly finds its way to the mind's contemplation. Some frequencies carry the refined qualities of the soul into the contemplation. Some frequencies are little refined, but still contribute to the contemplation. Because the light frequencies for the contemplation come from the conscious body, they resonate perfectly with the vibration of the person and her mind from the start.

In addition to the soul's light frequencies, Spirit Quartz works with a breadth of other light frequencies. A six-sided clear quartz crystal[2] normally projects six primary light frequencies into its environment. The six-sided clear quartz point at the core of Spirit Quartz has six such primary frequencies. As well, its encrustations of tiny quartz crystals also brings an abundance of the full range of all white light frequencies. Spirit Quartz provides the soul's light,

---

1   The consciousness, mind, intellect, and intuition need to be distinguished from the conscious body. Because there is some complexity to how the consciousness incorporates each of the parts mentioned, please see the discussion on the consciousness in *The Story of Light, Through Heaven's Gate*, Chapter 14, entitled: "Consciousness".

2   For the discussion to clarify the workings of the six-sided clear quartz crystal, please see the discussion in the subsection in this volume entitled: "Clear Quartz Terminated Crystals" under the section entitled: "Quartz".

the six primary frequencies, and the full range of white light to empower the mind's contemplation.

The quartz encrustations have a further role to play. The incoming light frequencies from the soul first come into the intuition of the mind. Once the intuition has been empowered, Spirit Quartz uses its encrusted matrix of quartz crystal to provide strong amplification of the light being used in the contemplation. These amplified frequencies then move beyond their usual subtleness to become strong beacons for illuminating the person's vision of her contemplation. This 'lighting up' gifts the mind with conscious reach into frequencies that are normally too subtle for the mind to work with.

Spirit Quartz' encrustations have an even more important role. They solve an immediate problem facing the mind. Light arriving from the higher dimensions is not always adjusted to the third dimension into which it has come. As well, the mind has a limited range of frequencies, which it can process readily. Unadjusted, higher dimensional light is beyond the mind's ability to convert into the concepts, ideas, and symbols that give understanding within a third dimensional context. That is, the implications of sixth dimensional light frequencies do not conform to the frames of reference of the third dimension. Spirit Quartz' encrustations serve an interpretive function. They translate the language of light. They take the soul's high and subtle light frequencies and convert them into the concepts, ideas, and symbols that a person's third dimensional mind can grasp. Further, the translation is unmistakable because of the amplification of the light frequencies by Spirit Quartz. Amplification ensures that the mind receives strong and well processed raw materials with which to work. Instead of having to do the preliminary work of strengthening, processing, and translating the light frequencies that make up the contemplation, the mind merely assembles them. With Spirit Quartz, the mind functions at a significantly deeper level of awareness than without it.

The particular Spirit Quartz crystal that was used to obtain the wisdom and information for this channel possessed a further feature of interest. The crystalline base, upon which the Spirit Quartz grew has a tinge of pale blue. It is a mild variation of the Angelite vibration. Because the vibration is Angelite[3], it works to open and recondition light receptors. The receptors involved include receptors within the third eye, crown, and throat—the upper chakras. Reconditioned chakra light receptors open first to the higher light frequencies that are immediately available from the person's etheric magnetic field. Second, reconditioning sets up the receptors to reach into the higher dimensions to attract heavenly light frequencies directly. Meditation, contemplation, and the mind's awareness each benefit in untold ways from the access an Angelite vibration gives to the light of the higher dimensions.

Spirit Quartz is a divine gift. It brightens the mind's contemplation with inter-dimensional realizations that can be applied on Earth. Spirit Quartz is the crystal for increasing consciousness and for advancing humanity's inventory of enlightened wisdom.

---

3   Please see Angelite in this volume.

Stilbite

Scientific Properties: (official name Stilbite-Ca)

Crystallography: Monoclinic
Chemical formula: $NaCa_4[Al_9Si_{27}O_{72}]\text{-}nH_2O$
Mohs hardness: 3.5-4
Density: 2.19(1) g/cm^3
Colour: (all variations) white, colourless, red, light yellow, light to dark brown, cream, orange, pink

Peach Stilbite

The Healer of Broken Hearts

The human heart is fragile and can be easily broken by the rigours of difficult interpersonal relationships. Sadness within the heart, and the pain of the emotions that go with it, can often render a person depressed and unable to thrive within his social sphere. With a broken heart, a person's love may be withheld from others until his heart is once again healed.

Whenever the broken human heart suffers the horrific pain of emotional imbalance, the soul rejoices knowing the benefit. The person's will to alleviate the pain attracts the lessons that the soul needs in order to continue its conscious evolutionary experience on Earth. Pain, however, is not necessary, and is not the soul's intended means of learning. Pain results from the imbalance that arises from the soul's will to set the course of its incarnation's life in the face of the unaligned and resistant emotional body of the Earthly heart. Until the soul and its incarnation come into alignment and balance, pain in the human heart is likely. Pain intensely motivates the Earthly spirit to seek relief through alignment with its soul. When the heart chakra aligns with the heart of the soul, the pain subsides. Peach Stilbite is most assuredly a stone of heartfelt loving grace, bestowed upon the emotional body to help bring about a balanced alignment with the soul.

The loving, soft, delicate, and genteel Peach Stilbite offers the grace of its harmony, complete with love from its watery origins. Through the rays of its pink and peach coloured frequencies, the emotions of the heart receive soothing frequencies of light. Peach Stilbite's purpose is to bring forth a most refined, cooling, pacifying ray of love to heal the heart. In the event that the pain of the heart reaches into the soul, Peach Stilbite works to overcome the ache.

The means, by which Peach Stilbite brings the light forth, arises from the spirit of the sea—the watery Neptunian confines of the liquidity of emotion. The sea brings a soothing vibration, which is offered gently through the Peach Stilbite. The characteristics of Peach Stilbite's love vibration are similar to Rose Quartz. However, its frequencies are significantly more refined and delicate, and the light moving through the stone originates from a very high vibrational source. The crystalline matrix of Stilbite is also similar to that of Selenite. Both Stilbite and Selenite work with very high vibrations.

Naturally-formed Peach Stilbite often has a fan shape. This indicates the movement of significant amounts of divine light into the stone's physical form in a short frequency pattern. The 'liquid' emotions in their highest frequencies, still on the enlightened side of the physical plane, flow across the third dimensional threshold into physical density in an abrupt manner. Abrupt in this sense is in reference to the flow of celestial vibrations and not to the rate of densification as perceived on the Earth plane. Once Peach Stilbite's vibration enters the Earth plane, it almost pours into its fan-like shape. It appears to freeze upon entry past the threshold of the third dimension. Peach Stilbite is usually cloudy, and looks like frozen orange juice. The tens or hundreds of years that go into the creation of Stilbite are exceptionally fast. It crystallizes onto the Earth very quickly relative to the speed of its flow in the celestial realms.

The emotional energy of the soul and the emotional body of the soul's incarnation come together to share a specific vibration rate. The vibration of the union corresponds to the vibration of the light frequencies of Peach Stilbite. The stone's vibration originates within the emotional energies of the soul's heart. Peach Stilbite brings the light of the soul to heal the broken heart.

Peach Stilbite helps the emotions in the human heart to unite with the high, subtle, and refined emotional energies in the soul's own heart. The presence of the soul's emotional light frequencies, and their union with the person's emotional light frequencies, bring about the alignment of the soul's emotional energy and the person's emotional body. Once the alignment is in place, the exchange of light between the soul's heart and the person's heart perfects the vibratory resonance and generates an even greater alignment. Peach Stilbite's offering of grace is the alignment of the physical and heavenly emotional energies. The healing given to the emotional body[1] of the person's heart chakra is created by the balance that results from the light frequencies that come with the alignment. When the human heart is aligned enough to reflect the vibration of the soul's heart, all is well. The broken heart mends, and the pain subsides.

In addition to the healing that takes place within the emotional body of the human heart, Peach Stilbite also works to enhance the conscious awareness. From the light of the soul, the frequencies of knowledge and wisdom that correspond to the divine will enter the mind's intellect. Because the strength of the divine will is supreme, the alignment of the emotions is most desirable. Without alignment, the mind suffers illusions, which lead to pain and suffering. The individual is most vulnerable to the illusions of false perceptions that are fuelled by the emotions and driven by the

---

1 The emotions and emotional body are different concepts. The discussion of the emotional body is better understood if the reader is familiar with the design, structure, purpose, and operation of the emotional body. Please see Chapter 15 entitled: "The Emotional Body", in *The Story of Light, Through Heaven's Gate*.

mind. Stilbite's vibration soothes and aligns the emotions. As a secondary feature, Stilbite gives the intellect the grace of conscious awareness. As the healing light emerges from the heart into the chakra distribution system and finds its way to the denser levels of the mind, the intellect receives light to illuminate the knowledge of divinity's will. When the mind consciously knows the directions of the soul's will, its Earthly will can contribute to the healing of the broken heart.

Peach Stilbite's speedy manifestation into the physical plane is slow in another way. It is slow because it works to gently sooth the emotions. In the very long process of celestial time, the balance of the emotions occurs towards the end of the soul's evolutionary journey. The emotions are a vibration of exquisite refinement, but usually begin as base and coarse—mundane anger, for example, as distinguished from graced anger[2], or belligerence. The emotions evolve progressively upward and eventually embrace the emotion of love. When the energy of the emotions is focused through divine grace, it provides the driving force that catapults love to the forefront of an individual's raison d'etre.

The need to involve the emotional part of the soul in the progress of emotional evolution comes with appropriate timing. If the soul possesses a warrior essence, for example, the lessons of emotional balance only come at the very end of the soul's Earthly contract. The reason is that a warrior needs to back up his threats to his enemies with the energy of unbridled emotions, without interference from the mind and intellect. An emotionally charged threat is perceived by the enemy as a credible danger. Consequently, an emotionally empowered warrior is far more potent than one who is emotionally static. In contrast, artistic expression often manifests entirely through consciously working with the emotions. The incarnation of an artistic soul needs to be in touch with his emotions early in his soul's lifespan on Earth.

---

2   The differences and implications of mundane and divine anger are discussed in this volume in the section on Red Garnet.

In this great celestial moment, when bondage to the Earthly contract is waning, and as ascension from the Earth plane approaches, the alignment and balance of the emotional body of the heart is taking place within scores of individuals. The will of the soul is to complete the lessons that balance the emotions, and in turn consciously bring about a most refined sense of love. Alternatively, to leave the emotions in a state of imbalance continues the pain suffered by the heart.

The emotional energies of the soul's heart are given passage to come to Earth through Peach Stilbite. In response, the emotional body of the physical heart accelerates to align with the soul's emotional energies. By placing Peach Stilbite on the heart chakra, the alignment and the re-balancing that occurs initiates healing. Peach Stilbite is the healer of broken hearts.

White Stilbite

Aligning the Highest Emotions

Scientific Properties: (see Stilbite, Peach)

Emotions!
Emotions of the heart, mind, and body!
White Stilbite carries the full scope of the human body's emotional energies. None are left out. White is the all-encompassing colour vibration. It includes all colours and all light frequencies. As every part of the human body possesses an emotional body component, and as the emotional body encompasses all light frequencies, White Stilbite can work with all aspects of the emotions. Further, the white variety of Stilbite is in close touch with the crown chakra implying that the very highest of energies are possible through this lovely and beautiful stone. White Stilbite works with all light, and especially with the highest frequencies of

the body and mind.

So what does White Stilbite do?

As the peach variety of Stilbite helps align the emotional body of the heart in the heavens and on Earth, the white variety works to align the emotional body of the crown chakra. The crown chakra that is open and aligned with the higher-self allows a greater flow of the highest light frequencies to shift into a person's physical body. The alignment of the crown's emotional body with the higher dimensional self means that the attraction for light that is set up in the crown is amplified significantly. Stilbite does not enhance or strengthen the emotional body, but it does ensure that the alignment is in place.

With the emotional body of the crown chakra in alignment with the heavens, the natural attraction of the body and mind for light brings desirable frequencies without impediments or blockages. If the person using Stilbite expresses the will to achieve a goal of some kind, and then contemplates that goal sufficiently to show the universe that the goal is serious, the universe will open and send its light energies to help fulfill the goal. The use of Stilbite ensures that the light of the goal has an alignment to follow. Consequently, light does not have to contend with blockages or repulsion from the person's etheric magnetic field.

Because Stilbite elevates the physical vibration of the person using it, the person's vibration accepts and comes into harmony with the high and subtle light frequencies of divinity from the heavens quite quickly. The physical body accepts light frequencies directly from Stilbite. Because the emotional body is also involved in the process, the flow of light does not stop when the body's need for light is satisfied. The emotional body continues to push light past the etheric field and into the physical form. Frequencies that cannot be used or processed immediately saturate the body's form. The abundance of light dominates the physical body, but still comes from White Stilbite. The emotional body forces light into the body, and Stilbite makes sure that it goes to the right place.

Beyond the point of saturation, some light leaks out of the body, but because so much light is continuously coming into the body, the body is always topped-up.

White Stilbite is especially useful in bringing high, specialized, and subtle light frequencies into the body. It is also useful for accelerating the physical form to a higher vibration without going through the slower process of waiting for the right light frequencies to arrive. As White Stilbite works to bring the person and her crown chakra into alignment, the mind, the emotional body, and the source of divine light in the heavens, collectively fall into alignment quickly. Thereafter, significant amounts of high and subtle light flow from the heavens.

Cavansite on Stilbite

Pathways to the Higher-Self

Scientific Properties of Cavansite:
Crystallography: Orthorhombic
Chemical formula: $Ca(VO)Si_4O_{10} \cdot 4H_2O$
Mohs hardness: 3-4
Density: 2.21-2.31 g/cm^3
Colour: transparent, greenish-blue to blue

In the mineral world of science and geology, Starry Stilbite is known as Cavansite on Stilbite. Cavansite Stilbite consists of a White Stilbite base, upon which roundish bursts of blue Cavansite, often in ball shapes, form. From the Heavenly Hosts, who offered the information for this channel, this exquisite angelic crystalline presence is given the grace of its truth with the name of Starry Stilbite.

The explanation for Starry Stilbite begins with a hierarchy of vibrations. The base chakra has the lowest vibration. Each higher chakra carries successively higher vibrations. The crown chakra carries the highest vibration of all the physical body's chakras. Within each chakra, vibrations also fall on a scale from low to high. The highest vibration within each of the chakras is its emotional body. The chakra's emotional body also carries vibrations to which the scale of low to high is applicable. Love is a high emotional vibration; anger is a low emotional vibration.

Further, within the mineral hierarchy of vibrations, Stilbite corresponds to the highest and subtlest of the light frequencies within the highest ranges of frequencies of the emotional body. While the peach-pink-orange coloured Stilbite corresponds to the heart chakra's emotional body, the uncoloured or white variety corresponds to the emotional body of the crown chakra, and in particular, to the highest light frequencies therein. White Stilbite, which forms the base for Cavansite, has a place among the purest of the white light frequencies.

Using the hierarchical scales just mentioned, White Stilbite works with the highest frequencies of the emotional body of the crown chakra. Therefore, it works with the highest frequencies within the human body. The presence of the emotions within the crown are, at times, less recognizable than the emotions of the other chakras. The effects of the emotions in other parts of the body are localized, specific, and may produce dramatic emotional outcomes. The emotional energies of the crown chakra are distributed throughout the entire physical body. Consequently, the exquisite light frequencies from White Stilbite are pervasive, but not concentrated. White Stilbite provides its delicate and subtle influences in a most divine manner—as love. Acquisition of a quality piece of White Stilbite, along with the vibration it gives off, permits the user to radiate the very refined and subtle frequencies of love's own sweet and loving vibrations. Exquisite are the user's emissions of love's emotion.

The bright blue to dark blue Cavansite aspect found in Starry Stilbite also has a unique and important role. Cavansite often grows into the shape of star bursts or ball formations that take up residence on the White Stilbite base. Each blue starry formation is precisely symmetrical with clearly shaped projections radiating out from the centre in all directions.

The bright, deep-blue star on Starry Stilbite has no natural resonance with the original system of seven chakras or with the new age system of eleven chakras[3]. As such, Starry Stilbite's blue vibration cannot be explained with reference to the throat chakra, as being the sky-blue light of truth, nor can it be explained with reference to the deep, cobalt-blue light of the third eye chakra, as being the light of consciousness. Rather, Starry Stilbite's blue star is the lighted angelic beacon for the way home. It is the gift from the universe to the enlightened beings of Earth of a lighted pathway to use to journey to the highest places within one's higher-self or Light Body, or to the realms of the Angelic Hosts. The blue colour of the star is the vibratory frequency that resonates with persons, who are attracted to it, and who are ready to connect with their higher-selves. The person on Earth can use the pathway to send her vibration into the realms of the beyond.

The angelic pathway, created by Starry Stilbite's deep blue stars, reaches up from the physical body of the crystal's user on Earth all the way to the highest level of the higher-self in the highest dimensions of the beyond-the-beyond. The connection of the person on Earth to her highest levels of self could only follow from the person's highest Earthly vibration. White Stilbite allows the highest aspects of the person's emotional essence to pervade the aura through the crown's distribution of light. The blue star, embedded in White Stilbite, shares this same high emotional vibration of the crown chakra. Stilbite's star is the lighted pathway to the stars—the enchanted road to the Godhead. The person's highest frequency of love moves through the highest aspect of her emotions

---

3   The new age has given rise to the recognition of four chakras, which are additional to the physical body's original seven chakras. Please see "The Eleven Chakra System" in this volume.

in the highest part of her physical body (the crown chakra), then journeys consciously (with or without awareness) into the starry realms along the blue star's angelic pathway.

The gift of the light of the heavens is available to the user of Starry Stilbite, who can then offer her highest, joyous, emotionally-charged, love vibration in return. The very high vibrations of love from the person on Earth and from the heavens flow in both directions along the pathway created by Starry Stilbite. Using it only in moments of serenity to enhance the light frequencies within the body is sufficient to justify its place in a person's life.

There is another way to use Starry Stilbite. Starry Stilbite provides a pathway to the highest places in the lighted universe and to the highest aspect of one's higher self. It does so for whoever is in near proximity. Using it in a crystal layout, the connection between the practitioner and the client needs to be certain. By using Starry Stilbite, placed near the forehead on either side of the supine client, both persons' vibrations reach into the upper dimensions. Both vibrations coalesce at the level of the higher-self, thus ensuring the integrity and security of the connection between them. Starry Stilbite can be counted upon to provide the pathway to establish the connection.

The Councilate of the Ascended-Light, who is the channel source for the enlightened understanding of the Starry Stilbite and this book, offers an invitation for the users of Starry Stilbite:

> *"Come experience the love that we might offer to you—your love and ours—the highest Earthly love and the love of angelic being merged into the One that we all can experience together. Your place with these vibrations is a path of the highest exquisite nature. Our love awaits to be as One with yours."*

Sugilite

Imposed Serenity for Soul Healing

Scientific Properties:
>Crystallography: Hexagonal
>Chemical formula: $KNa_2(Fe,Mn,Al)_2Li_3Si_{12}O_{30}$
>Mohs hardness: 6-6.5
>Density: 2.74 g/cm^3
>Colour: purple, light brownish-yellow

Sugilite has come to serve the new age. For the person owning Sugilite, its possession is an affirmation of the blessings of the spiritual path.

The mind's connection with the higher self is, at times, unaligned, blocked, or clouded. Sugilite overcomes these problems by offering the mind a fast and definitive experience of healing. It does so by moving the mind into a place of absorbed serenity. Sugilite imposes serenity. It injects an overwhelming amount of its purple ray into the mind, thus completely surrounding and enveloping the mind. It displaces and, thereby, removes any light frequencies within the mind's consciousness with its own frequencies. Once the mind is captivated by Sugilite's influence, its contribution to its user comes under the control of the will of the soul.

Sugilite's healing involves the temporary realignment of the dominant influences within the mind itself. First, the mind is enveloped by Sugilite's imposed serenity. This effectively eliminates the mind's conscious control of its thought patterns. Once the mind is cleared of light frequencies that could interfere, the soul can begin its work of healing. The soul's own energies are directed into the mind. The soul 'reads' the vibration of the person using Sugilite, then assesses not merely her consciousness and mind, but the needs of the physical body as a whole. From its assessment, it determines which light frequencies can best serve the purpose of healing. The soul then reaches into the heavens, acquires the necessary light frequencies, and sends them to the body. As is always the way of healing, light does the work of restoring the physical form to its healthy state.

Sugilite is best placed on the third eye chakra where the work of healing can begin with the mind—mind over matter. However, if the bodily organs and parts respond harmoniously to the vibration of Sugilite's range of purple light frequencies, it can be placed directly on those parts to do its healing. Importantly, the flow patterns of Sugilite's magnetic energy need continuity. If the soul is to participate in the healing process, continuity of the flow of light and of the person's vibration is mandatory. If the above conditions are fulfilled, Sugilite's light frequencies work to offset the problematic flow of energies related to a diseased organ or body part. By dominating the mind or body part upon which it is placed, Sugilite imposes its serenity, which makes room for the soul's choice of healing light. The energies that created the problem or disease are then displaced by the soul's healing light, and the diseased part is brought into balance.

Sugilite is a special vibration of healing that needs to be honoured by its owner. Sugilite is the royal crystal. By offering it a place of reverence in a crystal collection, its strength is reinforced. Sugilite then works for the user out of the joy of its purple love and intensifies the healing it brings.

Sugilite's domination of the conscious mind to allow the soul to bring the light needed to do the work of healing is its trademark feature.

Sunstone

'See-Me' Sunbeams

Scientific Properties: (Member of the Feldspar Group)

Throughout Earth's long history, the seed-light of the soul that was planted into the base chakra has been only a tiny speck in the sea of light[1]. Light was not plentiful in the beginning. The ability of the Earth's inhabitants to attract light from beyond the planet, either from the physical plane or from the higher dimensions, was quite limited. Lack of light did not give rise to being noticed by the angelic beings who were caretaking the Earth. However, primarily through meditation practices, a few of Earth's more adept spiritual devotees succeeded in illuminating their inner seed-light well enough to be noticed. Sunstone helps with the illumination.

Because the tiny speck of an individual's seed-light most often went unnoticed, the need arose to brighten the seed-light, along with the person's overall vibration. Raised vibration had the affect of attracting other light vibrations. The Heavenly Hosts, as well as, illuminated individuals in near proximity were drawn to the person with a higher vibration. When the Heavenly Hosts were drawn, the light they brought to bear made a person's Oneness even brighter. When another individual was drawn, sharing light became possible, but was still limited to the quality of the vibration of the individuals involved. In either case, more light became available and spiritual growth quickened.

---

1   For some religions the seed-light (or kundalini energies) is compared to the sesame seed or to a grain of sand. The analogy is that the seed or sand is a tiny speck in the grand scheme. For example, "the seed-light of the soul within the base chakra is like a single grain of sand on the beach of infinity". The discussion about the seed-light of the soul, its design, and the role of the base chakra can be found in *The Story of Light, Path to Enlightenment*, Chapter 3, sections 3.3 through 3.5.

Sunstone attracts light from its surroundings, which include frequencies that have found their way into the user's etheric magnetic field (aura), and from the user's immediate geographical location. It also picks up light generated from within the user's own Oneness. However, the primary source of Sunstone's inventory of light frequencies is the sun, hence the name. From each source, Sunstone collects light frequencies from the range of the divine golden ray.

The presence of tiny flecks of Hematite, found within the crevasses of Sunstone, have a significant role. First, they facilitate the grounding of light. Hematite's shiny black surface is also reflective, and therefore, gives off light from the mixture it attracts. The light first attracted by the Hematite, and then given off, becomes available to the individual using the stone, to her chakras, and to persons in near proximity. The user benefits from Sunstone's golden ray by wearing the stone, because her vibration brightens. The chakras benefit from the empowerment they receive. Other persons in the vicinity benefit, as they are attracted to the empowered person's light and vibration, of which they acquire a portion. The vibration of the seed-light of the soul within the base chakra benefits from the greater presence of light within the individual. Light reflected outward from Sunstone by its Hematite inclusions carries frequencies from the user's aura, and therefore, carries the characteristic personal vibration rate inherent to the user. Each benefit contributes to the overall brightness of the individual's personal beacon of light to which the Heavenly Hosts are attracted.

Once the Heavenly Hosts are involved, the quality and amount of light that the individual receives improves significantly.

Tiger's Eye

Navigating Spirituality in the Dark

Scientific Properties: (Variety of Quartz)
Crystallography: Trigonal
Mixture of Quartz, Limonite, and Riebeckite
Mohs hardness: 7
Colour: yellow-brown

Tiger's Eye is an ancient seer's stone. It is the gaze of the staring cat, and while it has similarities to the Hawk's Eye, there are also significant differences.

Its construction consists of the same cavernous patterns as Hawk's Eye with an iridescence throughout. Light receptors also line the stone's cavernous walls. Similarly, each receptor works with a specific frequency, amplifies its energy, and passes it on to higher groupings of frequencies[1].

Tiger's Eye is a golden mass within which there are black bands. The banding consists of several shades of dark mass, which create layers of contrast. Contrast is necessary for Tiger's Eye's version of seeing. The light receptors within the black aspects of Tiger's Eye ground light and hold it. Within the black ranges of frequencies, the higher and lower vibrations of black light frequencies are sorted out and amplified, thus making them easier for the mind's intuition to discern or read. The golden hues do not offer a grounding effect, and do not work with the black range of frequencies. Rather, they work with the golden range of frequencies and encourage the flow of light through the stone. The black light shows the dark and low vibrations that exist on the spiritual path, while the golden rays show the higher and creative vibrations.

1   Please see the section on Hawk's Eye in this volume for the foundation discussion on the construct of the matrix and hierarchy of light receptors related to this type of iridescent stone.

The golden light is processed by the individual light receptors in the mass of the stone in the same way as both the light flowing in the Hawk's Eye and the light entering the receptors of Tiger's Eye's black bands. Golden light frequencies enter the receptors of the gold-coloured bands where they are amplified and begin the aggregation process. Tiger's Eye's light is presented to the third eye chakra with differentiations between the unified aggregate of all frequencies, the groups of frequencies, the sub-groups, and the individual frequencies. Amplification and grounding make seeing the contrast between the various shades possible.

The hawk soars high in the air offering the vision of distant and broad landscapes in great detail. The tiger, however, stalks the midnight path through the jungle. Tiger's vision is limited to the darkness immediately ahead. The Tiger's Eye stone, then, illuminates the darkness that haunts the spiritual path.

There is no need to see much past the next tree in the forest or the jungle. The overgrowth makes the path quite dark and immediate, especially at night. On the darkened pathway, then, Tiger's Eye picks up the presence of whatever light is available. The many shadows that fall upon the spiritual path and that impede a person's vision do not result in absolute darkness. Even the darkness has some light that a seeker may use.

The contrasts from shadow to shadow, in the jungle or on the spiritual path, are not likely to be discernible to normal vision. Consistent with the tiger's nocturnal nature, Tiger's Eye works with the most subtle of light differentials for frequencies that are very low in vibration. The contrasts between frequencies, that are apparent when individual frequencies are amplified within Tiger's Eye, light the way to navigate the spiritual path through the darkness.

Tiger's Eye provides a landscape of contrasts by picking up the subtle nuances of light frequencies generated by the mind's contemplation. The frequencies of the contemplation are amplified by the stone's individual light receptors. The desires and directions of the will, as expressed by the contemplative mind, then return from the stone to the contemplation as energetically enhanced light frequencies. The directions, to which the will would lead a person, are revealed with greater clarity.

Tiger's Eye's light receptors accept light frequencies, which resonate with the golden frequency band. The golden band is the highest range of light frequencies picked up by the stone's colour pattern. It is also the highest light vibration available from among the darkened shadows of the path at night. The stone's light receptors select, ground, amplify, and reflect light, thus making it discernible to the conscious mind. In conjunction, the golden ray brings a higher vibration level of frequencies, which are needed to provide contrast to ensure that the lowest levels of available light are still readable.

Because Tiger's Eye brings the golden ray, the focus of the stone's power is the Earth's abundance. The golden ray empowers the creative force of the navel chakra. It offers the gift of a greater and more creative vision of the way life on Earth ought to be.

With the higher golden frequencies and the amplification of frequencies within the stone, the picture of the darkened scene becomes available to the mind. Particular aspects of the scene can be accessed in a more defined manner. The darkened areas are brought into closer view, thus allowing the discernments needed to read the shadows. Aspects of the path that are lighted stand out in sharp contrast against the darkness. As the picture ahead unfolds, a person can see to walk his spiritual path.

By providing the contrasts from among the shadows, the stone brings the spiritual path into focus. It exposes the darkness and the light, and hence the openings, curves, and dips that exist on the path. The person is given the information needed to choose the best direction to take en route to enlightenment. The stone also improves the seeker's vision by which to see the openings, curves, and dips, which lead him past his Earthly blockages.

While the dark aspects of the path are transient, they surround and confine the initiate until the way clear is chosen. The stone offers the much enhanced night-vision needed to prevent a person from stumbling through the otherwise blinding darkness. Given the necessary vision, the person using Tiger's Eye traverses the dangers along the way and, in due course, emerges into the light of day.

Topaz

Aligning with the Creativity of the Higher-Self

Scientific Properties:
>   Crystallography: Orthorhombic
>   Chemical formula: $Al_2(SiO_4)(F,OH)_2$
>   Mohs hardness: 8
>   Density: 3.4 - 3.6 g/cm^3
>   Colour: transparent, translucent, colourless, white, pale blue, light green, yellow, yellowish brown, or red

Topaz has been on the Earth since the most ancient of times. It has come through a number of metamorphic changes, as have most vibrations on Earth. During Earth's earliest times, Topaz worked with the human body's chakras, such as they were[1]. The design of the human form along with the design of its chakras has changed, and so has the way they offer and receive light. The original chakra designs were of course inferior and met with their end.

Once the human body was capable of accepting light, however little that might have been so long ago, Topaz made its contribution. Along with the changes that took place in the way light was organized in the chakras, so too did Topaz change. In today's world, Topaz' orange colour resonates with the upper frequencies of the second chakra, and at times, with the lower frequencies of the third chakra.

The divine Creator gave Topaz the grace to open the creative juices, the rasa, or life-force of human existence since the very beginning. One might well imagine that there was a great need dur-

---

1   The human body has had seven major chakras for many millennia, but this was not always the case. In the beginning, there were no chakras. For the full discussion about the evolution of the chakras, see *The Story of Light, Path to Enlightenment*, Chapter 3.

ing the early millennia to bring creative energies into the human form. By the acquisition of the power to create, the quasi light-entity of early Earth adapted to, or adapted, his immediate surroundings. The power to create, however, did not make life more comfortable in any significant way. Even though comfort was essential to basic survival, the presence of the creative power had another purpose. It permitted the higher-self and soul to manipulate light to a greater degree.

The limitations of the human body's ability to assimilate light were soon realized, and the need for improvements became apparent. The body was overhauled and redesigned. The role of Topaz, at that early stage, was to serve as a vibratory home for greater quantities and higher qualities of light. With more light, the soul's energies gained access to the way light was manipulated on the physical plane. During these early stages, the angelic ones did not yet know how light adapted to a third dimensional vibration. Adapting light to Earth is the essence of our mission on Earth, but the knowledge of how to do so lay ahead.

When Topaz first brought the power to create into the existing chakras of early man, seven chakras did not exist. At first, there was only a single chakra. Soon after, there were three chakras—the base, the heart, and the crown chakras. Topaz resonated with the crown chakra and, to a lesser extent, with the other two chakras. At this early point in history, the differences between the chakras was inconsequential. As such, any stone that could resonate with one chakra, resonated with all three chakras. The crown was somewhat more advanced, because the initial work to bring any available light into the body was done in the crown.

The distant past has now come to the present.

In the last few millennia, Topaz continued its work to bring forth the creative energies of the higher-self. To some extent, Topaz still brings forth light in the current new age, and still retains some ability to work with more than a single chakra. However, its ability to crossover between chakras is limited to the second and third chakras only. The second chakra resonates with light frequencies in the darker orange range of colours, as does the usually darker orange Topaz. These are the frequencies, which carry the body's sexual energies. The higher vibration of the navel chakra, which is the chakra of creative power, is a lighter shade of orange, but primarily golden-yellow. Topaz is also capable of empowering the lower ranges of the navel chakra to some degree.

When a person uses Topaz, his higher-self can participate to ensure the proper alignment between the chakras and the heavens, whenever the creative power is used. The higher-self directs the expression of the chakras by bringing the higher frequencies from the soul, which correspond to the frequencies indigenous to the chakras. Topaz gains a reputation for its contribution to the sexual and creative energies of the second and third chakras, but these are not the only vibrations enhanced by Topaz.

Once the soul and the physical plane align with each other, the increase in the amount of the soul's creative light energy coming to Earth is significant. Thereafter, the light frequencies acquired by Topaz work to further empower the chakras' energies and powers of creativity. With more creative energy, the chakras provide an even more welcoming environment into which more of the higher frequencies of the soul descend. Topaz helps create a place for the soul's creative forces to come.

Returning to the discussion of the second chakra, during the early millennia, the reproductive energies resided in the base chakra. The alignment created by Topaz between the base chakra and the soul was the primary means to bring the sexual creative forces into the human body. Consequently, the soul could more easily manipulate sexual reproduction by joining physical forms of specific quality. It had great control over the selection process of reproduction.

Today's base chakra is much changed. In the modern era, some of this type of soul-directed guidance is still possible by using Topaz. Again, Topaz of the darker orange variety resonates with the higher sexual energies of the pelvic or second chakra. It helps to open the second chakra to receive the creative frequencies of the soul. Once opened, the will of the soul is asserted with greater effect upon the sexual drive of the individual in question. While one might prefer to deny that species selection takes place in this way, the soul looks upon the process as a valuable tool for combining two persons with desirable qualities. The process of sexual selection, similar to how it worked in the earliest of times, is based primarily on the individual's ability to accept the soul's light into his body.

If the striated piece of Topaz also has a natural termination, it is most valuable to the way that Topaz offers its light.

Tourmaline

Gift of the Angels to Appreciate Love

Scientific Properties: (Tourmaline group)
Borosilicates of the Cyclosilicate Superclass.
Crystallography: Trigonal
Chemical formula:
$(Ca,K,Na)(Al,Fe,Li,Mg,Mn)_3(Al,Cr, Fe,V)_6$
$(Si,Al,B)_6(BO_3)_3(O,OH)_3(F,O,OH)$
Mohs hardness: 7
Density: 2.9 - 3.1 g/cm^3
Colour: translucent, transparent, green, pink, aqua, black

Tourmaline is an angelic gift from beyond the stars. It comes to Earth from the Angels. Tourmaline brings love to the physical plane, and makes it visible to persons who are most unacquainted with love. Under Tourmaline's influence, love in all its splendor is recreated into a vibration that lends itself to the understanding and knowingness of those whose ability to work with love is most limited. The accelerated vibration of the person who uses Tourmaline is unmistakable for the expression of love's own quiet, soft, and delicate manner.

The coming of this new age of Earth's accelerating vibration heralds the acquisition of a new approach to the inter-relationships between human beings. Existence within the heavy, ponderous, physically-bound, third dimensional, gravity-laden density on Earth has incarcerated the joyous expression of love. Love's path to the heart has been arduous. The weight of density is being lifted by the coming new higher vibrations that are now crossing Earth's path. To prepare for the beginning of this new and liberated expression of love, Tourmaline has emerged in unison with the Angelic Hosts.

So how does it work?

As the Angels implore, Tourmaline presents love to the physical plane with the splendor and vibrance of its own glorious gracious vibration of love from the heavens. With love, transformation takes place. Tourmaline gives love a radiant expression. When combined with the frequencies of the heart—Rose Quartz and Kunzite crystals, for example—Tourmaline shapes the love vibration most exquisitely. However, unlike Rose Quartz, which draws love into the heart, and Kunzite, which causes love to flow from the heart, Tourmaline gives expression to love in the external world.

Under the influence of Tourmaline, third dimensional dense light frequencies vibrate faster, and high and subtle angelic light frequencies vibrate slower. Their vibrations converge. Love is truly the middle way. Higher and lower vibrations come together, as the myriad of minor frequencies affected by Tourmaline merge. By increasing the vibration of the third dimensional person's essence of love, his divine qualities become more apparent to all persons with whom he comes in contact. Through the influence of Tourmaline, of whichever colour, the stone's user assumes the qualities of an angel, and is a delight to be with. The individual's love is not altered. Rather, the united vibration of the person and the angels increases the frequency rate of the love imbibed into the person with Tourmaline, as compared to the person without Tourmaline.

Colour Diversity

The shades and colours of Tourmaline have an affect on the corresponding chakras. Pink Tourmaline, for example, enhances the vibration of love within the heart chakra. Black Tourmaline enhances the love inherent to the base chakra. Green Tourmaline, as a healing stone, is not chakra-specific. It enhances all aspects of the healing process that the soul wishes to endear upon an individual. Led by the soul, the healing process defers to the increased availability of divine intervention and light to restore love within the afflicted parts of the human body and mind.

Love has many manifestations and numerous ways by which it might be expressed. Because love is so diverse, there needs to be some distinctions made between the ways that different coloured Tourmaline crystals help to express love. Each colour enhances a different side to love, and allows a person to express and receive love in different ways. While highly evolved spiritual beings easily work with love, lesser evolved individuals need help. In accordance with Tourmaline's mandate of divine service, the colours ensure that Tourmaline's vibration resonates with even the narrow-minded and inflexible individual. They, too, are worthy receptors of love and the grace of God.

Each chakra works with a specific colour of Tourmaline, love itself works through the different colours, and individuals also work with specific colours. Some persons resonate with the love of Tourmaline's black vibration, others resonate with the pink, and still others the green. Some persons are receptive to all of the colour bands. The divine will to move love into the denser regions of the planet necessitates the accommodation of persons who can receive only one set of light frequencies, hence the variety of colours to accommodate everyone.

Angelic love is resident within Tourmaline of any colour. Tourmaline offers this love in any place and throughout its colour spectrum. The quality of its expression of love carries the full range of the love of the angels. The stone's coloured frequency bands provide emphasis of a particular strength associated with love.

Individuals, who sense the angelic vibration in all its forms: the form of the universal, the form of Oneness, and the form of love itself, must be reasonably evolved spiritual beings who are already well established in the acquisition of light. Not all persons are reasonably evolved, however. Most individuals are evolved enough to work with only the most common light frequencies. Nonetheless, the will and intent of the angels is to offer their love to the full spectrum of Earth's inhabitants. The Angelic Hosts perceived that some additional strength, variation, and emphasis was needed to ensure that the light frequencies of love found their way into the mass of the Earth, to which the bulk of Earth's inhabitants tended to gravitate. Pink dominates the love vibration; black dominates the survival function; aqua dominates the consciousness; and green dominates the path towards greater healing.

Within its frequency range, each distinct Tourmaline colour accentuates the love vibrations that are available to the more enlightened individual, plus the added emphasis that is needed to penetrate the denser, less accessible vibrations, characteristic to the unenlightened individual.

Black Tourmaline

To Black Tourmaline, the Angelic Hosts offer their greatest respect. Its role places it within the darkest places on Earth. Because it resonates with the base chakra, it offers love at the lowest and densest levels, where the physical plane harbours significant negative energy. Love is challenged again and again. The person, for which Black Tourmaline was designed, travels among lower and non-evolved persons. In the face of such negative vibration, the qualities of Black Tourmaline offer the necessary fortifying qualities.

Black Tourmaline's energies manifest in two ways. On the one hand, it offers the love of the angels, inherent to all Tourmaline. On the other, dealings with the basic elements of unevolved persons, dense locations, and negative energies are accomplished through its ability to move basic (black) light frequencies into those venues. By taking care of the lower and denser energies, primarily through deflection, as well as, rerouting some energies into places where it can do no harm, the stone's user is then positioned to offer his raised love vibration in locations having little or no love.

Essentially, the stone creates a protective environment, from which love radiates forth.

The method behind Black Tourmaline's protective function needs further explanation. First, Black Tourmaline possesses a grounding capability. The negative energies and frequencies, found in the local environment, and to which Black Tourmaline is exposed, are drawn into its physical form. Then, the stone's striations, which run its length, carry this energy and light at very great speed through the stone and out again at its termination. The presence of a termination ensures that the flow is consistent, enters the stone from the base end of the piece, and has directional momentum as it exits at the point of the termination. Negativity is processed as it travels through Black Tourmaline.

Because Black Tourmaline is in service to the light, it has the inherent ability to 'see' where negativity exists, as well as, where negativity might manifest in a harmful way. For example, the negative energy generated by a heated argument between two people may lead to physical violence. The stone pulls the negative energy and light that is fueling the heated argument from the environment for processing within its crystalline structures. Given that the negativity is present in a reasonable quantity and is not overwhelming, and given that the stone is of reasonable size and quality, the negativity is rendered harmless.

How so? Wherever negative energy exists, it carries a vibratory frequency rate that is synchronized with its immediate surroundings. Negative energy is an inherent part of the harmony of its surroundings, thus giving it the power to do harm. For example, if unchecked, the violence caused by a heated argument could lead to bodily injury. Once negative energy is absorbed into Black Tourmaline, the first benefit is that of removal from the surrounding environment. The principle benefit is derived when the negativity moves through the stone.

While traveling through Black Tourmaline, the vibratory frequency rate of the negative energy and light is altered. It enters the stone in harmony with its environment at one frequency rate, and leaves the stone at a different frequency rate. The new and different frequency rate reenters the local environment, but quite out-of-synchrony with that environment. No synchrony means no harmonization and, therefore, no power to do harm. Black Tourmaline does not destroy negative energy, but renders it harmless by changing its vibratory frequency rate.

Negativity is attracted to love, as negativity is prone to be. When it is drawn by Black Tourmaline into the realm of love, it moves so fast that its potential to do harm is removed. Although the stone renders negativity out-of-sync and harmless, there is a caution. As mentioned, the effectiveness of Black Tourmaline is dependant upon its quality and size in the face of negative energy and light that is not so abundant as to be overwhelming. The caution is that every piece has a limit to the amount of negativity it can process.

Green Tourmaline

Green Tourmaline is a divine and precious gift of healing love. It is a classic healer: it works to accelerate, and thereby, raise vibration to open the physical body, thus allowing light to enter and do its healing. By raising the vibration of the physical body's individual molecules, light can penetrate further into existing blockages and density. Continued use of Green Tourmaline to accelerate the body's vibration enables more light to enter and to penetrate deeper and deeper, and thereby, continue its healing.

Green Tourmaline brings the Oneness energies of the person using the stone into balance. Acceleration of the movement of the body's molecules and atoms results in greater balance. Each faster moving molecule shifts more easily into its natural place in the body, according to the push and pull of its polar charge, thus precipitating balance. When individual molecules or groups of molecules vibrate at frequency rates that are in balance, ever greater quantities of light frequencies come into the body, and into deeper parts of the body. Balance serves the purpose of helping the person attract the light needed to create the wholeness necessary for a healthy physical presence. When each molecule of the body comes into balance, health is certain.

The best place to position Green Tourmaline on the physical body is over the localized area of the diseased or dense vibration. Placing the stone elsewhere is still quite effective, because the chakra distribution system (ida, pingala, and sushumna), along with the etheric magnetic field (aura), carry light from one location to another. The stone offers healing to all parts of the body, regardless of its placement.

Green Tourmaline, as does any other classic healing crystal, works within a specific range of frequencies. Within its own range, a crystal provides its optimal benefits. Green healing crystals that work directly to heal damage and blockages within the range of the physical body's vibration rate include Green Adventurine and Peridot, for example. Green Apatite works within the range of frequencies that directly heal the chakras. Bloodstone's range of vibration works within the lowest levels of the physical body's vibration to clear the most obstinate blockages found in the etheric magnetic field. In contrast, Green Tourmaline is a very high angelic vibration.

Unless the vibration of the person using the stone is quite low to start with, Green Tourmaline's focus of healing does not involve diseased body parts. As a high vibration, Green Tourmaline's 'healing' is better understood as working to raise the vibration of areas of the body that are not keeping up with the rising vibration of the rest of the body. The stone is most beneficial when the body's vibration is approaching enlightenment. When a person does the spiritual practices that eventually lead to enlightenment, to the ascension, and to receiving the Light Body, some areas of the physical body will lag in vibration. Areas that lag are only *relatively* lower in vibration. Although the lagging vibrations are truly quite high, they need to be as high as the rest of the body, otherwise they are likely to prevent the invocation of the Light Body. Green Tourmaline's range of healing frequencies is optimal for the high vibrations of the physical forms that are lagging and not quite high enough to receive the truly high and subtle frequencies of the Light Body. Green Tourmaline is a preparation stone for the invocation of the Light Body.

Green Tourmaline is best used with persons who are approaching the conclusion of their spiritual paths in anticipation of enlightenment, the ascension, and receiving the Light Body. Because love is the key to raising any vibration, Green Tourmaline's role of preparing the physical body for the invocation of the Light Body is best served by placing it at the heart chakra.

Pink Tourmaline

The pink variety of Tourmaline brings exquisite refinement to the love vibration. Because more of the most subtle of the angelic vibrations are connected to Pink Tourmaline than the other colours of Tourmaline, its light frequencies are an elevated form of the Tourmaline frequency itself. While there is a common, accelerated, raised vibration that reflects the angelic gift of love in any piece of Tourmaline, the pink variety brings a greater and higher range of this same angelic presence of love.

Within Pink Tourmaline's range of frequencies are the highest, most subtle frequencies offering the most exquisite tastes and sensitivities that love could provide. Pink Tourmaline brings love within range of the conscious acceptance of those individuals on Earth who resonate with the romantic, soothing, warmth of the gentle flow of love's joy, impassioned with all-encompassing grace. Pink Tourmaline's vibration is of the finest quality of love available on Earth.

The heightened vibration that comes through a person, who is wearing Pink Tourmaline, creates a love presence of exquisite quality. Any person in the immediate vicinity is touched by the love projected from the wearer's aura. If the wearer's personal attention is also offered to the other person, that other person experiences a sensation of love at even higher and subtler levels, whether or not he is consciously aware.

Pink Tourmaline acts as a generating station. It causes both the transmission and reception of the highest levels of love to both the person wearing the stone and any person or persons within the wearer's range of projection. The physical limit of such a projection is usually 20'. Any person within 20' of a person wearing Pink Tourmaline will be touched by love. Love will flow to and from both persons.

Because Pink Tourmaline's love vibration is among the highest levels of love possible on Earth, it can be received by the other person's soul. The soul receives the wearer's love vibration in the heavenly realms, exclusive of the conscious awareness of either the wearer or the receiver. The receiver's soul then reciprocates by returning its own vibration of love through the heart chakra of its incarnation. The reciprocated love offering is then received by the wearer of the Pink Tourmaline, and again, whether or not reception involves conscious awareness.

The response of the soul of the non-wearer is not necessarily as accepting, forthright, and straight forward as might be hoped. First, the lessons from the soul of the non-wearer are in play, and may cause reactions that are not consistent with the reception of love. Life-lessons may take priority over the exchange of love, especially if the experience of love might interfere with the lesson. Second, negative reactions, which are directed at the wearer by the non-wearer, are generally unlikely to happen, and, if they do happen, are very tempered. There is no need to tarry on the point about inappropriate responses. Wherever vibrations are bright, high, and so very loving, the truth attached to persons having dark and ill intention is too exposed for them to remain for any time within the wearer's range of projection. Persons possessed by darkness are more likely to promptly dismiss themselves and leave. The only exception might occur in the face of shadowy characters possessed of energy with excessive strength, and only if the wearer's aura displays a serious dis-ease vibration or some weakness that dark forces could leach onto. Essentially, Pink Tourmaline clears a person's space of other negative persons[1].

Pink Tourmaline is reserved for the most finely attuned souls, whose work and appreciation of all love offers to them the grace of this special love vibration. It is a stone, whose effect, is not consciously perceived by most persons who are exposed to it. Pink Tourmaline's frequencies resonate with relatively few. Anyone, coming into close proximity to the wearer of Pink Tourmaline, experiences an elevation of his vibration, as both souls mutually reciprocate the light of love, which affects all it touches.

Aqua Tourmaline

Aqua Tourmaline's influence is greatest on the third eye. It enhances the intuitive connection between the third eye and the realms of the higher-self. The subtle blue and aqua hues of Aqua Tourmaline bring the high and subtle light frequencies of consciousness into the human mind. Specifically, Aqua Tourmaline brings the light frequencies of divine vision. Coming from the Eye of One that pervades the heavens with consciousness, the light frequencies of divine consciousness pass into the intuitive side of the third eye. The person using Aqua Tourmaline then sees with the greater inner vision of the higher-self.

---

1 The comment needs to be made that Pink Tourmaline is not intended for the purpose of removing negative individuals from the wearer's space. Purchasing a piece with this intention precludes being loving. An unloving person is not likely to find an acceptable quality piece of Pink Tourmaline to purchase. His vibration will not harmonize with the venues, i.e., shops and booths that sell crystals, within which such a piece is available. Judgments of others cannot trump love.

Aqua Tourmaline helps the light of the higher planes to make a speedy crossover into the third dimension, and into the consciousness of the recipient's mind. As light arrives on Earth from the heavens, it experiences the trauma of crossing into the third dimension[2]. The shock of passing through the dimensional barriers and into the density of the third dimension causes damage to individual frequencies, and especially to the frequencies of consciousness. Most of a frequency's higher aspects are too high to enter the density of the physical plane and split off. A portion of the light frequency remains in the heavens, and a portion comes to Earth. The frequency is partial, not whole. Other aspects of individual frequencies come with distortions, warps, or portions missing.

Especially when the consciousness is involved, help is needed to bring light into the physical plane. Aqua Tourmaline elevates the general vibration of the third eye, which then resonates much better with the frequencies of consciousness coming from the higher-self. By creating a stronger, less resistant, connection to the higher-self, the crystal ensures that the intuitive aspect of the mind receives the in-coming light simultaneous to its arrival. The stone both prepares the mind and serves as a bridge between dimensions. The shock and trauma experienced by the in-coming light frequencies is significantly reduced. Light arrives intact in a gentle flow with no distortions.

The use of Aqua Tourmaline brings a clear flow of the high-quality, divine light of consciousness from the heavens directly into the consciousness of the person using it. What insights, visions, realizations, and awareness are in-store for the blessed owner of Aqua Tourmaline?

---

2   The principle that governs the flow of light from the heavens to the Earth is only briefly discussed here, and only enough is said to allow an understanding of Aqua Tourmaline. The foundation discussion regarding the difficulty in bringing light to Earth is found in *The Story of Light, Path to Enlightenment*, section 1.9, entitled: "Innovating Physical Duality".

* * * * *

The primary feature of Tourmaline is the angelic qualities that it imparts to its user. Among his contemporaries, those in the user's space will warm to him. They will feel a certain joy in his company, but are not likely to attribute their elevated feelings to anything tangible. Beyond the angelic influence, each specific colour of Tourmaline adds to the user's ability to be in the venue most enhanced by that colour. Black Tourmaline shunts negativity aside and opens dark places to light. Green Tourmaline brings the spiritual devotee into the raised vibration needed to achieve enlightenment and the invocation of the Light Body. Pink Tourmaline orchestrates the reciprocation of love, not just on the physical plane, but also between souls. Aqua Tourmaline helps the third eye and consciousness to bring its vibration into alignment with the consciousness light frequencies coming from the Eye of One in the heavens, and helps to ensure that the passage of those frequencies into the third dimension is easy and takes place with minimal damage.

Rainbow or Watermelon Tourmaline incorporates some or all of the stone's primary colour variations, and in varying quantities. The individual primary colours make their specific contributions, exclusive of the other colours present, but work together with them as well. The combinations of Tourmaline's colours moderate the emphasis offered by any one colour. While emphasis is not as strong in any one colour, the influence of the combination brings flexibility to the expression and exchange of energies with other persons. With flexibility, the user of Watermelon Tourmaline can touch a much wider range of individuals with his love.

Tourmaline is a gift of the angels.

Turquoise

Stone of Truth

Scientific Properties:
Crystallography: Triclinic
Chemical formula: $Cu(Al,Fe)_6(PO_4)_4(OH)_8 \text{-} 4H_2O$
Mohs hardness: 5-6
Density: 2.6 - 2.8 g/cm^3

Colour: transparent, translucent, opaque
bright blue, sky-blue, pale green, blue-green, turquoise-blue

Truth is[1]. It needs expression.

Turquoise is truth. Turquoise, the stone of spoken truth, was the initiate's stone among the great lamas of Tibet. It is also a well known icon of the First Nations of the American southwest. This crystal of deep and brilliant sky blue vibration brings steadfast, unswerving wisdom at the throat chakra.

Turquoise is an Earth stone that resonates within the framework of third dimensional concepts that are understood by the human mind. Once concepts are whole and complete, they constitute the principles of wisdom—the pearls of knowledge. Turquoise vibrates in the throat chakra as the pearl itself. Turquoise is a principle of wisdom, complete and whole, and most beautiful to know. What of this pearl, this principle of wisdom, brought to Earth in the framework of a concept and a crystal? The concept is truth. The truth behind the concept of truth is that Turquoise

---

1   Truth is! Truth is all that is, as opposed to that, which is not. Nothing exists outside of truth. Conversely, if something is not truth, it is not something. It is nothing, or more accurately, a negation of what is.

carries the light of the original divine source of light—the light of the Godhead.

Communication of divine wisdom on the Earth begins in the heavens at the original source of light, the Godhead. For divine light to enter the physical plane and manifest as a third dimensional vibration, it assumes the form of truth. Divine light converts to truth. The throat chakra translates divine light into truth in the form of concepts, ideas, and symbols, which can be interpreted by the intellect. The divine light, then, steps down into the words or expressions of communication that convey truth. Turquoise brings light to the throat chakra. Thereafter, the stone's user expresses himself through his alignment with the divine light of truth and the Earthly speech that follows.

Each full and complete, spoken truth may be subdivided into units. Each unit is composed of, first, the spoken word, which constitutes the story of the parable. Second, the truth of the story in its conceptual form. And third, the presence of the essence that constitutes the light frequencies of that truth. The light of the truth expressed, as it makes itself available to the human intellect, comes complete with a cast of additional supporting frequencies. Each additional frequency contributes its piece of the truth. All of the pieces make a whole and complete truth. If any of the pieces are missing, the vibration of truth is not aligned with the Godhead. While missing pieces do not necessarily constitute an untruth, a whole truth requires all of the pieces.

Turquoise is a throat chakra stone, which resonates specifically with the mid-range of the throat's frequencies. It is, therefore, intimate with the centre of the throat chakra's essence and purpose. Because the mid-range carries the strongest intensities of the throat chakra's vibration, the throat is significantly empowered by the divine light brought forward by Turquoise.

Turquoise brings the sanctity of truth from the heavens. This means that the flow of its divine light comes protected from the perils of negative vibration. Turquoise brings clean, untainted frequencies. So how are the divine Turquoise frequencies protected as they descend to Earth? Turquoise, as truth, has an alignment that originates from the highest levels of the Godhead. Its connection to the Godhead is maintained—for the full duration of its frequencies' journey from the Godhead, through the enlightened upper universe, through the lower dimensions, and to the Earth—without breaking. On arrival within the third dimension, Turquoise brings not only the core light frequency[2] of the Godhead, but also the core light frequencies *of truth* of the Godhead, along with the primary light frequencies[3] for the throat chakra's *empowerment*.

Turquoise works to make truth possible on Earth. It does not bring, and is not of itself, a variation of the truth. Truth can take many forms. Turquoise brings truth only as a gift directly from the Godhead, along with empowerment frequencies for the throat chakra. Turquoise is exclusive to the throat chakra. It cannot resonate with any other parts of the body, because its light includes only the Godhead's core frequencies and the frequencies of empowerment exclusive to the throat.

The Godhead core frequencies include the 'core' light frequency itself, as well as, the 'core light frequency *of truth*'. The Godhead's core light frequency, intended for the throat chakra, is limited to the throat chakra, but the Godhead core light frequency *of truth* is not limited to the throat chakra. The Godhead core light frequency *of truth* arrives in the throat first, and is then distributed to the body through the chakra distribution system. A Godhead core frequency is intended for only a single body part, and resonates only with that part. The core frequency that belongs to the left elbow stays with the left elbow. The core frequency that belongs to

---

2   The 'core light frequency' is a specific type of frequency that is discussed in *The Story of Light, Through Heaven's Gate* in Chapter 4, sections 4.1 and 4.2. Protection is afforded by the 'frequency channel pathways' and the 'pathfinder vibrations', also discussed therein.

3   Both 'preparatory' and 'primary empowerment' light frequencies are discussed in *The Story of Light, Through Heaven's Gate* in Chapter 12, sections 12.2.1 and 12.2.2.

the sternum stays with the sternum. However, the core frequency *of truth* is universal to all that is. Therefore, it resonates with every part of the physical body.

A word on core frequencies...

The core frequency that initiates the enlightenment of any unlit form is the one and only frequency that resonates with that form. The core frequency *of truth* is additional to the core frequency. It takes its place on the first ring of light and surrounds the core frequency. It is a core frequency, but of the core of truth. Whereas, the initial Godhead core light frequency brings the unlit physical form or body part into the light and initiates the growth of Oneness, the core light frequency *of truth* makes the form or body part whole and congruent with its original purpose.

The throat chakra works to distribute the core frequencies *of truth* as a means of their expression, or it works to distribute them to the body parts to which they belong. Similar to the Godhead core light frequency, the throat chakra's primary *empowerment* frequencies remain with the throat. Primary empowerment frequencies arrive with Turquoise's complement of light and do not resonate elsewhere.

When the core frequencies *of truth* assimilate into the body part for which they were intended, the body part comes into alignment with the Godhead with no particular agenda attached. This means that the alignment does not fix itself on the acquisition of light intended for the body part as a matter of course. Rather, the alignment opens the door to the larger universe—the Godhead in particular—and although light can flow, it takes its lead from the body part. For example, the ankle of the right foot aligns with the Godhead through Turquoise's distribution, via the throat chakra, of the ankle's core frequencies *of truth*. The alignment of itself does nothing more than establish a connection. The flow of light to the ankle begins with the etheric magnetic field emanating out from the ankle. The ankle's etheric field attracts light. Its attraction draws light to itself through the connection established by the alignment. Thereafter, the core frequency *of truth*, which finds its way into the ankle and establishes its presence, adds to the empowerment of the ankle to attract ever higher frequencies for further empowerment.

The role of the throat chakra in this process is simple. It is the first line of attraction for the core frequencies *of truth*. It filters out frequencies coming from the Godhead that are not purely the core frequencies *of truth*. It allows only the pure core frequencies *of truth* to pass, and only if connected to the Godhead. Other frequencies cannot resonate with the throat chakra and, therefore, are not part of the flow. The role of Turquoise is to facilitate the flow to the throat chakra of the core light frequencies of the Godhead, the core light frequencies *of truth* of the Godhead, and the primary empowerment frequencies for the throat chakra.

Ulexite

Purveyor of Heavenly Grace

Scientific Properties:
Crystallography: Triclinic
Chemical formula: $NaCa[B_5O_6(OH)_6]\text{-}5H_2O$
Mohs hardness: 2.5
Density: 1.955 g/cm^3
Colour: transparent, colourless, white

Ulexite Then

When first introduced to me by the Councilate of the Ascended-Light some two decades ago, Ulexite was not a crystal that could be used by human beings in any significant manner. Its vibration was too high and not adjusted to the physical plane. Further, humanity was not ready to receive it. Ulexite offered to the inventory of light on Earth the highest frequencies of loving white light that had yet to manifest into the third dimension. Since then, changes have taken place, and Ulexite has begun to fulfill its purpose on Earth.

Initially, I received a very fragile Ulexite specimen. Its structure consisted of delicate, long, and extremely fine, silvery striated filaments. The filaments were unprotected and could not endure even the gentlest of movements without damage and fragmentation. Its purpose in coming to the Earth then was to participate in the experiment to bring the extremely high and subtle ranges of frequencies it heralds onto the physical plane. The caretakers of the universe were attempting to introduce a light vibration that was previously unknown to the Earth, and that was unable to descend into physical form. Through Ulexite, the initial wave of these very high and subtle frequencies were being given a home of sorts in physical form.

Because Ulexite was so very high and difficult to bring into physical form, it needed the help of quartz. Ulexite's vibration manifested between two foundation layers of clear white quartz. The foundation pieces, of necessity, were of very good-to-excellent quality in their construction. The configuration of the foundation was patterned somewhat differently than regular quartz. It fanned out in a circular fashion, thus allowing the transiting Ulexite frequencies to enter at the centre point and radiate outward. Without the quartz serving as an intermediary bridge between the physical plane and the higher realms, Ulexite's manifestation was not possible.

When my specimen of Ulexite first reached into the third dimension, it gravitated to the high quality quartz foundation, where it temporarily took up residence and accumulated. The method, by which Ulexite's frequencies moved onto the physical plane, required that the foundation quartz incorporate a bridging function of its own. The quartz created not simply the alignment and means for the flow of the highest of light frequencies into Earth's density, but also created the physical environment into which the light enters the Earth plane. The local space into which Ulexite's light came had to be clean. It also had to be free of any negative presence, and well protected and insulated from any incursion of negative light vibration. The presence of tainted light frequencies severely diminished the possibility of bringing Ulexite's other-worldly vibration into the third dimension. Within the foundation quartz, Ulexite was pure light, but not yet manifest form.

Because Ulexite was among the highest of the light vibrations currently on Earth, numerous Angelic light-workers were involved in its densification process. The angels took the process to the next step by generating a magnetic charge within the piece of foundation quartz, which was located opposite to the piece to which Ulexite's light first came. The two pieces looked somewhat like a sandwich. The charge drew the light across the space between the two foundation pieces, and thereby, suspended the vibration of Ulexite within the third dimension. The polar action of the quartz foundation was comparable to making snowflakes[1] in terms of the delicacy of its polar attraction.

Ulexite's polarized light frequencies are drawn from the heavens into the quartz of one side of the foundation, then across the third dimensional threshold in their opposite polarity. They then enter the quartz of the other side of the foundation. Vibration switches polarity as it transits from the heavens to Earth. Once Ulexite's light frequencies start flowing between the two foundation pieces, they complete a circuit. The circuit begins in the heavens. It descends into the first side of the quartz foundation, then crosses to the second side of the quartz foundation, and then reverts back into higher vibration, which exits the physical plane and returns to the heavens. During the transit from the first quartz foundation to the second, Ulexite's vibration enters the density of the physical plane.

Light flowing in circuit does not immediately result in manifest physical forms of Ulexite. The flow instead creates the magnetic field for the attraction of more Ulexite frequencies. With more light and the resulting intensification of the flow, greater quantities of Ulexite's frequencies mingle with third dimensional vibration. A most significant amount of its light passes through the circuit before enough of it can actually enter the third dimension. An even more significant amount must pass before Ulexite actually precipitates into physical form.

By having great quantities of light passing through the circuit, other frequencies are displaced. This ensures that the environment is absolutely pure and untainted. The negativity-free foundation, upon which Ulexite relies, can then receive the light, as it is, in

---

1 Snowflakes are intimate with manipulating light frequencies through their inherent magnetic charges. The creation and purpose of snowflakes is discussed in *The Story of Light, Through Heaven's Gate*, in Chapter 8, section 8.5, entitled: "The Contribution of Atmospheric Gases".

its high state of vibration. With a purified space and the intense flooding of that space with Ulexite, some frequencies are slowed by the congestion and unable to flow out of circuit. The circuit cannot accommodate the flow of the light once saturation has been reached. The light then stops flowing. At a point when the circuit is super-saturated, precipitation onto the physical plane begins to occur. Ulexite's light frequencies enter physical density. Once conditions are truly perfect, densification takes place over a relatively short time period. The tiny threads of flowing light energy 'sweat' or condense into the filaments that give Ulexite form on Earth.

As previously mentioned, Ulexite was an experiment involving the highest light frequencies yet to descend onto the Earth. The foundation quartz itself is most pure and not of the usual Earthly variety. Its radiating fan-like configuration is indicative of its very quick arrival. Fast entry into Earth's density reduces the potential for the attachment of negative vibration. Further, the angelic ones planted the foundation quartz within geographical areas of purity. Further still, to create the appropriate structural configuration, the foundation quartz arrived as a series of individual quartz deposits in tandem. Adjacent and separate formations serve as light stations for the disembarkation of Ulexite's light frequencies, and for setting up opposing polar charges in preparation for the creation of the circuit.

Ulexite's light frequencies were unique. The light offered by most crystals anchored itself within the physical body as intended, but not so with Ulexite. There was no place for these high frequencies within human essence at the time I received my first specimen. The highest of Earth's enlightened beings may have been capable of directing some of these light frequencies into their own bodies, but more likely, the light passed through without sustaining a presence. For the person who handled Ulexite and received the grace of awareness and vision, the benefit was almost certainly coming from the clean, pure, and high-quality quartz of the foundation, and not from Ulexite's filaments.

The purpose behind the Ulexite experiment is that of communication with the higher realms of existence. The physical plane is intended to move in-concert, in all time and space, with the Oneness of the heavens. Whether or not the Earth remains on the third dimension after the ascension of its soul's presence, its physical potential will always be available to manifest its spirit in physical form. As part of the communication with the heavens, pathways to areas of the enlightened universe that are, as yet, untapped are being offered to the souls of persons, who have achieved the ascension, but have also chosen to remain on Earth. The mission to enlighten the Earth cannot be complete if its inhabitants cannot travel, at will, to all parts of the Oneness of the vast infinite universe.

Because of the state of Earth's evolution, when I received my first Ulexite specimen, there was no need to explain the relationship of the enlightened universe that opened through its grace. A basis of understanding of these highest realms of the heavens needed to be established prior to embarking upon journeys there. Consciousness on the third dimension had no basic framework of symbology, which could translate the language of the light from Ulexite and from the universe beyond, into recognizable third dimensional terms. The accumulation of Ulexite frequencies and the development of the wisdom of its nature was assured, and yet, lay ahead awaiting the passage of Earth time. The person, who owned Ulexite, might consciously journey to the uncharted areas of the beyond-the-beyond, but these places were also beyond the potential of the human being's conscious body. There was no means to assimilate the light involved, nor to bring back any part of the experience.

Two decades ago, the reader had to be content with knowing that, as the light of Ulexite accumulated, the process of acquiring the greatest wisdom yet known to Earth had begun.

Ulexite Now

Over the past twenty years, Ulexite has modified its vibration. Initially, Ulexite was barely able to find its way onto the Earth. The circuit it created allowed some sweating of its vibration into physical form, but most of its essence returned to the heavens after only a brief exposure to the physical plane. Brief as it was, exposure brought a modified vibration of Ulexite back to the heavens. The returning essence, no matter how little the exposure, contributed to the understanding of its place on the Earth, as well as, of the requirements needed to modify its vibration to be suitable to the Earth.

In addition to the changes taking place within Ulexite's crystalline essence, the human body, for those who have pursued the spiritual path, has also changed and evolved. The body is now working with a significantly higher, deeper, and broader range of light frequencies.

Ulexite's role has begun to take shape. Ulexite changes the frequencies of the crown chakra within a select set of light receptors. The purpose is to bring them into alignment with a particular portion of the higher-self of the person using it—exclusive of other persons. Each piece of Ulexite attunes to the user's frequency rate once held in-hand or in near proximity. In the same way as Selenite, Ulexite's vibration rate takes on the user's vibration rate. A single person can attune to Ulexite's vibration exclusive to others, if that is the intent. However, Ulexite is not entirely exclusive. It can take on the vibration of a group of individuals, if certain conditions are fulfilled. The conditions include:

1. The consciousness of the group using Ulexite must be quite developed and high. Being on the spiritual path is not enough, for example. Each person or group must possess a high vibration that is above the threshold below which a person or group cannot establish a connection to Ulexite.

2. The members of the user group must be in harmony with each other. Again, the level of harmony must be quite high to sustain the consciousness needed in the first requirement.

3. The group needs to work with conscious intent through their awareness. They must know their purpose and what they are doing. Using Ulexite requires that they be aware of their actions and agree to a common intent.

4. The direction of the intent must focus on an outcome or achievement that is worthy.

Intent is subjective and the propriety of the user(s). If they intend to send light and healing to some person, place, or group, Ulexite works to bring the light frequencies for healing. If the intent is to solve an engineering problem, Ulexite establishes a connection that brings the light for solving the engineering problem. If the mind can be involved, and the will is appropriately oriented to an higher vibrational outcome, Ulexite can be a participant.

To begin its work, Ulexite needs to be in near proximity to the user or group of users. Some measure of calm and serenity needs to be established for the purpose of allowing the stone to reach into the regions of the heavens that could contribute light or empowerment frequencies to the outcome. Ulexite, as does Selenite, remains in a state of dormancy until its vibration is reprogrammed to the user's vibration. Reprogramming permits Ulexite to shift its vibration to that of the user's intent. Ulexite then conforms to the will that is being created within the contemplation of the user's mind. Its vibration creates an harmonious connection between the user and the exact place in the heavens that stores or creates the specific light frequencies needed to fulfill the user's contemplation. Per the examples previously mentioned, Ulexite can reach into the heavens to bring healing light in the quantity and quality needed, or to bring light to solve engineering problems related to specific topics. There is no limit to appropriate intentions and no limit to the light Ulexite can access. Again, Ulexite works only when vibrations are adequately high and well intentioned. Therefore, it is not likely to work with anyone, except the most adept of spiritual persons whose place is already well established with the heavenly hosts.

Some suggestions about Ulexite's use may include the wilful bringing of light into places of darkness. To that end, it can be used to extend forgiveness where needed, to bridge communication gaps for worthy outcomes, and to give insights to help a person overcome shortfalls in perceptions. It can bring the light needed for evolving one's understanding of perplexing ideas, concepts, or relationships. Ulexite can help the user to communicate with deceased loved ones or other beings on the enlightened side of the universe. Importantly, a person or group can use Ulexite intentionally to bring light frequencies from the heavens to raise the vibration of a place, a house, or a locale.

It can also be used to thwart negative actions imposed by others. Ulexite and the enlightened universe from which its influence comes do not directly interfere with a person's will to do unsavoury acts. Rather, Ulexite protects its user by orchestrating light frequencies that help in any number of ways to redirect the user away from places of negative vibration, given that the negative action is inappropriate and not among the user's life-lessons.

As long as the vibrations, intent, and participants are high enough, Ulexite can be reprogrammed to the user's frequencies and reach into the area of the universe where the frequencies of fulfillment exist. It can then bring those frequencies back from the higher planes along the threads of connections between the users and their higher-selves.

For the future, Ulexite's adaptation to the physical plane is improving steadily. The vibrational threshold, below which it can participate, is steadily dropping to accommodate lower and lower vibration, thereby expanding the range of individuals, who can effectively use Ulexite. The trade-off with making its use possible with individuals having lower vibration is that the Ulexite can reach up only as high as the vibration of the user, to whom it is reprogrammed. The more spiritually adept the user(s), the higher will the stone reach into the heavens.

Unakite

Love Connection Stone

Scientific Properties:

Unakite is an altered granite composed of pink orthoclase feldspar, green epidote, and generally colorless quartz.

Colour: various shades of green and pink and is usually mottled in appearance

Unakite is aptly named for its role in unifying light with light. It is an Earth crystal, but not among the truly indigenous stones. It is not a new age piece either. Unakite has had a presence on Earth for many hundreds of years.

From the beginning of Earth time, enlightened beings from the heavens have visited the planet to ascertain its state-of-affairs. With the help of the enlightened visitors, Earth's enlightened inhabitants determined the need to infuse certain light frequencies onto the planet. Such frequencies came. By using the new frequencies, the progression of Earth's lighted path continued. Unakite was and still is an example of a crystalline vibration that the enlightened ones added to the inventory of vibrations on Earth. The enlightened ones determined that the need for Unakite's contribution to the Earth was sufficient to make it available for use by individuals.

Unakite's primary role involves uniting the light vibration of the user with other sources of light. The user's Oneness and the Oneness of the vibration upon which the user is contemplating are brought together within the stone. The responsibility then rests with the user to offer love to remove any obstacles that might deny access to the Oneness of the stone. Thereafter, the merged Oneness within the stone is released to be incorporated within the user's consciousness.

Using Unakite is not complex. It has the ability to bring love forward to be shared. The user's Oneness is placed into the stone by affirmation of her will. The Oneness of the being or object at the centre of the contemplation is also placed within the stone. The user then offers love to the union of the combined Oneness. With enough love, the combined Oneness is released. The user then unites with, or shares with others, the Oneness of the contemplation through the combined Oneness.

There is no limit to the Oneness a person might contemplate and unite with. An individual's lover is a legitimate light source with which to unite, as is the light of a new pair of roller skates, a new house, or any other object of desire. The divine Oneness of a person's contemplation is the vibration that enters Unakite. Love for the divinity of that Oneness (e.g., the roller skates), on the part of the person using Unakite, results in the release of that Oneness into the person's life. The means by which the union manifests on the physical plane then unfolds. The materialization of an object for the sake of simple propriety is not considered to be love enough to bring release. However, for those things and persons that are the focus and quest of a person's heart-felt love, Unakite does its job. Unakite brings the Oneness at the core of the love object—person or thing—and offers it to the stone's user.

Unakite is of the heart. Its Oneness is released only by the love of the heart. Unakite is also a stone of contemplation. When using Unakite, it is placed first at the third eye chakra to affirm the user's desire, and then at the heart to affirm her love. The user does not need to undergo any arduous process of intense contemplation. Rather, the user makes her affirmations to the stone by holding it to the third eye and heart. It may then be cleared with the sun and water for a short while[1], after which it is ready to use again.

---

1   Please see the section on clearing and cleansing crystals in this volume. In this instance, 'a short while' means to place Unakite in a window in the Sun for a half-hour or so. Placing it in a crystal goblet in water is also helpful.

The gift of the stone is the acquisition of the combined Oneness, which makes its way into the user's body and essence through love. An actual physical presence or manifestation of the Oneness vibration may or may not accompany this gift. For example, the roller skates may come as a 'find' at a garage sale. As another example, the person to whom Unakite's user is directing her love may send a letter or email to say 'hello'. If the user truly wants and loves another person or a material object, the love is very likely to result in its physical manifestation. The love object or person materializes for the user's enjoyment. Love brings love; the form has no limit.

About the Author

Roger Joyeux is the incarnation of a soul that has been on Earth since time began. In this lifetime, his core truth is to bring forth the body of knowledge that is the story of divine light. *The Crystal Textbook* is his third book. The first two books are *The Story of Light, Path to Enlightenment*, and *The Story of Light, Through Heaven's Gate*.

Roger began channelling spirit guides in the mid-70s. In the 1990s, he awakened to his spiritual path starting with a trip to the Siddha Yoga Ashram in Ganespuri, India. In 1990, Roger began channelling the angelic cadre called *The Great White Brotherhood*, and soon after, *The Councilate of the Ascended Light*. He is also a conscious channel for the Ascended Masters.

Roger works extensively with crystals, conducts workshops, and offers personal sessions. His mission, passion, and divine purpose on Earth is to spread a conscious understanding of the nature of crystals and divine light, and to help individuals complete their paths to enlightenment so they may consciously participate in the divine co-creation of our physical world and achieve the promise of the ascension that this new age brings.

CPSIA information can be obtained at www.ICGtesting.com
Printed in the USA
LVOW04s2331271114

415888LV00027B/926/P

9 780968 652138